Nordiska Museets Handlingar: 4

SLEDGES AND WHEELED VEHICLES

Ethnological studies from the view-point of Sweden

By

GÖSTA BERG

1935

Astragal Press
An Imprint of Finney Company

All rights reserved. No part of this publication may be reproduced or transmitted in any form or by any means, electronic or mechanical, including photocopy, recording, or any information storage and retrieval system without the written permission of the publisher.

Copyright © 2015 Astragal Press

ISBN: 978-1-931626-34-7

Astragal Press
An Imprint of Finney Company
www.finneyco.com • www.astragalpress.com

Facsimile of volume originally published:
UPPSALA 1935
ALMQVIST & WIKSELLS BOKTRYCKERI-A.-B.
35198

CONTENTS

	Page
Illustrations	6
Preface	12
Chapter I. Before the sledge	15
» II. The built-up sledge	35
» III. The simple runner-sledge and the origin of the built-up sledge	74
» IV. The double-sledge for timber and other transportation	90
» V. The cart	99
» VI. The slide-car and the origin of the cart	129
» VII. The wheel-sledge	144
» VIII. The waggon	150
Literature	173

ABBREVIATIONS

E. u., Ethnologiska undersökningen (Ethnological survey) at the Nordiska museet.
UUB., University library, Uppsala.

ILLUSTRATIONS

Plate I.
1. Water-transport with guide-runner. Tåsjö, Jämtland.
2. Guide-runner. Östmark, Värmland.
3. Guide-runner. Idre, Dalarna.
4. Guide-runner. Idre, Dalarna.
5. Plough-runner. Folkärna, Dalarna.

Plate II.
1. Hollowed-out trunk-sledge. From Pajala, Lappland.
2. Hollowed-out trunk-sledge from Lapps in Frostviken, Jämtland.
3. Runner for transporting tent-poles. From Lapps in Arjeplog.

Plate III.
1. Hunters trailing shot seals on the ice. Runö, Esthonia.
2. Hay-transport on boughs. Mármaros, Hungary.

Plate IV.
1. Ski-sledge with nails on either side of the posts. S. Finnskoga, Värmland.
2. Hay-sledge with nails on either side of the posts. Tydal, Sör-Tröndelag, Norway.
3. Sledge of "east-Finnish" type. Nederkalix, Norrbotten.

Plate V.
1. Sledge from Kola Peninsula, Russia.
2. Seal-hunter's sledge. Runö, Esthonia.
3. Conveyance from Torne district. Finland.

Plate VI.
1. Detail of a sledge as seen on 2. Mora, Dalarna.
2. Sledge for transporting wood for charcoal. Leksand, Dalarna.
3. Sledge for wood-transport. Ödsköld, Dalsland.
4. Hay-sledge with nails on either side of the posts. Dalsland.

Plate VII.
1. Dung-sledge from Aruland, Sogn-Fjordane, Norway.
2. Dung-sledge from Ore, Dalarna.
3. Sledge from Lillerupsholm, Jutland, Denmark.

ILLUSTRATIONS

Plate VIII.
1. Sledge with semi-cylindrical body, used for hay-transport. Venjan, Dalarna.
2. Hay-sledge from Tjörn, Bohuslän.

Plate IX.
1. Conveyance from Bredared, Västergötland.
2. Conveyance from Orsa, Dalarna.
3. Conveyance from Oppmanna, Scania.

Plate X.
1. Sledge for carting stones, from Kullerstad, Östergötland.
2. Sledge for carting stones, from N. Ny, Värmland.
3. Simple runner-sledge, used for water-transport. Sorunda, Södermanland.

Plate XI.
1. Sledge, used at wolf-hunting. Västergötland. Detail from a drawing 1849 by Fr. v. Dardel.
2. Timber-sledge from Åsele, Västerbotten.
3. Sledge from Frändefors, Dalsland.

Plate XII.
1. Timber-trailing without runners. Ytre Rendal, Sör-Tröndelag, Norway.
2. Timber-transport with a short-sledge only. Häggenås, Jämtland.
3. Timber-transport (the man is wearing snow-shoes). Frostviken, Jämtland.

Plate XIII.
1. Short-sledge for timber-transport. Kisa, Östergötland.
2. Short-sledge for timber-transport. Idala, Halland.
3. Short-sledge for timber-transport. Venjan, Dalarna.
4. A pair of sledges, for timber transport. Norrbotten.

Plate XIV.
1. Double-sledge. After a drawing by Fr. v. Dardel.
2. Double-sledge for hay-transport. Silvberg, Dalarna.
3. Double-sledge for timber-transport. Central Småland. After a sculpture by C. A. Rolander.

Plate XV.
1. A pair-drawn ox-cart, as seen on an engraving in Suecia Antiqua.
2. Cart from a rock-sculpture at Rished, Askum, Bohuslän.
3. Cart from a rock-sculpture at Rished, Askum, Bohuslän.
4. Wheel, bog-find from Lilla Mellösa, Södermanland.

Plate XVI.
1. Cart with disc-wheels. Älvdalen, Dalarna.
2. Cart with disc-wheels. Röros, Tröndelag, Norway. After a drawing by J. F. L. Dreier.
3. Dung-cart with disc-wheels. Älvros, Härjedalen.

Plate XVII.
1. Corn-cart with wheel-guards. Svärdsjö, Dalarna.
2. Corn-cart with wheel-guards. Järvsö, Hälsingland.
3. Hay-cart. The surroundings of Falun, Dalarna.

Plate XVIII.
1. Hay-cart. Norum, Bohuslän.
2. Hay-cart. Söderbärke, Dalarna.
3. Hay-cart. Nårunga, Västergötland.

Plate XIX.
1. Hay-cart. Hudene, Västergötland.
2. Cart, as seen on an engraving from Gothenburg, by Elias Martin, 1787 (?).
3. Hay-cart. Vilhelmina, Lappland.

Plate XX.
1. Slide-car on its way to the mountain dairies. Ore, Dalarna.
2. Slide-car for collecting the hay. V. Vingåker, Södermanland.

Plate XXI.
1. Transport of the dead in the Oviken mountains, Jämtland.
2. Slide-cars in Ukraina. After a photograph in the Hungarian National Museum, Budapest.

Plate XXII.
1. Sledge with attached slide-car. Svinhult, Östergötland.
2. Sledge with attached slide-car. Borgsjö, Medelpad.
3. Sledge with attached slide-car for wood-transport. Säter, Dalarna.

Plate XXIII.
1. Trailing a plough. Hällstad, Västergötland.
2. Plough slide-car from Fågeltofta, Scania.
3. Slide-car for turf-transport. Antrim, Ireland.

Plate XXIV.
1. Wheel-sledge for hay-transport. Ed, Dalsland.
2. Wheel-sledge with a single runner at the fore. Ström, Jämtland.

ILLUSTRATIONS

Plate XXV.
1. Wheel-sledge for corn-transport. Nysätra, Västerbotten.
2. Wheelbarrow used for hay-transport in the swamps. Fagerhult, Scania.
3. Draught-pole. Tystberga, Södermanland.

Plate XXVI.
1. Draught-pole. Mangskog, Värmland.
2. Wheeled-pole. Burs, Gotland.
3. Wheeled-pole. Leksand, Dalarna.

Plate XXVII.
1. Waggon from a rock-sculpture at Rished, Askum, Bohuslän.
2. Waggon from a rock-sculpture at Långön, Tossene, Bohuslän.
3. The Dejbjerg waggon. About 100 B. C. National Museum, Copenhagen.

Plate XXVIII.
1. Waggon with "nailed" beam-construction. Burseryd, Småland.
2. Waggon with "cylinder" beam-construction. Svinhult, Östergötland.
3. Waggon with supports from the back wheels and with two poles and shafts. Västerstad, Scania.

Plate XXIX.
1. "Trein-waggon" for hay-transport, with solid front-wheels. Nössemark, Dalsland.
2. "Trein-waggon", probably from the north of Scania.
3. Hay-waggon from Hede, Härjedalen.

Plate XXX.
1. Waggon from Rackeby, Västergötland.
2. Waggon from Landa, Halland.

Plate XXXI.
1. Waggon from Tving, Blekinge.
2. Waggon with gate in the rails. Runö, Esthonia.

Plate XXXII.
1. Dung-waggon. Algutsrum, Öland.
2. Conveyance from Sällstorp, Halland.

		Page
Fig. 1.	Boat-sledge. Bog-find from Ragunda, Jämtland	17
» 2.	Boat-sledge. Bog-find from Delsbo, Hälsingland	17
» 3.	Boat-sledge. Bog-find from Laukaa, Tavastland, Finland	17

			Page
Fig.	4.	A fisherman with his sledge. Kuolajärvi, Finland	19
»	5.	Boat-shaped sledge from Korpiselkä, Finland	21
»	6.	Seal-hunter's sledge from Esthonia	21
»	7.	The fore-end of a boat in Hille, Gästrikland	23
»	8.	Dug-out trunk-sledge of the Samoyed-Ostyak	25
»	9.	The distribution of the guide-runner in Sweden	27
»	10.	The skin-sledge of the Västerbotten Lapps	31
»	11.	Sledge-runner. Bog-find from Gråträsk, Piteå, Norrbotten	37
»	12.	Sledge-runner. Bog-find from Kuortane, Finland	37
»	13.	Sledge-post from the Gorbunowa-find, Russia	39
»	14.	Reconstruction of a sledge of the Gråträsk-type	41
»	15.	The distribution of the younger sledge-runners in Swedish bog-finds	43
»	16.	Sledge-runner. Bog-find from Grundsunda, Ångermanland	45
»	17.	Sledge-runner. Bog-find from Lycksele, Lappland	45
»	18.	Sledge-runner. Bog-find from Nederkalix, Västerbotten	47
»	19.	Sledge-runner. Bog-find from Stensele, Lappland	47
»	20.	Sledge-runner. Bog-find from Junsele, Ångermanland	47
»	21.	A pair of sledge-runners. Bog-find from Hammerdal, Jämtland	49
»	22.	Sledge-runner. Bog-find from Vilhelmina, Lappland	49
»	23.	Sledge-runner. Bog-find from Björna, Ångermanland	49
»	24.	Sledge-runner. Bog-find from Vilhelmina, Lappland	49
»	25.	The post-construction from a Chukchee sledge	51
»	26.	The cross-bar construction on a sledge from Norsjö, Västerbotten	55
»	27.	Sledge with treenails on either side of the posts. Sogn, Norge	57
»	28.	The distribution of sledges with semi-cylindrical body in Sweden	67
»	29.	Detail from a painting with sledge-driving from Mora, Dalarna	71
»	30.	Conveyance from Rättvik, Dalarna	72
»	31.	A fork-shaped sledge from Fågeltofta, Skåne	76
»	32.	The distribution of the fork-shaped simple runner-sledge in Sweden	77
»	33.	Simple runner-sledge from Falster, Denmark	78
»	34.	The distribution of the method of trailing the timber on the ground	91
»	35.	A guide-runner, used as trailer for timber-transport	94
»	36.	Pair-drawn ox-cart from Karinainen, Finland	101
»	37.	The Dystrup wheel. Bog-find from Örum, Jutland, Denmark	103
»	38.	The most southern distribution of carts in Sweden	107
»	39.	One-horse cart. Engraving on a copper cross from 12th century	115
»	40.	The distribution of disc-wheels on carts in Sweden	117
»	41.	Wheel-guard of hazel-wood from a hay-cart. Central Småland	123
»	42.	Cart with disc-wheel and semi-cylindrical body. Älvros, Härjedalen	124
»	43.	The distribution of the semi-cylindrical body on carts in Sweden	125
»	44.	The distribution of slide-cars in Sweden	131
»	45.	Comprised Tatarian slide-car for the transport of wood	141
»	46.	The most northern distribution of the waggon in Sweden	152

ILLUSTRATIONS

	Page
Fig. 47. The distribution of the "cylinder"-construction and of the "nail"-construction in Sweden	160
" 48. The distribution of outer rail-supports on waggons in Sweden	166
" 49. Detail of a waggon with projecting rails. Torsås, Småland	169
" 50. The distribution of waggon framework with upward lengthened openwork sides in Sweden	170
" 51. Waggon with gate in the railed-side. Gotland	172

PREFACE.

The object of this Work is to investigate certain problems connected with the history of vehicular transport from a Swedish point of view. The idea is not to create an encyclopedic more all-round collection of facts. On the contrary. Necessity has forced me to an almost exaggerated concentration in order that a general survey, including the Swedish phenomena in its rightful and justifiable connection, might be forthcoming. The Work is based upon the apprehension that "no historical problem can be understood and solved with any hope of success by limiting our attention to one particular culture-sphere to the exclusion of all others, and even in the minutest specialization of our work we must never be forgetful of the universalistic standpoint."[1]

Apart from principal lines, in the Swedish development have details rarely been touched upon. Philological phenomena have not been taken into consideration either as regards the descriptive, or in the employment of terminology from a culture-historical point of view. Here with certainty lies an opportunity for the execution of very successful work if carried out on principles other than those used by myself. In this connection it may not be esteemed out of place to draw attention to the importance which a knowledge of transport-methods plays in the judging of the expansion of culture as a whole, and culture, as the individual element. It is well-known how this fact has been pointed out and emphasized by various Scholars amongst whom may be included Gudmund Hatt, Clark Wissler, Paul Descamps and others.

One of the Author's aims has been to scientifically include the Northern subject-matter which concerns the origins and expansions of both sledges and wheeled-vehicles. Moreover I have also endeavoured to maintain a general view of the historical aspect of the culture of North Europe which, thanks to continued research verifies itself more and more. The North European culture-zone appears to have been originally and intimately related to that of North Asia, but at an early date it was strongly influenced by impulses from the Mediterranean and by internal culture-innovations. To an enormous extent have these forces made tabula rasa with the old culture and

[1] Laufer, 1931, p. 536.

it is at the periphery especially that one must seek for relics upon which to reconstruct to some extent the earlier stages on which the later evolutions were based.

Without further procrastination may be said, that it was a mistake to treat the Lapps independently as the connecting link between Europe and the North of Asia, but ethnological North European research on this wider basis is only yet on its threshold. The Scandinavian subject-matter as derived from research, as well as that from Ireland and Scotland and to some extent from East Europe must necessarily be of an entirely eruptive nature. In some special instances I have endeavoured to prove that such is the case.

In conclusion I should like to express my gratitude to all those who in any way whatever have contributed to the carrying out of this Work. It is unhappily impossible to mention all by name.

Ten years ago, Professor Sigurd Erixon at the Nordiska Museet awakened my interest in the history of transport and on many occasions has given me excellent advice and information in connection with my studies.

The late Professor K. B. Wiklund, Uppsala, kindly allowed me free access to his rich collection of excerpts touching on the history of reindeer breeding.

Dr. Erik Granlund of the Geological Survey, Stockholm, has bestowed a great deal of disinterested labour on ascertaining and precisioning the dates of several of the bog-find runners mentioned in this Work.

Dr. Nils Lid of Oslo rendered invaluable assistance by publishing and distributing a list of questions bearing on sledges and wheeled-vehicles, from which list were received over a hundred answers, from various parts of Norway.

The compiling of the Work has been facilitated by a grant from the "Humanistiska fonden" which, in 1932, enabled me to take a leave of three months' absence from my duties. I wish to thank Professor Sigurd Curman, King's Custodian of Antiquities for appreciation shewn for my work. In 1930, thanks to a grant from the "Längmanska kulturfonden," I was able to study much of the subject-matter quoted here, in the various Collections of Central Europe.

The Director of the Nordiska Museet, Professor Andreas Lindblom, has facilitated my work in every conceivable way and has shewn special confidence by including it in the Museum's Proceedings.

The publishing expenses have been essentially derived from the interest on the "Sundbornsprostens donation" (foundation) which is at the disposition of the trustees of the Nordiska Museet.

My colleagues at the Museum and at the Royal Armoury have shewn great interest in the Work by rendering assistance in every direction. This with particular reference to my wife and Dr. Sigfrid Svensson, without whose encouraging help the book had never been realized. The assistants at the Ethnological Survey have collected much of the Swedish data. Herrar Ola Bannbers and Sam Owen Jansson have made a valuable contribution by kindly reading through the proofs.

I am indebted to Mrs. J. S. Herrström for the English translation.

Nordiska Museet, March, 1935.

GÖSTA BERG.

CHAPTER I

BEFORE THE SLEDGE

The method of transporting a burden by carrying it on the head, the back, or by hand is a prevalent and easily found custom in the human being's every stage of culture. "The man as a beast of burden," to avail oneself of Otis Mason's expressive utterance has, at an early stage, however, endeavoured to ease his labours by means of divers more or less ingenious expedients. His methods display a skilful differentiation, which has left its mark on implements and which can be made use of in this connection. May be the development of methods of transport, as far as land-transport goes, can distinctly be said to characterize the North Eurasian culture-area. Also, it seems to be by the aid of research-material from this part of the world, that we shall by degrees, get a survey of the origins and connections of these transport methods and implements.

In later times this area was characterized especially by the occurrence of the sledge, but there must lie behind, a precursory stage, a period before the sledge which, of necessity, contented itself with other and more primitive vehicles. In Chapter III we shall find that the simple runner-sledge was an implement belonging to this class, which can be traced to pre-historic time in the history of man. Theoretically at least, however, there is discernible still another period in which the simple sledge with two runners is unknown. It is inconceivable that such a culture period without the simple runner-sledge existed everywhere. The space of time we are tolerably well able to survey evinces, on the whole that, both, or all three forms appeared simultaneously. Kaj Birket-Smith has also emphasized and rightly so, that "there is nothing self-contradictory as ancient and primitive types can of course continue alongside more highly developed types."[1] In the following, those forms which theoretically may have existed before the simple two-runner sledge will be treated coherently.

Northern prehistoric finds prove to us that already in prehistoric times there was in Sweden a clearly defined single-runner sledge. Amongst the oldest

---

[1] Birket-Smith, 1929, 2, p. 168.

wooden objects found in the regions of the North is included the keel of a sledge which was discovered in a bog during some railroad work in 1885, "on the northern side of the one-time outlet of the Ragunda sea, in Gedungsen" (a waterfall, also called Storforsen). The runner, illustrated in Fig. 1, is mentioned here as the "Ragunda runner" after the district in which the find was made. In its present mutilated condition, it is 120 cm. long,[1] and hewn in wood with two grooves running lengthwise; it is pierced by holes, eleven pairs in all, and at one end, probably the rear, is a pair of perpendicular holes. Dr. Erik Granlund, of Sweden's Geological Survey, Stockholm, has made a pollen-analytical investigation and the result of the examination proves that it dates from a time which corresponds to the Younger Stone Age in the south-Swedish culture-area. There is a prehistoric bog find of a similar character from Delsbo, Hälsingland. It is called the Delsbo runner and is seen in Fig. 2. This runner was found when digging a dyke on the Sävholm estate about 1913. As it appears now it is about 243 cm. long, but the thin fore-ends were badly damaged when it was being excavated and taken up.[2] It has the same length-wise grooves running almost to the ends, and towards the fore are the same eleven pairs of holes whilst those at the rear end are missing. The runner bears signs of wear and tear, and cannot therefore be regarded as an incompleted implement. It is now in the Historiska Museet, where it has been conserved unfortunately without previous pollen-analytic treatment. An examination of this kind made at the place of the find, on my initiative, has proved it to be likely that the runner dates at least from the Bronze Age.

To these two Swedish finds may be added one from Laukaa, in the north of Tavastland, Finland. This runner, Fig. 3, which is in a good state of preservation has a length of about 450 cm. Nearly the whole of the upper-side is hollowed out to a depth of about 4 cm. and there are seventeen pairs of pierced holes which slope from the inside downwards. At the one end, as on the Ragunda runner, are two perpendicular holes.[3] To my knowledge there has been no pollen-analysis made in connection with this runner. Though differing in detail, these three finds must be grouped together and reconstructed on mainly the same lines. U. T. Sirelius has led the way through bringing forward a group of "hunting sledges" of the single-runner type which are in general use as a snow-vehicle in north and east Finland.[4] As regards the Laukaa runner, he is of the opinion that it once had sides of thin boards, held together

---

[1] All length measures in this book are taken from the under-side of the object (not in projection).
[2] Hillgren, 1925, pp. 32—35.
[3] Sirelius, 1928, pp. 949—951; I am indebted to Dr. T. Itkonen for the excellent drawing of the runner.
[4] Sirelius, 1913 (a).

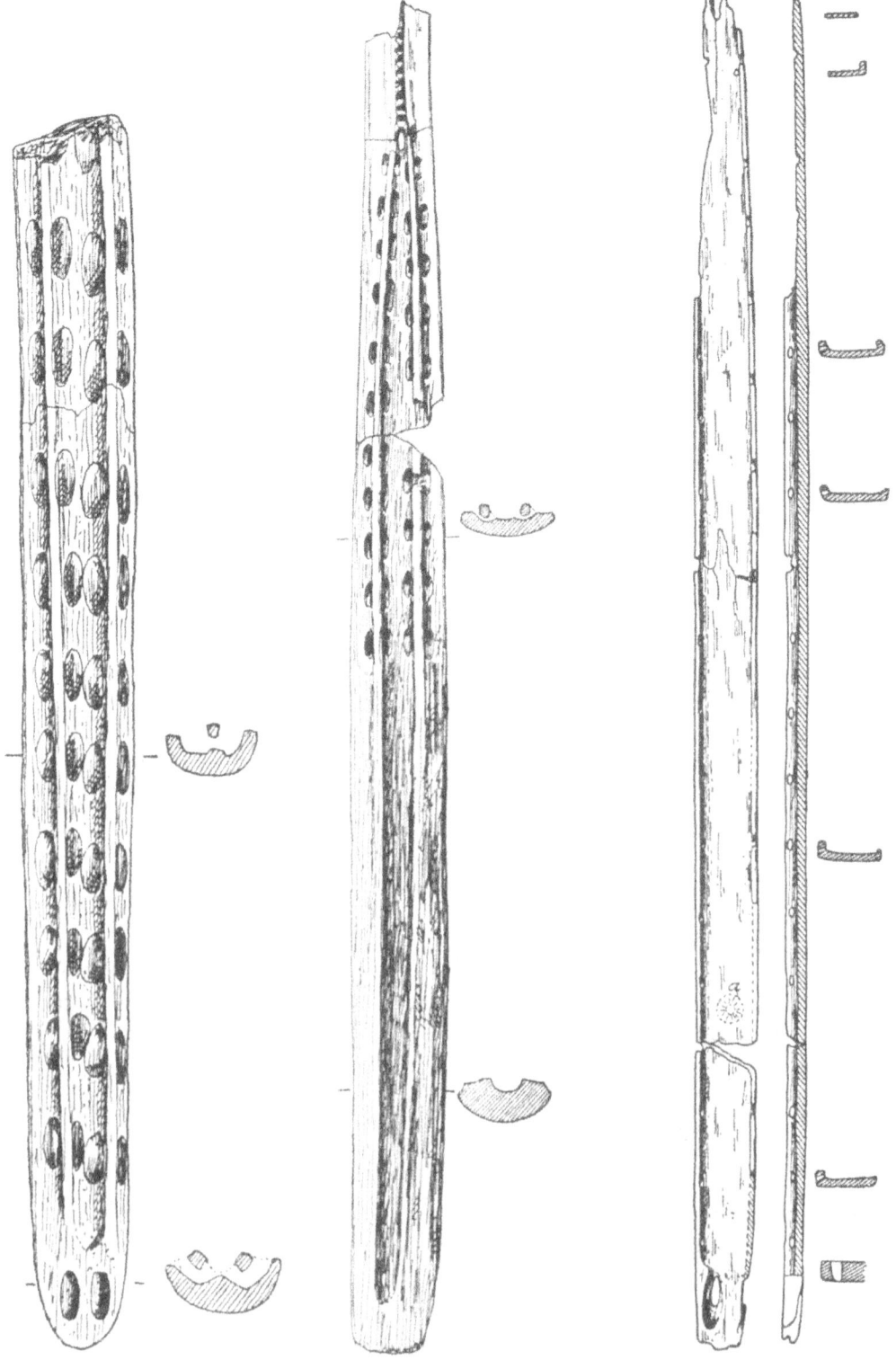

Fig. 1. Boat-sledge. Bog-find from Ragunda, Jämtland.

Fig. 2. Boat-sledge. Bog-find from Delsbo, Hälsingland.

Fig. 3. Boat-sledge. Bog-find from Laukaa, Tavastland, Finland.

by osiers or strips of skin, as seen on one type of the hunter's sledge, Fig. 5. In one of his earlier works has Sirelius treated several other forms of this implement and it is evident that both the Ragunda and Delsbo runners can be explained in like manner.[1] An observation made at the excavation of the Ragunda runner is of interest in connection with the former. In the Museum inventory it is stated that "before the earth fell away from the holes in this wooden implement, large black spots had been noticed, one in each hole, which appears to be the remains of thick rope which had once been inserted".

The pairs of holes at the one end of the Ragunda and Laukaa runners are worthy of note. As far as I can see, the preserved parts must have belonged to the rear ends. The standards which had once occupied the holes may have served to hold the back ends of the two sides of the body together. One is obliged to await enlightenment from further finds in order to learn how the traces were attached. In the meantime, one might assume that the ends of the side-boards were lashed together with osiers, or by other means which, at the same time served as a hold for the traces. This method is to be met with now and again, later, on the hunting-sledge.[2] It is extraordinary, however, that on the Delsbo runner itself, which is undoubtedly the fore-part of a sled, are no signs of hauling arrangements whatever.

Though only one runner of this group is dated with certainty one should be able to ascribe all to the Stone or Bronze Age. For the present however, the material is far too scanty to allow of any wider-reaching conclusions. It would not seem out of the way to believe that the vehicle was man-hauled and that it was chiefly used for bringing home the hunter's bag, all of which coincides with the younger hunting-sledge we are about to investigate later. Like the latter it has also undoubtedly been used in connection with the ski, an implement which both in Sweden and Finland most certainly dates archaeologically from a time corresponding to that of the Ragunda runner.[3]

Noteworthy is the relationship established already at a period so remote between North Sweden and Finland. The archaeological circumstances of North-Swedish provinces are too little investigated to enable the placing of these mutual affinities in their historical coherence, a state of things mostly due to the rare occurrence of ceramic in prehistoric finds. However, I have endeavoured to point out that the conformity of the oldest skis, on either side of the Gulf of Bothnia must be reduced to one common culture basis. This

---

[1] Sirelius, 1928, p. 951. — A similar construction from a later time shews the upper side-boards of the sledge of the coopers used in Malung, Dalarna. The boards are threaded with osiers through vertical holes — according to Herr O. Bannbers.

[2] Cf. Sirelius, 1913 (a), Fig. 4.   [3] Berg, 1933 (a), pp. 144—149.

Fig. 4. A fisherman with his sledge. Kuolajärvi, Österbotten, Finland. After U. T. Sirelius.

basis as far as the Baltic districts are concerned was a "Bone" Culture, predominant there during the Ancylus Period, which had spread, already at that time, far north into Sweden — at least, to Jämtland and to North and Central Finland.[1] Our knowledge of this culture is derived chiefly from carefully preserved Danish finds. It seems to consist of hunting and fishing elements of a type whose nearest analogies should be sought, for instance, amongst various Northern Indian tribes.[2] Dwelling places lay along the shores of the Sea, where fishing and mammal-hunting was carried on during the hot season. But in all probability hunting expeditions far into the forests have set forth from these dwellings. The greater number of implements contained in the finds are made of bone and horn, as also Professor Sune Lindquist has indicated in the impressive term "Bone Age" which he applies to the epoch in question.[3] It is reasonable to suppose that skis and runner-sleds were used on these hunting occasions in winter and, for a life of this kind, in such a climate as that of the North, they may be said to have been indispensable. Besides, it is only a matter of natural sequence that the primitive hunting-fishing culture which archaeologically appears in the Mullerup-Kunda Culture, far north in Scandinavia and Finland survived during later periods and was traceable amongst the newer methods, and innovations, and novelties found in the implement inventories of the time.

Types of sleds more or less akin to prehistoric forms have up to modern times been employed in North and East Finland as well as amongst Lapps

---

[1] Berg, 1933 (a), p. 153; Childe, 1931, p. 329.
[2] Jenness, 1932, p. 47.   [3] Lindquist, 1918.

in neighbouring parts of Sweden.[1] I know them from Pajala,[2] by the name of "veturi", and they are used by the residents in Vittangi,[3] and Jukkasjärvi.[4] It is worthy of note that from Bjurholm in Ångermanland is mention of a hunting-sledge called "attja" but in this case it is made from a hollowed-out portion of a tree-trunk.[5] It specially came into use on the far-away hunting expeditions to the desolate forest-tracts to transport the food and carry home the bag. Sirelius has in a most instructive manner described these ancient hunting methods and indicated what an important part they played in the people's economy.[6] Without doubt they splendidly illustrate conditions which prevailed earlier in the greater parts of most Northern Europe. There are several old notices from Finland telling of the hunting-sled. In 1520 mention is made of some men who went out into the wilds with such a sled ("ackebotten").[7] An account from 1620 describes how the huntsman hauled the sled with a line drawn over one shoulder, across the breast and under the other arm. Sirelius has published a still more detailed account from a document dated 1663, from Paldamo in North Österbotten.[8]

The runner-sled had its uses in Finland also as an implement of agriculture, whilst the latter was still in its primitive stage. When denshired land was being cultivated, it served to transport food, seed, and also undoubtedly to bring home the threshed grain.[9] In addition to the many Finnish evidences, Sirelius has produced others from Further Carelia.[10]

In many instances are these sleds, and this refers to those of Sweden too, of a more developed type, the distinguishing feature being the firmly contrived ribs which hold the boards together. I shall return to the development of this construction in the following. The implement in each case is drawn by the hunter himself. The same may be said of the sled which is used by the hunters east of Archangel[11] and of the one known as the "ahkja," Fig. 6, employed in the north of Esthonia. The latter deviates considerably as to type, and according to Leinbock it "may be a Finnish loan."[12] From the northern

---

[1] Hatt, 1915, p. 263.
[2] E. u., notes and photog. from B. Laqvist.
[3] Nordiska Mus. 195,684.
[4] According to Dr. Ernst Manker, after the late R. Pappila, Lapp-bailiff.
[5] E. u. 3307. [6] Sirelius, 1913 (b), 1919—1921, 1, pp. 34—37, 1933, p. 21—23.
[7] Hist. Aikakauskirja, 1913, p. 375.
[8] Sirelius, 1913 (a), p. 13. Sirelius has omitted to mention that although the document dates from 1663, it was not printed before 1777.
[9] Grotenfelt, 1899, p. 187.
[10] Sirelius, 1913 (a); cf. Paulaharju; 1923, p. 168, 1927, p. 160, Vilkuna, 1930, p. 8.
[11] Borisov, 1906, p. 10. After Wiklund, 1918, p. 267.
[12] Leinbock, 1932, p. 34. I am indebted to Dr. Leinbock for information and picture-subject of this interesting implement. It is used for transporting nets and fish to the shore.

Fig. 5. Boat-shaped sledge from Korpiselkä, Carelia, Finland.
After U. T. Sirelius.

Fig. 6. Seal-hunter's sledge from Kuusalu, Esthonia.
After the photograph of a reconstruction in the National Museum, Tartu.

parts of the Carelian Republic in the White Sea districts, it is said that dogs are used as draught-animals: "Without them are neither fish nor seal caught out on the ice, to which, nets and other implements, in a sort of 'ahkja,' are transported by dogs, each wearing about his neck a round collar. The dogs are large and so strong that one man can ride behind each dog."[1]

One might presume that the employment of dog-traction in the north of Further Carelia superseded the older stage of man-haulage, in which the huntsman trailed his vehicle after him. Further information may be had from J. Fellman. The traces seem to have been copied directly from the harness worn by man. The use of the draught-dog for the single-runner sled as in the White Sea districts, probably constituted the idea of the dog as draught-animal for the built-up sledge (cf. Chapter II), and is at the same time one of the few survivals of the use of the dog in this capacity on European soil.

The employment of the reindeer by the Lapps, as draught-animal, suggests probable knowledge of dog-traction. The sledge used by the Lapps is, as is not unknown, fundamentally a single-runner sled of the type now investigated. Gudmund Hatt avers that it was never drawn by dogs but by the hunter himself.[2] The harness of the reindeer reverts, in its old form, to the manner in which the huntsman trailed his sled,[3] but as we have recently seen, the same may be said of the dog-harness. Hatt has tried to explain the employment of draught-reindeer by the Lapps as Samoyed influence,[4] but as the Samoyed always drives pair-draught, and the sledge of the Lapps is driven by

---

[1] Fellman, 1906, 1, pp. 506 (1829), 535. Cf. Castrén, 1855—58, 1, pp. 146, 153.
[2] Hatt, 1919, p. 110.   [3] Wiklund, 1918, p. 258.
[4] Hatt, 1919, p. 119. Cf. Tanner also, 1929, pp. 257, 414.

single-traction, this is obviously impossible. The tame reindeer as draught-animal is probably an independent culture-element of the North, whether one will or will not assume a stage between, when the dog alone served man in this capacity. Fritz Flor has indeed proposed that the tame reindeer, even as draught-animal, was domesticated as early as the Bone Age and Ancylus Period. But there is no evidence with which to support this hypothesis.[1] One cannot here go into closer details concerning the lengthily treated and contested questions as to the first occurrence and date of the tame reindeer amongst the Lapps, but this much is obvious, in any case, that any actual employment of the reindeer here is of relatively late date and must have occurred under strong influence from the peoples of the North.[2] As far as research is concerned at present, it would seem highly probable that the Lapps had used the reindeer for hunting purposes previously to their immigration from the South to the regions of Northern Scandinavia.

In consideration as to how the idea of using the reindeer as a draught-animal originally occurred, one would seem inclined to call to mind the earliest known employment of the single-runner sled in its connection with hunting expeditions. Sirelius has shewn how the tame reindeer was also originally and extensively used as a decoy in wild reindeer hunting.[3] With the dog as traction for the hunting-sled, or as the help-mate of man on draught occasions, the idea to substitute the decoy-reindeer in this capacity, was obviously very handy.

The boat-sledge of the Lapps not only indicates progress as regards the solving of the draught problem, but evinces an enormous advancement when contemplated side by side with the single-runner sled.[4] I have already mentioned that on many of the hunting-sleds which Sirelius has reproduced and described, the side-boards are fastened to ribs, which in their turn are nailed to the runner. The Lapp sled is constructed in the same way.[5] It would not seem out of the way to believe and, indeed, several Scholars have stated that, in this modification of the sled we are met with influence from the boat.[6] As Hatt has described the Lapp sled, the sled of the Västerbotten Lapps, it has normally four ribs, which are fastened to the keel with treenails. Similar ribs are used

---

[1] Flor, 1930 (b), pp. 143, 150; cf. Menghin, 1931, p. 231. — Birket-Smith, 1931, pp. 605—606; cf. Gandert, 1930, pp. 61—62.

[2] Cf. Wiklund, 1918.

[3] Sirelius, 1916, pp. 4—11.

[4] Ilmari Manninen's proposition that the Lapps, at an earlier date, used a double-runner built-up sledge, seems to me to be supported by no palpable reason, 1932, p. 312. The author is informed that Toivo Itkonen is of the same opinion as Manninen.

[5] See Hatt, 1913, and others.

[6] See, for instance, Byhan, 1923, p. 311; Hallström, 1926, p. 256.

Fig. 7. The fore-end of a boat in Hille, Gästrikland.
After a photograph by Ernst Klein.

in small boats in North Sweden. They are fastened to the keel with treenails in square holes. Generally three boards comprise the sides of the built-up sledge, though a reproduction by Hatt shews four. From the Lule Archipelago I have records of boats with four.[1] Most remarkable also is the coincidence regarding the extraordinary pointed ends of the sled which are attached to the keel and into which the side-boards are inserted. This also goes under the name of "snibb" (point) when met with on boats in Ångermanland and Hälsingland for instance, in North Sweden, Fig. 7.[2] It is quite conceivable that the ribs were of earlier occurrence in Lapp culture than was the treenail. Hatt has given reasons for such an assumption,[3] and should this be so, then most probably the side-boards have from the beginning — as were the stern-boards in later years — been sewn to the frame with sinews, as in the case of the Lapp boat. A group of Swedish and Finnish bog-finds leads us to hope that by degrees we also may come a little nearer the truth. Sirelius has published a floor-plank of a hunting-sledge found in Pihtipudas, in Tavastland, which shews signs of having been sewn to a frame.[4] From Sweden are similar floorboards known from Gråträsk[5] and Lappträsk,[6] in Norrbotten and in Gåxsjö in Jämtland,[7] but of a different form. Quite lately Toivo Itkonen has published five such finds from Finland, namely, from Alajärvi and Övertorneå in Österbotten, from Enare in the Lapp Territory, from Kankanpää in Satakunda and from Sonkajärvi in Savolaks. To these may be added three Finnish finds of sledges without ribs, but with boards which had evidently been fastened to the runners, similarly, as we presumed were those of the Ragunda, Delsbo and Laukaa finds. The latter originate from Haapavesi and Esse in Österbotten and from Tövsala in south-western Finland. As Itkonen says, it is extra-

---

[1] Högberg, 1926, p. 11. The Lapp boat (sewn) had often three boards, Drake, 1918, p. 76.

[2] I am indebted to Dr. Ernst Klein, Nordiska Museet, for valuable information concerning these boats; cf. Högberg, 1926, p. 12. It is noteworthy that Dr. Klein met with such boat "points" in Weichsel, and as, far south as the southern Danube which great distribution should support the antiquity of this construction.

[3] Hatt, 1913, p. 142.   [4] Sirelius, 1913 (a), pp. 9—10.

[5] Vitterhetsakademien, 1926, Fig. 45 c.

[6] Berg, 1934. The ribs have probably been fastened to the runners with nails.

[7] In Jämtland's Museum, Östersund. — The runner is closely related to the Sonkajärvi runner, Itkonen, 1935.

ordinary to come across such sledges in finds from western and south-western Finland, indeed as far south as the Åbo Archipelago which are nowadays only known from northern Österbotten and Carelia.[1] This should dispense with any possible suspicion of this being a Lapp sledge.

Kaj Birket-Smith has rejected Sigrid Drake's hypothesis that it was the inhabitant of the North who used the boat-shaped sledge, and "that it spread from there to the Lapps and the people of Österbotten and Carelia."[2] Her reasoning is philological and from this basis alone would such an assumption be highly improbable.[3] However, thanks to subject-matter which has been brought to our notice, matters appear in quite another light. I need only call to mind that both the Ragunda and Delsbo runners originate from areas where Lapps to all appearances were unknown in remote times.[4] When, in addition, the Finnish finds of this group, mostly occur within areas where hitherto there is no evidence of Lapp settlement, must undoubtedly the boat-shaped sledge be presumed as having been employed by other than Lapp-inhabitants. Lapp culture must be freed, more than ever before, from the idea of its being an off-shoot of the circumpolar culture areas of the East. Instead, it should be regarded as a substratum of an older Arctic culture which spread over greater parts of most Northern Europe and, which, in its turn should be coupled with the culture-area just named. Later on have newer culture influences diffused the older development in other parts of the North and the Lapp culture has obviously become, in many instances, at least, a distinct kind of its own.

Before Sirelius drew attention to the single-runner hunting-sled had Hatt essayed to prove that the Lapp-sledge evolved from a sled, a dug-out tree-trunk, similar in form, and in some way or other related to the monoxyle boat. Hatt was able to shew sledge types of this kind amongst the Lapps.[5] It is not unlikely that we are dealing here with a form of the single-runner sled belonging to the type of the prehistoric finds and the Lapp sledge. It is not only amongst the Lapps,[6] Pl. II: 1—2, that we meet with the trough-sled if I may so call it. A similar sled was used to transport manure to the fields in summer-time in

---

[1] Itkonen, 1935. — Itkonen assumes the possibility that the sledge from Sonkajärvi had no ribs, but that the side-boards had been lashed together with sinews.
[2] Drake, 1918, pp. 84—85. Cf. Wiklund, 1918, pp. 267—268.
[3] Birket-Smith, 1929, 2, p. 166.
[4] Concerning the migration of the Lapps to Jämtland in the 16th century see Wiklund, 1928.
[5] Hatt, 1913, p. 140.
[6] A similar trough-sled is known to Hallström amongst the Lapps in Utsjoki, in Finnmark, Norway. Hallström, 1926, p. 255; cf. with a similar sled from Ångermanland, p. 20.

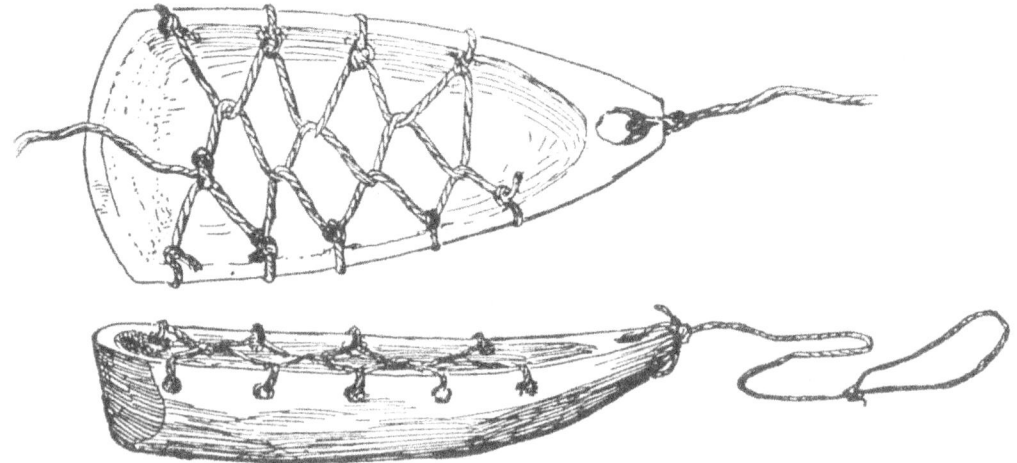

Fig. 8. Dug-out trunk-sledge of the Samoyed-Ostyak. After K. Donner.

the south of Österbotten, north Satakunda and east Tavastland, Finland.[1] It was comprised of a dug-out tree-trunk about 3 m. long, with an osier line for hauling attached to the ends. It was drawn by the horse. Gösta Grotenfelt states that it was used especially on clayey and marshy ground, where it ran fairly easily. Tradition tells that the trough-sled was used to trail out manure also in Vestlandet in Norway.[2] In Hungary, a similar trough-like implement drawn by the horse was employed to carry grain to the mill, over very bad roads.[3] It was also used for trailing manure out to the field.[4] As to whether one is justified in coupling herewith, information from Berchtesgaden in southeast Bavaria, which stated that in the out-house were manure-troughs ("misttrogn"), as well as manure-sleds, I am not in a position to say.[5] As a conclusion to this group should be mentioned Ebeling's indication of the occurrence of the trough-sled in Spain.[6]

In spite of the fact that these accounts of the occurrence of the trough-sled in Europe are very sporadic, and the possibility that they may be more or less incidental forms, there exist reasons, however, which favour the belief that they may exemplify an earlier stage in the development. Some similar trough-sleds are also known from amongst Siberian peoples namely, the Ostyak-Samoyed,[7] Fig. 8, the Yurak-Samoyed[8] and the Soyot.[9] They are used as hunting-sledges. The small Cheremiss ice-sledge reproduced by

---

[1] Sirelius, 1919—21, I, pp. 261—262; Grotenfelt, 1915, pp. 8—15; Kuusanmäki, 1928, p. 54.
[2] Information from enquiries, from Hareid in Möre and from Selje in Sogn-Fjordane.
[3] Banner, 1912.   [4] Gönczi, 1895, p. 172; Ecsedi, 1934, p. 274 (illustration).
[5] v. Schulenberg, 1896, p. 75.   [6] Ebeling, 1932, p. 53.
[7] Donner, 1919, pp. 94—98.   [8] Schrenk, 1848—54, p. 530.
[9] Donner, 1919, pp. 94—98.

Sirelius[1] should not be omitted here. The scanty material unfortunately renders it impossible to come to any conclusion as to the trough-sled's early history.[2] Moreover, the types are so indifferently developed that one is unable to count, with any certainty, on their genetic connection. On the other hand, such a connection cannot be denied, and therefore it should be applicable even to the North-American toboggan in its various forms.[3] The Chukchee use a trough-like toboggan made of baleen.[4] Most natural would it seem, to suppose the runner-sled and trough-sled as variations of one common and very primitive basic form, a form which must unquestionably be of very High Antiquity. It is probable that it was diffused over the whole of the Northern Hemisphere and that it, in conjunction with the skin-sled and the snow-shoe, from the very beginning was, may be, a product of a culture element from the remotest of times.[5]

A strikingly clear indication of the one-time importance of the runner-sled in the Northern culture zone may be gathered from other single-runner implements which were still being used in later times. Gudmund Hatt has drawn attention to a similar runner-implement called the "push-runner" (skjutmede) which was employed in many of the rural districts of North Sweden for the purpose of transporting water from the well or sea, up to the house, Pl. I: 1—4. It was generally made of pine, like a ski, with a slightly up-turned fore. At this end was sometimes a hole for the hauling-line and two persons could take part in the transport. The runner is hollowed out to form a kind of platform for the vessel. A cask of a larger size is more commonly used.

In Sweden the push-runner or guide-runner is known from the following places: *Dalsland* (Vårvik, according to Herr P. H. Nilsson, with one or two ridges), *Värmland* (Blomskog, according to Herr P. H. Nilsson; Gräsmark, Nordiska Mus. 88,733, with one ridge, E. u. 4362; Östmark, E. u. according to notes of N. Keyland, Pl. I: 2; Bograngen, Nordiska Mus., Archives), *Dalarna* (Malung, according to Herr O. Bannbers; Transtrand, Jirlow, 1935, p. 30; Lima, E. u. 4142; Särna, Hatt, 1913, p. 144, one example in the Swedish Ski Museum, Stockholm, with one or two ridges; Idre, Nordiska Mus 173,303, 173,308, with one ridge), *Härjedalen* (Hede, Nordiska Mus. 173,630; Älvros, E. u. according to R. Jirlow, with one ridge), *Jämtland* (Gåxsjö, E. u. 4268; Hotagen, according to Herr E. Granberg; Klövsjö, with two ridges, E. u. 4115; Marieby, E. u. 5422; Laxsjö, E. u. 865; Revsund, E. u. 4268), *Medelpad* (Borgsjö, E. u. 4268; Holm, E. u. according to Levi Johansson), *Ångermanland* (Bjurholm, E. u. 3307; Graninge, E. u. 4167, according to Dr. Manne Hofrén, with one ridge; Säbrå, according to Dr. Hofrén, with one ridge; Tåsjö, according to Dr. I. Arwidsson; Viksjö, according to Dr. Manne Hofrén), *Västerbotten* (according to Dr. R. Jirlow, common in the

---

[1] Sirelius, 1913 (a), p. 18.
[2] In the Pitt-Rivers Collection, Oxford, is preserved a model of a trough-sled from British Burma used to transport plants from the nursery to the field.
[3] Cf. Birket-Smith, 1929, 2, p. 166.
[4] Bogoras, 1904—09, p. 107.
[5] Cf. Hatt's basical research, 1916, p. 249.

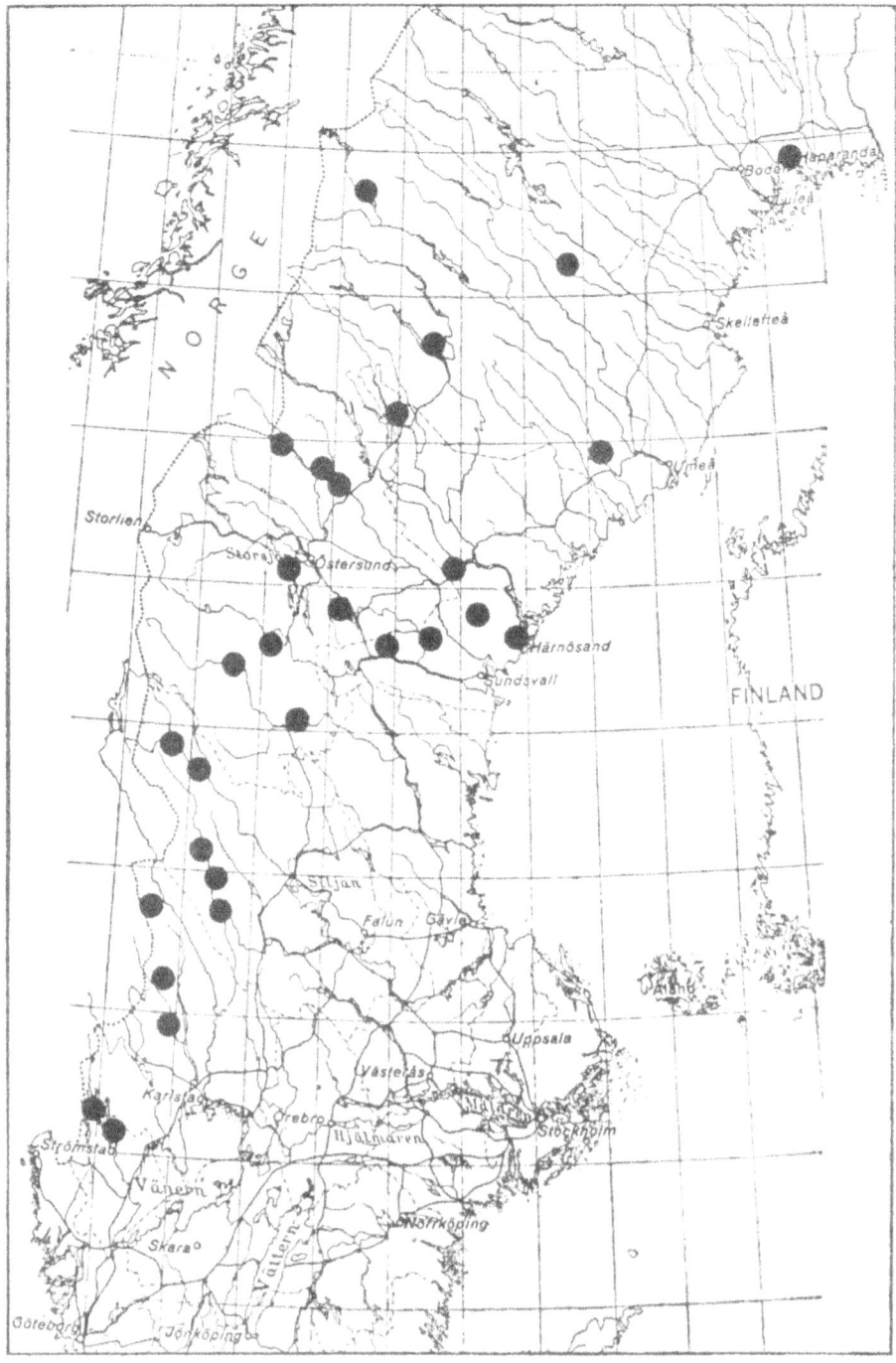

Fig. 9. The distribution of the guide-runner in Sweden.

province; Malå, E. u. 1110; Tärna and Vilhelmina, E. u. 645) and *Norrbotten* (according to Dr. G. Hallström is the guide-runner usual in Jokkmokk and Jukkasjärvi and eastwards; cf. Wiklund, 1926, p. 16).

From this brief summary, cf. map, Fig. 9, it appears that the guide-runner had a clearly defined expansion here in Sweden. Both types, the one having one ridge against which the vessel is placed and the other with two, one at the fore and one behind the vessel, seem to vary without exception throughout the whole of the area of its occurrence. Nowadays, the guide-runner seems to be intimately connected with the cask, but one can obviously presume this to be a later speciality. In order to judge the ethnological position of the guide-runner it is necessary to know something of its occurrence exterior to our country.

As far as I have been able to gather, it is used in all the western provinces of *Norway* from Finnmark in the North (cf. Hallström, 1926, p. 256). Thus it occurs in Nordland, Troms, N. and S. Tröndelag, Telemark, Buskerud and Hedmark. In most of these cases the runner is equipped with one ridge, but both from Finnmark and N. Tröndelag I am told there are some with two. From Vinje in S. Tröndelag I know of such a runner with a fore-end shaped like a ski. Further north, in addition to the transport of water, the implement is used for conveying the cooked cattle-food from the cottage to the cattle-shed. Dr. T. Itkonen has informed me that in *Finland*, the push-runner seems to be fairly common throughout the whole country (cf. Sirelius, 1913 (a), p. 21; Vilkuna, 1930, p. 6). It occurs also in *Russian* Carelia (Sirelius, 1913 (a), p. 13). To this expansion area must *Esthonia* be added, where it appears in the same identical form (Manninen, 1928 (a), p. 154; Rahvateaduslikud küsimuskavad 1931, p. 12; Leinbock, 1932, p. 34).

The geographical expansion of the guide-runner must of necessity be indicative of High Antiquity. It is out of the question to apprehend its expansion in Scandinavia as due to Finnish influence, as the implement occurs in provinces where no Finnish immigration took place during the years 1500—1700.[1] In several districts where Finnish influence is evincible in, for instance, certain parts of Hälsingland, south Dalarna and the mining districts of Västmanland, the guide-runner, on the other hand, is entirely absent. The conical-shaped summer-kitchen affords a parallel to some extent, which in a similar form appears in Jämtland. In olden times this kitchen-type, with variations, spread as far as Central Sweden. Sigurd Erixon is of opinion that this refers to a remote form of dwelling-place culture with prehistoric ancestry.[2] It may be that the guide-runner had a greater expansion in earlier times in North Europe, and that the base of its expansion, both as regards Scandinavia and East-Balticum—Finland is to be sought south of the Baltic Sea.

Wherever the push-runner originated, as to how it happened should not be difficult of apprehension. I. Ecsedi relates how the poor, in Hungary, push

---
[1] The author has maintained earlier his opinion to the contrary. Berg, 1925, p. 18. — Concerning Finnish dwellings in Sweden see Lönborg, 1907, with map, p. 83.

[2] Erixon, 1931 (a), p. 10, 1932 (b), p. 52.

their grain in a sack, before them, on a block of ice, over the frozen river.[1] Undoubtedly have all sleds and sledges in their proper sense obviously developed from such a primitive and indifferent primeval provenience.[2]

An implement very akin to the guide-runner is the simple runner on which in many parts of Sweden the plough was transported to the field. It is comprised quite simply of a piece of wood or a log which was bevelled at the front. The plough-share is placed in an indentation or a staple and steered along in an upright position, Pl. I: 5. Such sleds are known to me from Scania, Småland, Östergötland, Sörmland, Nerike, Dalsland, Bohuslän, Värmland, Västmanland, Uppland, Dalarna, Hälsingland and Ångermanland.[3] In the south of Sweden, other types, presumably from still remoter times have been common (cf. Chapters III and VI), and geographically they are associated with the occurrence in North Europe on the whole. The single-runner plough-sled is not confined to Sweden, however. It is known from Falster in Denmark[4] and it has also occurred in Latvia.[5]

There is a close connection between the guide-runner and the wooden-runner which is used on the islands of Hogland and Seitskär, in South Finland, for transporting boats for seal-hunting. This runner has a groove for the keel on the upper-side and an iron ring at the front to which the boat is attached.[6]

Lastly, it is not impossible that the well-known seal-shooting-runner used on the coastal districts of the Gulf of Bothnia has connections with the guide-runner. The implement resembles a very long ski with which the huntsman transports himself within gun-shot of the game. An iron-fork situated at the fore-end supports his gun, and usually a small white sail attached to the runner prevents him from being discovered by the seal.[7] Ernst Klein has associated this seal-shooting-runner with the guide-runner, but without any conclusions as to their genetical relationship.[8] Later on, Edvin Brännström, following an assumption of Gustav Hallström, endeavoured to trace it back to an implement which is supposed to have been used for hunting on land, and more especially

---

[1] Ecsedi, 1926, p. 144, 1934, p. 274 (illustration).

[2] Cf. how such an improvised sledge was used for amusement in London — according to an account from 1598, Herman, 1902, p. 219.

[3] Chiefly according to information in E. u.

[4] Grundtvig, 1909, p. 244.

[5] According to Professor Sigurd Erixon.

[6] Manninen, 1931—32, 1, pp. 83—84; Itkonen, 1923, pp. 25—26. — To shoe the keel of the boat with wood was on the other hand common in many parts in North Sweden (Högberg, 1926, p. 11; according to Dr. E. Klein), Norway (Ström, 1762, 1, p. 130), Finland (Rudenschöld, 1738—41, p. 23) and the Faroe Islands (Åkesson, 1911, p. 68) as well as in Esthonia (Manninen, 1931—32, 1, p. 82).

[7] Wiklund, 1928, p. 18, and see references. — Flor confuses this sail which is also used by the Samoyed, Eskimo etc., with real sails, Flor, 1930 (b), p. 147.

[8] Klein, 1929, pp. 143—144, 1930, pp. 146—147. Compare contrary opinion, Jirlow, 1930, pp. 94—95.

for wild-bird shooting.[1] Should this hypothesis prove to be correct the seal-shooting-runner may obviously be assigned to a great, though heterogenous, and in many respects closely related group of single-runner transport vehicles.

To this category belong of course such implements as the Lapp runner for the transport of tent-poles, Pl. II: 3, the runner mentioned in Chapter III which was used as a trailer for timber transport, the runner of the wheeled-sledge, Pl. XXIV: 2, etc.

A parallel to the single-runner sled which, probably to some extent is ethnologically referable to the same culture-group as the former, is the skin or hide sled.

Gudmund Hatt and U. T. Sirelius have drawn attention to a primitive sled met with amongst the Lapps which consists of reindeer or seal-hide by means of which the personal belongings were removed.[2] Hatt knows it from the Lapps of Västerbotten and Härjedalen. Here, it is covered with another hide and is trailed between two reindeer on the march, Fig. 10. In records from 1820, by the Rev. J. Nensén, the same vehicle from Lycksele, in the Lapp Territory, is mentioned as being used "in case of need, in the absence of sleds," sometimes drawn by reindeer, and sometimes by man-haulage, on skis.[3] Sirelius, quoting T. Itkonen, states that in Utsjoki, in Finnmark, in Norway, Lapps on skis trailed their belongings after them, in the whole hide of a seal.[4] There are accounts from Karasjok in the same province, of a similar sled of reindeer-hide.

According to Örjan Olsen the hide-sled is employed by the Soyot of the Sayan Mountains[5] and K. Birket-Smith has shewn that it is in use amongst several Eskimo tribes and North American Indians.[6] It is not unnatural therefore, that Fritz Flor, in his investigation, Haustiere und Hirtenkulturen, points to the skin-sled as one of the proofs that a product of a Samoyed culture formed a basis for further development throughout the whole of the North Eurasian area, and that this same Samoyed element was associated with a "proto-Eskimo" element.[7]

Side by side with this North Eurasian expansion we meet with a sporadic skin-sled further south. Ragnar Jirlow writes that on Holmön in south Västerbotten — in a district where Lapps are supposed never to have settled[8] —

---

[1] Brännström, 1934, pp. 282—284.
[2] Hatt, 1913, p. 139; Sirelius, 1913 (a), p. 1.
[3] Nensén's records, p. 302, Uppsala University Library; Drake, 1918, pp. 81, 83.
[4] Cf. Paulaharju, 1927, p. 160.
[5] Olsen, 1915, p. 71.
[6] Birket-Smith, 1929, 2, p. 71, 163 and Tab. B. 32.
[7] Flor, 1930 (b), especially p. 88.
[8] Wiklund, 1914, p. 10.

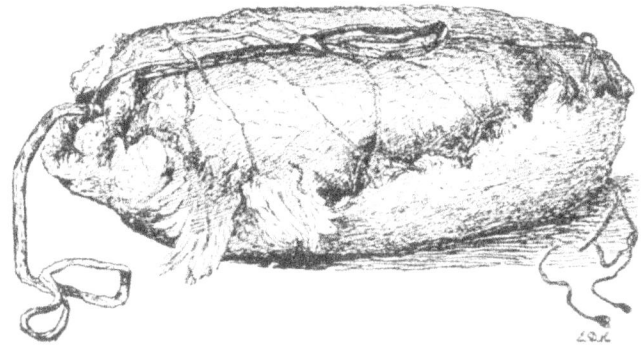

Fig. 10. The skin-sledge of the Västerbotten Lapps. After G. Hatt.

a sled of seal-skin was used to take up the hay from the marshes in olden times.[1] In the 16th century Olaus Magnus wrote from Sweden that "an elderly man who wishes to be conveyed down a steep mountain-side or hill, must seat himself on a bear-skin and be trailed along by the aid of his sons and serfs." On the accompanying illustration, which is wrongly delineated, in that the hair is portrayed as being upwards, the equipage is drawn by a horse.[2] There is no known analogy to this in our country, but in a recent publication from Jutland, in Denmark, is stated how in olden times it was usual to drive to the mills and the town on the hide of a horse, in severe winters, which was harnessed to the tractor.[3] In Germany, the condemned prisoner was dragged to the place of execution on a cow or swine-hide concerning which custom Karl von Amira has given accounts, dating from the 14th century to 1817.[4] There are many analogies in this connection, and the employment of such an old primitive vehicle undoubtedly serves as an extreme expression of contempt for the doomed one.[5] From Noricum, the Austrian Alpine Countries, there is a reproduction by Agricola, 1556, shewing how ore was trailed down the mountain-side in sleds of skin.[6] That the skin sled is not foreign to Asiatic sub-arctic regions

---

[1] Jirlow, 1931, p. 94.

[2] O. Magnus, 1555, I, p. 199. Professor G. Thörnell, Uppsala, has kindly informed me that the accounts appear to him, judging from "the contents as well as the wording, to be Olai Magni own."

[3] Hansen, Sprog og Kultur, 1932, p. 30.

[4] v. Amira, 1926, pp. 226—227.

[5] Cf. for example, Liebe, 1924, pp. 17, 83, 104 — Jews were dragged simply, or trailed on a board to the place of execution, 1694, 1475, 1642; cf. Grimm, 1854, p. 262; Heinemann, 1900, p. 107, Jena, about 1700; Hartley Elliot, 1928 (a), p. 55. — Woman with "breasts of stone" was dragged on a sledge; — as far as I understand the authoresses have misapprehended the illustration; New English Dictionary, under Sledge, — note, 1651—1828 on the sledge for transport of the delinquent to the place of execution; Schweiz. Idiotikon, under Schleiff, pp. 133, 134, 138, 147, Schlitte, pp. 767, 775. — Possibly the tendency to use simple and primitive vehicles in this connection may be explained in that these were tabooed and must be destroyed after the execution. On the other hand, to share v. Amira's opinion that the custom with skin-sledges in this connection was cultic, appears to be impossible.

[6] Agricola, 1556, p. 168.

is to be gathered from a reproduction by P. S. Pallas, shewing how a little boy trails charcoal into a Kalmuck tent, by means of such an implement.[1]

Here should undoubtedly be included Strabo's statement that the inhabitants of Caucasus went down the mountain sides "with their belongings lying on the hides of animals." Strabo also met with the custom amongst the Medes and Armenians (Strabo, XI, 5, 6).[2] I think the manner of movement indicated here must have been sliding. O. Herman tells that in his youth, about 1840, gypsy boys in the Hungarian towns, choosing a suitable incline, "just threw themselves on their dirty sheep-skin coats and slid at a good speed right down into the valley."[3] This particular custom cannot be isolated from sliding on implements of another kind. Seen apart from the toboggan of later times, examples are not unusual and are met with in divers and far distant places. I can mention sliding which has occurred in Sweden on stone, or on a piece of wood simply. It took place in the various south Swedish country-sides.[4] As a game it was known on the Faroe Islands[5] and in Switzerland[6] and France. Plutarch relates how the Teutons (Cimbri) during fights in the North of Italy, slid down the heights on their shields (Marius, XXIII). During the 19th century tobogganing became the fashion in the higher classes of society especially, to begin with, in Russia. In itself the sliding idea is not very far to seek and is excellently exemplified in the Hawaiian single-runner sleds, on which one slid down the mountain-sides at places made for the purpose.[7] Worthy of note is the way the idea is made use of, for practical purposes, at the gold-mines in Salzburg. The single-runner wooden sled is freighted with leather sacks of ore. The one in charge of the transport sits on the sled. Examples are to be found in Sammlung für deutsche Volkskunde, Berlin and, with more inventive brakes, in the Museum für Volkskunde, Vienna.

Obviously a culture-element so primitive and simple in character as the skin-sled need not necessarily be considered as genetically connected throughout the whole of its expansion area. Already has been indicated that the hide on occasions is nothing more than an incidental material which can be easily replaced by a stone or a piece of wood etc. It is told by Ragnar Jirlow that in Nordmaling, Ångermanland, a sled of bark was used for the same purpose as

---

[1] Pallas, 1776, Pl. 5.   [2] Cf. Markwart, 1930, p. 84.
[3] Herman, 1902, p. 227.
[4] For instance Bohuslän, Sarauw-Alin, 1923, p. 227; Östergötland, according to Dr. Sigurd Erixon: on the mountain "Skråhalla," in Söderköping; Småland, Ödman, 1830, p. 86 — on the Kase stone at Växjö; Göth, 1931, p. 156, and Gotland, according to Carl Franzén — on "Skoldrebacke" in Rute; also in Fardhem.
[5] Svabo, 1781—82, p. 134.
[6] Friedli, 2, p. 88, Rütimeyer, 1924, pp. 377—382. — Rütimeyer views the sliding on stones as belonging to magic cult.
[7] Arning, 1887, p. 125; 1931, p. 60; cf. Bogeng, 1926, p. 46.

PLATE I

1. Water-transport with guide-runner. Tasjö, Jämtland. Photog. I. Arwidsson.

2. Guide-runner. Östmark, Värmland. Drawing by N. Keyland.

3. Guide-runner. Idre, Dalarna. Nordiska Mus. 173,308

4. Guide-runner. Idre, Dalarna. Nordiska Mus. 173,308

5. Plough-runner. Folkärna, Dalarna. Nordiska Mus. 177,211.

PLATE II

1. Hollowed-out trunk-sledge. From Pajala, Lappland. Photog. B. Laqvist.

2. Hollowed-out trunk-sledge from Lapps in Frostviken, Jämtland. Nordiska Mus. 79,894.

3. Runner for transporting tent-poles. From Lapps in Arjeplog. Nordiska Mus. 192,564.

the above mentioned Västerbotten skin-sled. At Björkö in Österbotten, Finland, according to the same author, the implement was comprised of pieces of wood nailed together.[1] This method should be compared with the employment of boughs, which are used on marshy land to bring up the hay. I am familiar with this method from Kråkshult in Småland[2] and from Gotland.[3]

The bough as an implement of transport is known also exterior to Sweden, and is common in many places, Pl. III: 2. In *Norway*, there are evidences from Nordland, Sörtröndelag, Möre, Sogn-Fjordane, Buskerud and Hedmark. From Bjerkreim in Rogaland there is a joinered raft-like sled which seems to resemble the one from Västerbotten. It is said that in Dalsfjord in Möre, when cattle got hurt in the mountains they could be trailed home on such a slide-car-like sled (according to enquiries). It is further known to me from *Finland* (Grotenfelt, 1899, p. 263; Sirelius, 1919—21, 1, p. 383; Aaltonen, 1931, p. 62), *Esthonia* (Leinbock, 1932, p. 33), *Switzerland* (Stebler, 1903, p. 304; cf. Schweizer Idiotikon under Schleiff, p. 131; trailing of hay down mountain slopes, without platform), *Austria* (Haberlandt, 1929, p. 2, trailing down mountain-slopes) and *Hungary* (Ferencz, 1909, trailing on even ground).

For the moment I would not dare to give any definite opinion as to what connection these forms might have with the skin-sled. It would not seem unreasonable to believe that both forms, that is to say, the skin-sled and the bough-sled are variations of one and the same natural transport-method.

Gudmund Hatt has indicated how the origin of the skin-sled may be explained, if one takes into consideration other and still simpler methods of transport which came into use in about the same district. Should a reindeer die during the autumn migration of the Lapps, the body is cut open, the inside removed, and the former sewn together again. A trace is fastened through the nostrils and the deer is trailed last in the row on the march.[4] Almost a parallel is met with amongst the Northern peasants in Voss, Norway. In this instance, the fallen wild reindeer are allowed to remain after the internals have been removed till an opportunity occurs, when they are then trailed home on the snow.[5] Occasionally one meets with this method in Sweden today, on the elk-hunt,[6] and animals which have met with a natural or accidental death are often trailed home directly on the ground.[7] Even in connection with the transport of fish, on Gotland, has something similar occurred.[8]

Most common, however, is the trailing of the seal on the ice when the hunt

---

[1] Jirlow, 1931, p. 94.
[2] E. u. 5573.
[3] Säve, 1891, p. 45; cf. Rietz, 1867, p. 756 ("Trysa").
[4] Hatt, 1913, p. 139.
[5] According to Dr. Nils Lid; cf. Lid, 1930, p. 152. According to enquiries the same method occurred at Ringebu in Buskerud.
[6] According to Herr Adolf Rencke (Värmland).
[7] E. u. 240, Sjösås, Småland.
[8] Säve, 1892, p. 104.

is over as, for instance, in Gotland,[1] Runö in Esthonia,[2] Pl. III: 1, in Västerbotten[3] and Norrbotten.[4] Nowadays the seal is generally transported on a light kind of sled. A. G. Schrenk says that the Samoyed bundles the seal-skins and blubber together, and trails them along on the ice to the shore.[5] Amongst the Chukchee the dogs or the huntsman himself trails the seal home in the same way,[6] and many of the Eskimoes act in like manner.[7]

It is then to this sphere of culture that the skin-sled belongs, and with absolute certainty it should be ascribed to exceedingly remote times.[8] It may be, as the geographical occurrence in North America especially seems to indicate, as old as the snow-shoe. That it had a greater expansion earlier in our part of the world and was taken up by the Lapps from an older culture is probable.

Thus it is seen that the single-runner sled and the skin-sled may both be assigned to a prehistoric culture-element within the circumpolar regions. Evidence of their occurrence leaves much still to be desired as far as Europe and Asia are concerned and this scarcity of research-material renders it impossible to come to any safe and definite conclusions as to their mutual relationship and as regards other primitive transport implements. The main object here has been to draw attention to these forms as a group of implements which, probably before the more general expansion of the simple-runner sledge and the built-up sledge, may have served to fill a human need.

---

[1] Säve, 1867, pp. 51—52.
[2] Klein, 1924, p. 243; E. Klein and J. Österman, 1927, p. 73; cf. Manninen, 1931—32, p. 84.
[3] Jirlow, 1930, p. 83.
[4] Dahlbäck, 1926, p. 32; cf. from Norrland's coastal districts, Ekman, 1910, p. 239.
[5] Schrenk, 1848—54, 2, p. 414.
[6] Nordenskiöld, 1880—81, 2, p. 102; Bogoras, 1904—09, Pl. 10: 2.
[7] Stefansson, 1923, p. 208.
[8] Cf. Birket-Smith, 1929, 2, p. 163.

CHAPTER II

THE BUILT-UP SLEDGE

The built-up sledge differs from the simple runner-sledge in that, as regards the former, the freight lies elevated above the plane of the runner. This can be brought about in many ways, but most common is the raising of the platform by means of mortised supports or posts. This method appears to be very ancient, and is met with as the leading type in the oldest archeological finds of sledges, made not only in our country, but in Northern Europe on the whole.

Not a few ancient finds of sledge-parts have been made in Sweden and Finland, but these are almost exclusively runners. As no survey of this material has ever yet been published, either as regards Finland, it should not be considered out of place to treat the subject at some considerable length here.[1] To begin with is deserving of note, how these finds from prehistoric time, of easily perishable pieces of wood, have been rendered possible, by nature's own peculiar conditions and the preserving influence of humus-acids. Undoubtedly have peat-bogs played the same part in Northern Archeology as, for instance, have the dry sandy tracts in the Further Orient, Central Asia and parts of America. As concerns our part of the world, at least, may be added, that very significant means of dating known as the pollen-analytic method, which is based on the variations of the vegetable world itself and was worked out thanks to the penetrating judgment and circumspection of (especially) Lennart von Post. This method has made a comparatively accurate dating possible in numerous cases, and cautiously used, as it has been, has already rendered valuable aid to ethnological deductions.[2] Evident is it, however, that new finds render a necessary control possible and bring about a deeper knowledge of treated subject. New material comes along which, together with archeology's enlarged territory in general, is likely to throw new light also over the earliest history of the sledge.

In 1926 a find of various kinds of wood-objects was included within the

---

[1] A brief preliminary survey has already been published by the author, Berg 1933 (b).
[2] There is a brief survey of pollen-analysis, its aims and methods, by von Post, in Eberts Reallexikon, under Pollenanalyse. Cf. Godwin, 1934.

collections of Statens Historiska Museum, Stockholm. Amongst these was a unique broad sledge-runner, Fig. 11. The find was made at Gråträsk in Piteå, Norrbotten, but nothing further seems to be known concerning it, other than that it was discovered in a bog where the Tjeutjer stream flows into the lake of the same name.[1] A pollen-analytical examination has given the result that this runner dates back to the end of the Stone Age or the early part of the Bronze Age. It is younger than the Ragunda (Chap. I) but older than any other such Swedish bog find which has been investigated.[2] The runner has been very long. In its present condition it consists of three fragments, of which two could be put together. The length of these is about 150 cm., whilst the third part measures something like 90 cm. Its widest part is 21 cm. The under-side is plane and along the upper, runs a groove with a parallel ridge on either side, where pairs of holes are cut, some vertical and others having connection with the groove. Every fourth pair is of the vertical kind. Judging from Finnish parallels, the preserved end-piece should comprise the rear end of the sledge-runner. It contains two larger and coarser square holes, whilst two of lesser size penetrate the runner almost at the point, and shew a hollow on the under-side where, rope, or trace has laid embedded. The whole runner comprises a very thin board which as a rule is no thicker than 2·5—3 cm.

This Gråträsk runner, solitary hitherto of its kind amongst Swedish finds, has numerous Finnish analogies which enable a more conclusive opinion on the construction of sledges belonging to this category, and which should offer certain indications as to their position in general culture-history. U. T. Sirelius and T. Itkonen have published these Finnish finds in the form of smaller investigations, but as the material is so very diffused, it appears necessary to tabulate them in some way here.

The following are sledge-runners of the Gråträsk type which are known to me from Finland:
Kuortane, Österbotten: An almost complete runner 317·5 cm. long, in outward appearance

---

[1] Vitterhetsakademien, 1926, pp. x, xlix.
[2] The pollen-consistence in % on some of the Swedish runners, in order of date:

	Picea	Pinus	Betula	Alnus	Oak-mixed wood	Corylus
Ragunda	—	61·5	36	2·5	—	2
Gråträsk	1·5	71	26	1·5	—	—
Delsbo	17	32	46	4	1	—
Siksele, Lycksele	23	57	18	2	—	—
Storholmen, Stensele	19	54	26	1	—	1
Botesflon, Hammerdal	36·5	48	12	3·5	—	—
Malgonäset, Vilhelmina	25	68	7	—	—	—
Morjärv, Nederkalix	29·5	42	24·5	4	—	—
Rysjön, Björna	11	59·5	27	2·5	—	—

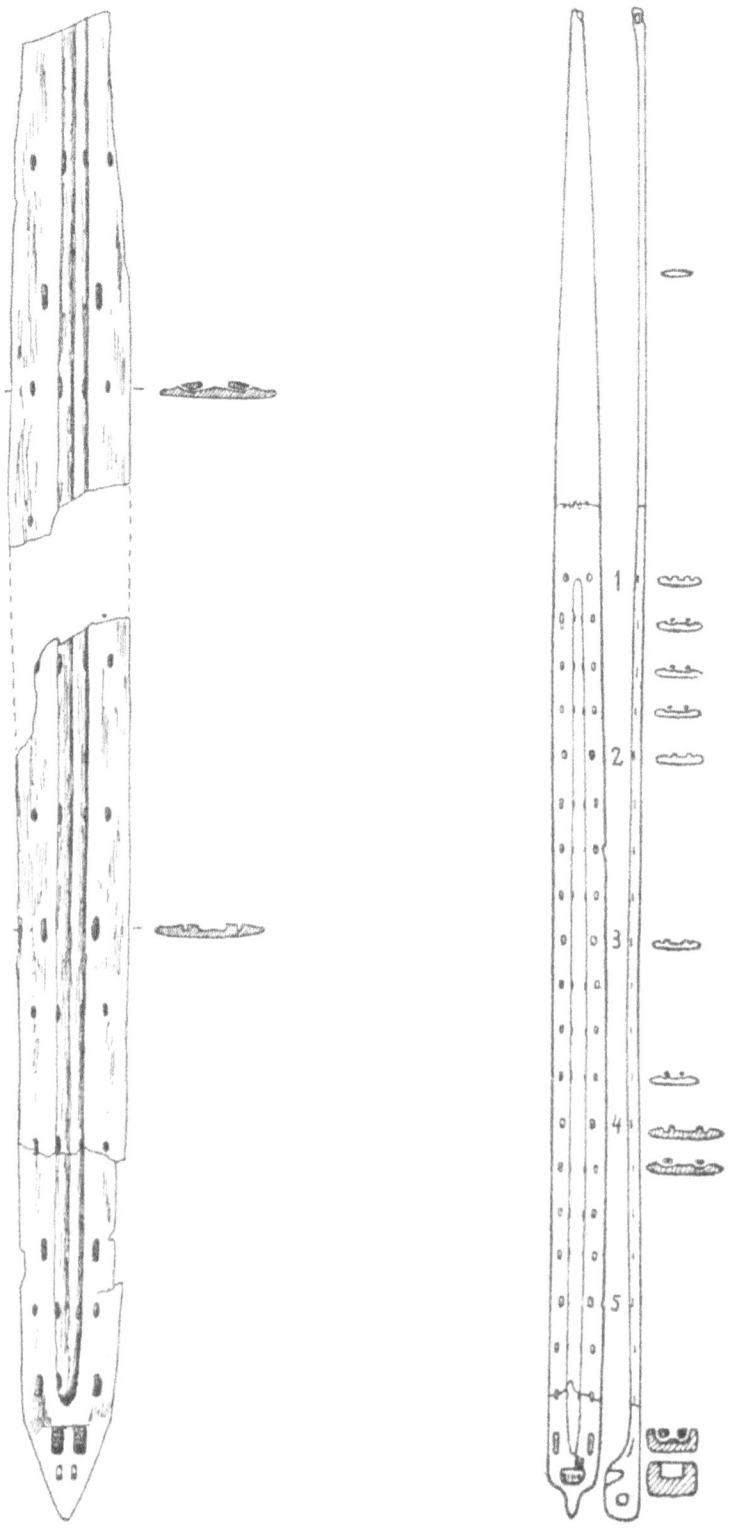

Fig. 11. Sledge-runner. Bog-find from Gråträsk, Piteå, Norrbotten.

Fig. 12. Sledge-runner. Bog-find from Kuortane, Finland. After T. Itkonen.

closely resembling the Gråträsk runner, Fig. 12. Its greatest width is a little more than 12 cm. and it is 2—2·5 cm. thick. National Museum, Helsingfors (Itkonen, 1931—32, pp. 59—61).

Ylistaro, Österbotten: Fragment of a runner (rear-end) of the construction with the central groove, National Museum, Helsingfors (Sirelius, 1913 (a), p. 14).

Evijärvi, Österbotten: An almost complete runner, 290 cm. long, of the construction with the central groove. Greatest width 11 cm., thickness, 2—3·5 cm. Österbottens Historiska Museum, Vasa (Itkonen, 1931—32, p. 61).

Pihtipudas, Tavastland: Fragment of a runner (rear-end). In construction it differs from the foregoing, in that, on the upper-side one meets with a ridge in place of the central groove, through which run horizontal holes corresponding to those in the other type which ended in the central groove. National Museum, Helsingfors (Sirelius, 1913 (a), p. 18).

Saarijärvi, Tavastland: Fragment of a runner (rear-end) of the same construction as the Pihtipudas. National Museum, Helsingfors (Sirelius, 1916, pp. 15—17).

Rautalampi, Savolaks: Fragment of runner (rear-end) of the Kuortane type. It is 76·5 cm. long and 8·7 cm. wide. Two pairs of post-holes are in preservation. Kuopio Museum (Itkonen, 1935).

Rantasalmi, Savolaks: Fragment of a runner (rear end) of the construction with the central groove. National Museum, Helsingfors (Sirelius, 1913 (a), p. 15).

Kiuruvesi, Savolaks: An almost complete runner, 412 cm. long, closely related to the Kuortane and Gråträsk runners. Its greatest width is nearly 12 cm. and it is about 3 cm. thick. The runner appears to be little, or scarcely at all used. National Museum, Helsingfors (Itkonen, 1930, p. 86).

In the National Museum, Helsingfors there is a preserved find with a central ridge. Its place of discovery is unknown. See Itkonen, 1930, p. 85.

Sirelius has stated, in connection with an investigation made in compliance with the request of the Finnish botanist, Harald Lindberg, that the above mentioned runner from Ylistaro should be dated to early Litorina time.[1] Several foreign scholars have inclined towards this opinion amongst whom may be mentioned Oswald Menghin and Fritz Flor who came to far-reaching conclusions due to this statement.[2] However, the investigations made were worked out in diatomacé calculation, and should be found unsatisfactory. In any case they admit of no assumption of such High Antiquity.[3]

A pollen-analytic investigation has lately been made of the Kuortane runner which afterwards was dated by Leo Aario to about 3,500 B. C. The dating, however, is due to Väinö Auer's theory as to the time when the fir migrated to Österbotten and one can probably be inclined to believe that the runner is somewhat younger.[4]

Sirelius has drawn wide conclusions on the probable assumption that the Ylistaro runner is built of cembra (pinus cembra), which tree, in our days, occurs no further west than north-east Russia.[5] It is not unknown, that other objects made of this wood, in Finland, are preserved from pre-historic time, namely two spoons, which most probably date from the Stone Age.[6] However, the

---
[1] Sirelius, 1916, p. 15.
[2] Menghin, 1931, p. 239; Flor, 1930, p. 52.
[3] According to Dr. Erik Granlund, Stockholm.
[4] Aario, 1933.   [5] Sirelius, 1916, pp. 16—18.
[6] Ailio, 1912, pp. 268, 277. Europaeus, 1929, pp. 83—84.

Fig. 13. Sledge-post from the find at Gorbunowa, Russia. Sketch by D. Eding.

cembra pine should have expanded much further west, far earlier, and therefore it is not possible with certainty to judge from the material itself as to its origin in the Ural-districts.[1]

Besides the foregoing Finnish finds, just lately, there has been a Russian find of essentially the same type as the Gråträsk runner. This find was made between the years 1926—1928, in Gorbunowa, a place situated west of Tobolsk, between Jekaterinenburg(Sverdlovsk) and Tjumen. The Gorbunowa runner belongs to the group with the central groove and is 240 cm. long in its present fragmentary condition. Both ends are obviously missing, at least, one can say they are in a mutilated state.[2] It is worthy of note that here also have been preserved objects of wood which the excavator, Dr. D. Eding, assumes to be sledge-posts, Fig. 13. These pieces of wood are not less than 52·5 cm. long and one could feel inclined to doubt, as to whether in reality sledges, with such thin runners, could have been raised to such a height.[3] But surely Eding is right. Other finds in Gorbunowa give Eding reason enough to assign the objects to the Stone Age, or to the early part of the Bronze Age.[4]

The investigations made by Sirelius have opened the way for a better understanding as to how these sledge-runners should be reconstructed in order to

---

[1] Map after A. Bode, Suomen Suku, 1, 1928, p. 145.
[2] Eding, 1929, p. 9; cf. Itkonen, 1931—32, p. 62.
[3] I am indebted to Dr. Eding who kindly gave me this information. Letter, 24.V. 1932.
[4] Eding, 1929.

give an idea of the sledge when complete.[1] Itkonen has also treated the problem and at several important points has corrected Sirelius' representation. Itkonen has sketched a reconstruction shewing his idea of the Kuortane runner in reality, Fig. 14.[2] So much is evident, that double rows of posts had been inserted into the vertical holes in the upper-side of the runner, and these had been strengthened by lashings of some kind, which were threaded through the intervening three holes. The rear-end posts had been still more firmly attached to the runner. The fore-ends had been very turned up and lashed to the foremost pair of posts. The pairs of posts must have been held together lengthwise, by means of side-rails, into which they were mortised.

It seems to me that the posts in Itkonen's reconstruction are quite too low and the Gorbunowa find would appear to confirm this opinion. Their form should be pictured in accordance with the find, that is to say, thicker in diameter than the holes themselves, but as being mortised into these. The long front ends of the runners devoid of posts then take on a more natural aspect, and one inclines to the idea of their having been considerably more upturned, even perhaps to the extent of curving backwards. We have no details whatever as to the appearance of the platform, but that can be thought of in many ways. Most appropriate would be an association with North Asiatic sledges of later time. It may have been constructed at a lower level than the upper side-rails, like, for instance, those newer forms of the Ostyak, Vogul, Zyryan and Lamut.[3]

The Gråträsk sledge has undoubtedly been of the Finnish and Russian type. It were impossible to isolate it from that culture which is marked by foreign finds. When it comes to the point of having to judge as to which this culture has been — in spite of the very faulty indications in connection with the dating — a certain degree of probability should speak for an association of the type with the comb-ceramic Stone Age culture. This question coheres, however, with the draught-problem of the vehicle.

Sirelius adopted the idea and, in my opinion, rightly, that such large sledges as these were not meant for man-haulage; instead he assumed that they were drawn by reindeer. This hypothesis formed one of the main supports of his opinion that the tame deer was a domestic animal, in Finland, already in the Stone Age.[4] When he, however, also considered them as being too large to be dog-sledges, Kai Donner came forward with the assertion that larger

---

[1] Sirelius, 1913 (a).
[2] Itkonen, 1931—1932.
[3] See Manninen for illustrations, 1934, pp. 226—229.
[4] Sirelius, 1916, p. 18.

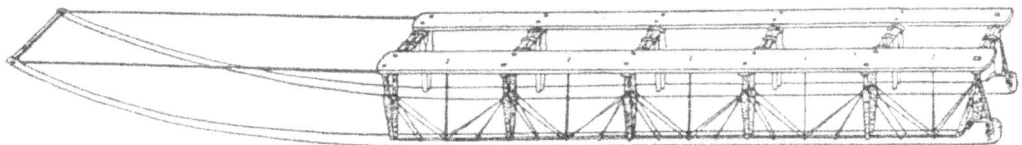

Fig. 14. Reconstruction of a sledge of the Gråträsk-type. After T. Itkonen.

vehicles of a similar kind were brought into use amongst the Eskimos.[1] Donner essayed on other grounds also, to prove that the dog in historic times had been the most important draught-animal in the Ural district, and Sirelius conceded later that his own hypothesis was uncertain.[2]

It would seem probable that Donner is right in his presumption that sledges of the Gråträsk type were drawn by dogs, or may be, by dog and man together. The illustrated dog-span as met with, for instance, in north-east Asia and amongst the Eskimos, is a demonstration of a secondary development. Under primitive living-conditions it should have been no easy matter to provide food for a lot of draught-dogs. The harness arrangements on these foregoing sledges afford little guidance. But it should be pointed out that scarcely is conceivable any other kind than that corresponding to the hauling-line used on the Siberian dog-sledge, which is attached to the runner behind the upturned ends, or the fan-like form of harness which is fastened to a curved attachment at the front.[3]

The domestic dog is known from bone-finds in the Mullerup-culture[4] and Oswald Menghin presumes that it is only by chance that it has not been met with in the Kunda-culture.[5] There is nothing to prove here, however, that the dog was used as draught-animal. In a valuable investigation from an archeological standpoint, O. F. Gandert has reviewed finds of tame dogs and sought to associate the dog as draught-animal in the comb-ceramic culture.[6] It is of interest in this connection that amongst the exceedingly scanty osteological material found within the comb-ceramic zone, there is a Finnish find from Pihtipudas.[7]

The comb-ceramic culture, especially in Finland, appears to us as a hunting and fishing culture, which had its settlements in the coastal-districts, and on the shores of inland seas and water-courses.[8] It must be remembered that hunting expeditions took place in winter-time, far away from home, a form of

---

[1] Donner, 1927, pp. 144; cf. Birket-Smith, 1929, 1, p. 176.
[2] Sirelius, 1928, p. 953.
[3] See Martin for instance, 1897, Pl. 16: 1—2.
[4] Nordman, 1927, p. 16.   [5] Menghin, 1931, p. 231
[6] Gandert, 1930.   [7] Gandert, 1930, p. 66.
[8] Europaeus-Äyräpää, 1930, p. 169.

sustenance which is known also to us from later times, in Northern Finland. It would not seem unlikely that these sledges were used just in this connection. There can have been no question of trade, to speak of. On the other hand, it must be emphasized that apart from summer communication by boat, the sledge, combined with the ski, had a great part to play, and in this sphere of culture rendered possible a means of livelihood, also in winter-time.[1]

There are good reasons for assuming that it was the draught-dog and sledge which were instrumental in bringing about that enormous expansion, which the comb-ceramic culture has to shew. J. Ailio has already expressed his opinion that such is the case. In his remarkable Work "Fragen der russischen Steinzeit" he has just drawn attention to the great importance of intercommunication in this connection.[2] "The means of communication of the Stone Age is a question which, with absolute certainty, needs special investigation, before one can understand the widely-stretched association of culture in connection with communication, already treated."

The relationship of this type of sledge to the comb-ceramic culture explains its wide distribution from Norrbotten in the west, to the Urals in the east.[3] As regards the Swedish find, there should be no cause for surprise, though no find of the essential "Leitfossil," the comb-ceramic, has hitherto come to light in our land. The sparseness of the appearance of ceramic in North Sweden on the whole is, in this connection, a matter of great consideration. There are sundry imported pieces, of Eastern character, from the later Stone Age in upper Norrland[4] and recently, I have tried to shew that a find of a pair of skis, together with a stick from Burträsk, in Västerbotten, evinces this same Easterly character.[5]

In addition to the foregoing Finnish runner finds, there are three which are of an essentially different type. They were made in Alavuus, Jalasjärvi and Saarijärvi, in the south of Österbotten. These runners, like those recently investigated, have two parallel rows of vertical holes, but they are plane on the upper-side and void of trace of any sort of lashing for strengthening the posts. The post-holes are instead, much closer. In the fragmentary Alavuus runner, which is now 130 cm. long, there are seven pairs. The runners are rather thin. They only measure about 3 cm.[6]

On the request of Sirelius, Lindberg made a botanic-palaeontologic inves-

---

[1] Cf. Berg, 1933 (a).   [2] Ailio, 1922, p. 69.
[3] Cf. v. Richthofen, 1932, p. 116: "the culture area of the pit and comb ceramic stretches from the district of the Oder to Siberia and from Ukraine to Finland and the most northern parts of East Norway."
[4] Hallström, 1929, p. 51.   [5] Berg, 1933 (a), pp. 144—146.
[6] Sirelius, 1913 (a), p. 23, 1916, pp. 14—15; Itkonen, 1935.

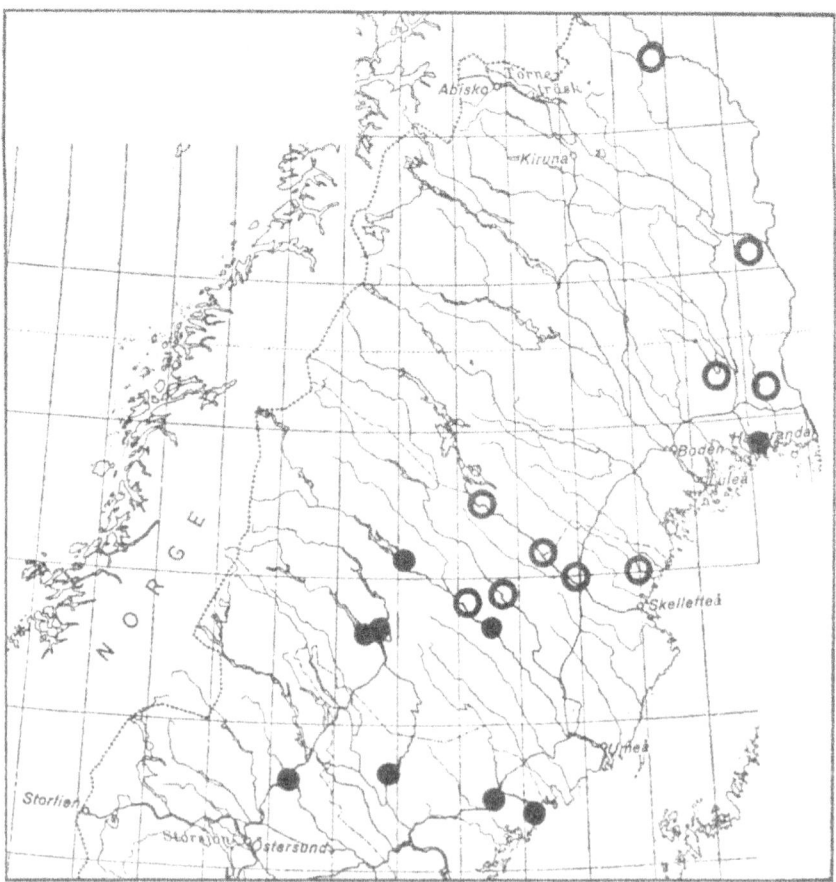

Fig. 15. The distribution of the younger sledge-runner in Swedish bog-finds. The open circles are finds of skis of the Bothnian type (after a map by A. Zettersten).

tigation of the above mentioned Saarijärvi runner, but with no other positive result than that the object was of High Antiquity.[1] After treating the timber, Sakari Pälsi and Sirelius too, decided that it had been hewn with a stone axe,[2] but this opinion has been rejected by several, and Itkonen also, considers it to be insufficiently supported.[3]

In spite of the fact that the posts on the Alavuus, Jalasjärvi and Saarijärvi runners are perpendicularly erected, it were impossible, with Sirelius, not to couple them with the Yurak-Samoyed sledge on which, as is known, the posts slope backwards, whereupon they are concentrated to the back part of the sledge.[4] In such case the Samoyed sledge may undoubtedly be considered

---

[1] Sirelius, 1916, p. 15.   [2] Sirelius, 1916, p. 18; Pälsi, 1916, p. 48.
[3] Ailio, 1917, p. 37; Itkonen, 1930, p. 89.
[4] See Lehtisalo, 1932, pp. 68—180, for Samoyed sledge. — According to Rytkönen, 1931, p. 109, it still occurs in Finland that "all or at least the foremost posts are placed in a backward sloping direction."

as a secondary development which brings the merits of the type, as far as flexibility and elasticity go, into their proper light. In all probability, this may have reference to its usage on naked ground.

All these sledges have once been equipped with pairs of posts. There are however, amongst the bog-finds, numerous runners with single posts having the same construction as those of our day. As a rule, these are smaller in size. One exception, is formed by two Finnish runners found, the one in Rantasalmi, Savolaks and the other in Viikinäis in Heinola, Tavastland. The Rantasalmi runner is in two pieces and these are happily in a complete state of preservation. It is 222 cm. long, and a somewhat deep groove runs along the greater part of the upper-side. In the groove are obvious marks of the wear and tear of the posts, which have been nine in number. They were lashed to the runner through vertical holes piercing the sides of the groove.[1] The Viikinäis-runner is still longer. It measures 246 cm. Toivo Itkonen considers it to be of greater age than the Rantasalmi runner.[2]

In the year 1911 a find of the fore-part of a runner was made in Morjärv, Nederkalix, Norrbotten. It was of quite a different type.[3] In its preserved condition it measures 186 cm., whilst it is not more than 8·5 cm. wide, Fig. 18. It is made of resinous pine-wood.[4] In the upper-side of the runner are two holes, both rectangular and vertical, the foremost is carved in the thickest part, whilst the one behind has two smaller holes, one on either side, which are pierced through to the central hole. Besides these, at the front-end there are one greater and two smaller, which are pierced quite through and each is rectangular. The under-side of the runner is convex. As the tract is little known from the "history of forests" point of view a pollen-analytic examination has only given the result that the runner belongs to "a comparatively late time, probably to historic time."[5]

In the find from Glommersträsk in Arvidsjaur, Norrbotten, which contained amongst other things a ski of Bothnian type, was included also the front-end of a sledge-runner, with a similar hole to that on the Morjärv runner. The end is scooped out on either side, so that it has acquired the appearance of a knob.[6]

---

[1] Sirelius, 1913 (a), p. 25, 1928, p. 951.
[2] Itkonen, 1935.
[3] The find was discovered by Herr A. Ekholm and was handed over to the Nordiska Museet by Dr. G. Ekholm.
[4] According to Dr. Carl Malmsten, Stockholm.
[5] According to Dr. E. Granlund.
[6] Cf. p. 23 and Berg, 1934.

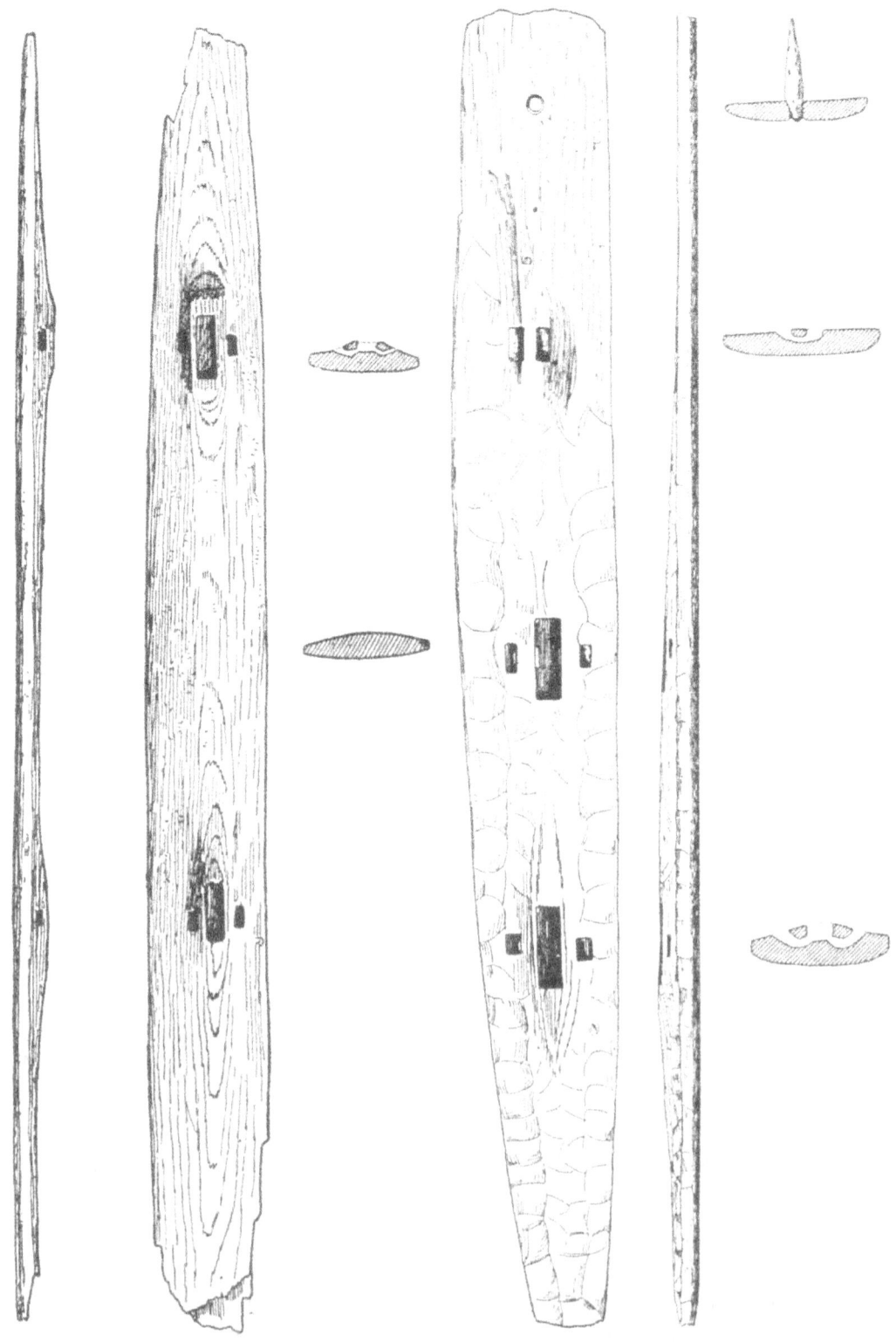

Fig. 16. Sledge-runner. Bog-find from Grundsunda, Ångermanland.

Fig. 17. Sledge-runner. Bog-find from Lycksele, Lappland.

A similar find was made in 1932 in Siksele, Lycksele, Västerbotten, and is preserved in the Historiska Museet. The runner, which is about 100 cm. long and 12·3 cm. at its widest part, has two holes of the kind we met with on either side of the latter hole on the Morjärv runner, Fig. 17. There is also a hole at the front-(?)end with a ridge, and a smaller round hole, into which a small round peg, also included in the find, seems to fit. According to the pollen-analytic investigation, the find should be assigned to the Late Bronze Age or Early Iron Age. "The most probable should be, one of the centuries before the Birth of Christ."

In 1923, on Storholmen in Storuman, Stensele, Västerbotten, the fragment of a runner illustrated by Fig. 19, was found. It belongs to this group and measures 155·5 cm. long. There is a hole resembling the foremost hole on the Morjärv runner, and at the front end is a rectangular hole pierced through, and some smaller ones. Pollen-analysis indicates a time corresponding to that of the Malgonäs runner which will be dealt with in the next paragraph and may with a certain amount of reservation be considered as prehistoric (Historiska museet).

The runner from Malgonäset, Vilhelmina, Västerbotten, was discovered in 1928 and is now in the Historiska Museet. It is not less than 247 cm. long, although the rear-end, at least, appears to be missing. The width, which is 7 cm. is, if possible, still less than that of all other runners in this group. There are two holes with raised edges, and at the front end is a vertical hole pierced through a thickened part, which hole should be compared with the foremost on the Siksele runner. Fig. 22 gives an illustration, and the pollen-analytic examination dates it to the same time as the foregoing.

A find of another runner was made in Vilhelmina in the year 1913, which was not taken care of before 1931, when it was included within the Nordiska Museet's collections, Fig. 24. This runner which, in its preserved state, is 214 cm. long, is of special interest because the two post-holes have each by its side, a round hole which penetrates the runner. These have obviously served to hold the runner and side-rail together, to which function we shall return later. There has been no pollen-analysis.

In Högen, Grundsunda, Ångermanland the middle part of a runner of the Morjärv type was found in 1934, Fig. 16. It is 143 cm. long. It is equipped with two holes and arrangements for lashing the posts. The same year, in Junsele in the same province still another runner was found, Fig. 20. This also, which is 157 cm. long has two post-holes similar to those seen on the Grundsunda runner, as well as one at the front, but here there are no arrangements for lashing the posts.

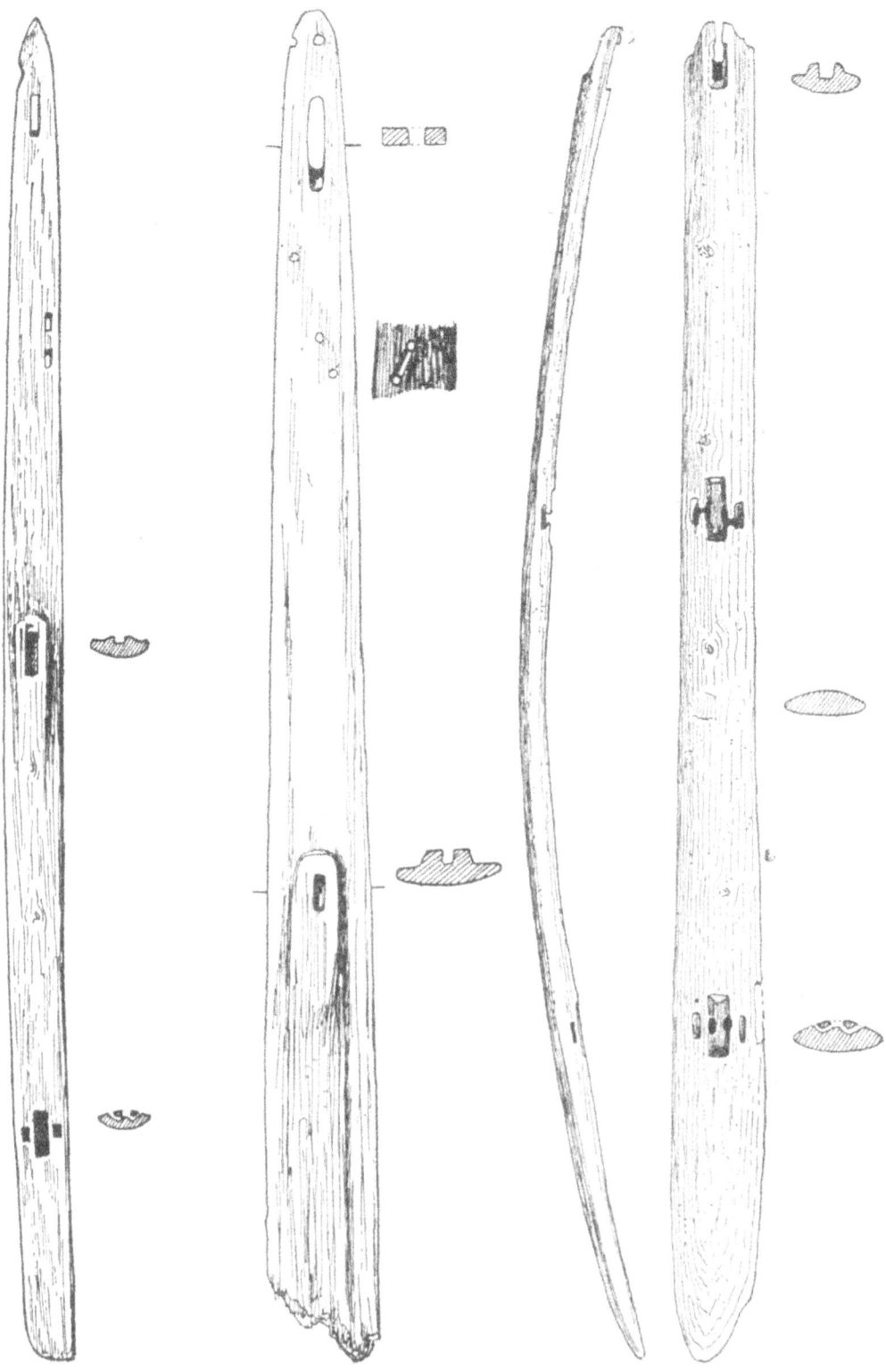

Fig. 18. Sledge-runner. Bog-find from Nederkalix, Västerbotten.

Fig. 19. Sledge-runner. Bog-find from Stensele, Lappland.

Fig. 20. Sledge-runner. Bog-find from Junsele, Ångermanland.

A find of two runners, forming a pair, has been made at Botesflon, east of Edesjön in Hammerdal, Jämtland. It is now preserved in Jämtland's Museum, Östersund. Both runners are in two pieces, but put together they are respectively 262 and 219 cm. long. Only a tiny piece is missing in the joint of each. The back-end in neither case is preserved. The widest part of the one measures 7·8 cm., and the other 6·8 cm., Fig. 21. The holes for the posts are partly pierced through and have raised edges, and are partly of the type met with on the Morjärv runner. At the fore-end, on the upper side of the runner, is a thin ridge which is pierced by a vertical hole. At the point of each is a small round hole. The pollen-analysis shews it to be of a somewhat younger age. It is impossible to make a more definite statement.[1]

Mention should also be made of a runner belonging to this group, which was found in 1916 on the shore of Rysjön, south-west of Björna Church, Ångermanland. It is in the Museum in Härnösand. The runner-fragment, which has fallen asunder, into three greater, and six lesser pieces, has a total length of 180 cm. As may be seen from Fig. 23, the preserved parts of the runner contain only one post-hole cut vertically with high raised edges. Though the object affords much difficulty in attempting its reconstruction, it belongs without doubt to this group. The pollen-analytic investigation refers it to a rather insignificant date.[2]

Finally, there is a remarkable find from Klevmarken, Dals-Ed, Dalsland. It was made in 1933. It is a similar object to the others and has arrangements in two places for lashings of something or other, which one assumes to be posts. This find has not yet been scientifically investigated.[3] It is of great interest, more especially as it was found so far southwards.

These sledge-types have been investigated through finds of runners known from Finland. To begin with I will make a group of Finnish finds.

Enontekiö, Lapp territory: A 72 cm. long, fragment of a runner with two holes, resembling the latter one on the Morjärv runner. Its greatest width is 13 cm. and thickness 2·5 cm. National Museum, Helsingfors (Sirelius, 1928, p. 951).

Sodankylä, Lapp territory: A runner of the same kind as the Morjärv and Enontekiö, 181 cm. long, with three post-holes. National Museum, Helsingfors (Itkonen, 1935).

Pielavesi, Savolaks: A runner about 1·5 meters long and a width of 5 cm. with two post-holes carved in thickened parts, as seen on the Botesflo runners. Between these two holes, in about the middle of the runner, are two smaller raised parts, beside each other. Through each of them is a vertical hole. There are vertical holes at both back and front ends. Ski Museum, Helsingfors (according to Dr. T. Okkola through Dr. Itkonen).

Sonkajärvi, Savolaks: A runner of the same type as the Malgonäs, 146 cm. long, with two post-holes penetrating the runner. National Museum, Helsingfors (Itkonen, 1935).

---

[1] According to Dr. E. Granlund.
[2] According to Dr. E. Granlund.
[3] Dr. G. A. Hellman has kindly given me information about the find, and also a reproduction of the runner.

PLATE III

1. Hunters trailing shot seals on the ice. Runö, Esthonia. Photog. G. Schantz.

2. Hay-transport on boughs. Mármaros, Hungaria. Photog. National Museum, Budapest.

PLATE IV

1. Ski-sledge with nails on either side of the posts. S. Finnskoga, Värmland. Nordiska Mus. 182,270.

2. Hay-sledge with nails on either side of the posts (beside, is the loading-rack lying on the ground). Tydal, Sör-Tröndelag, Norway. Photog. S. Erixon–O. Ekberg.

3. Sledge of »east-Finnish» type. Nederkalix, Norrbotten. Nordiska Mus. 76,839.

PLATE V

1. Sledge from Kola Peninsula, Russia. Photog. D. A. Zolotarev.

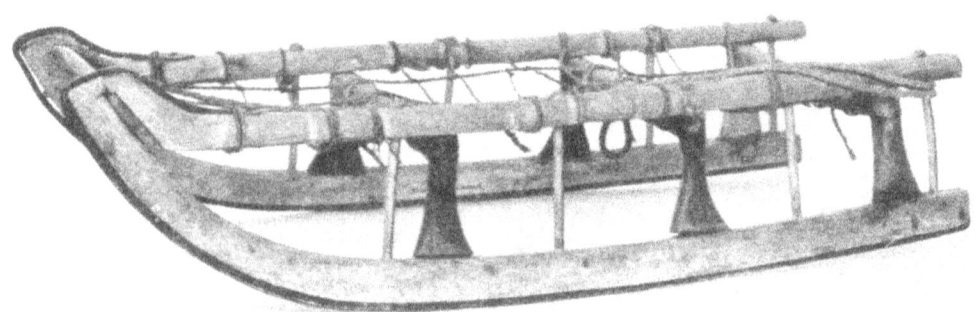
2. Seal-hunter's sledge. Runö, Esthonia. Nordiska Mus. 115,853.

3. Conveyance from Torne district, Finland. Nordiska Mus. 76,768.

PLATE VI

1. Detail of a sledge as seen on 2. Mora, Dalarna. Photog. S. Erixon.

2. Sledge for transporting wood for charcoal. Leksand, Dalarna. Photog. G. Berg.

3. Sledge for wood-transport. Ödsköld, Dalsland. Photog. N. I. Svensson.

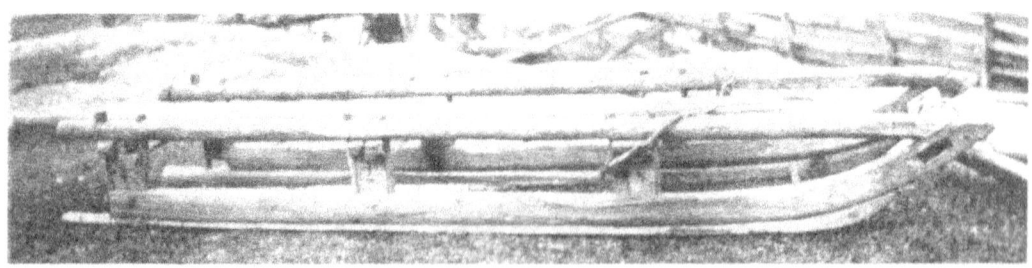

4. Hay-sledge with nails on either side of the posts. Dalsland. Photog. Gabriel Gustafson.

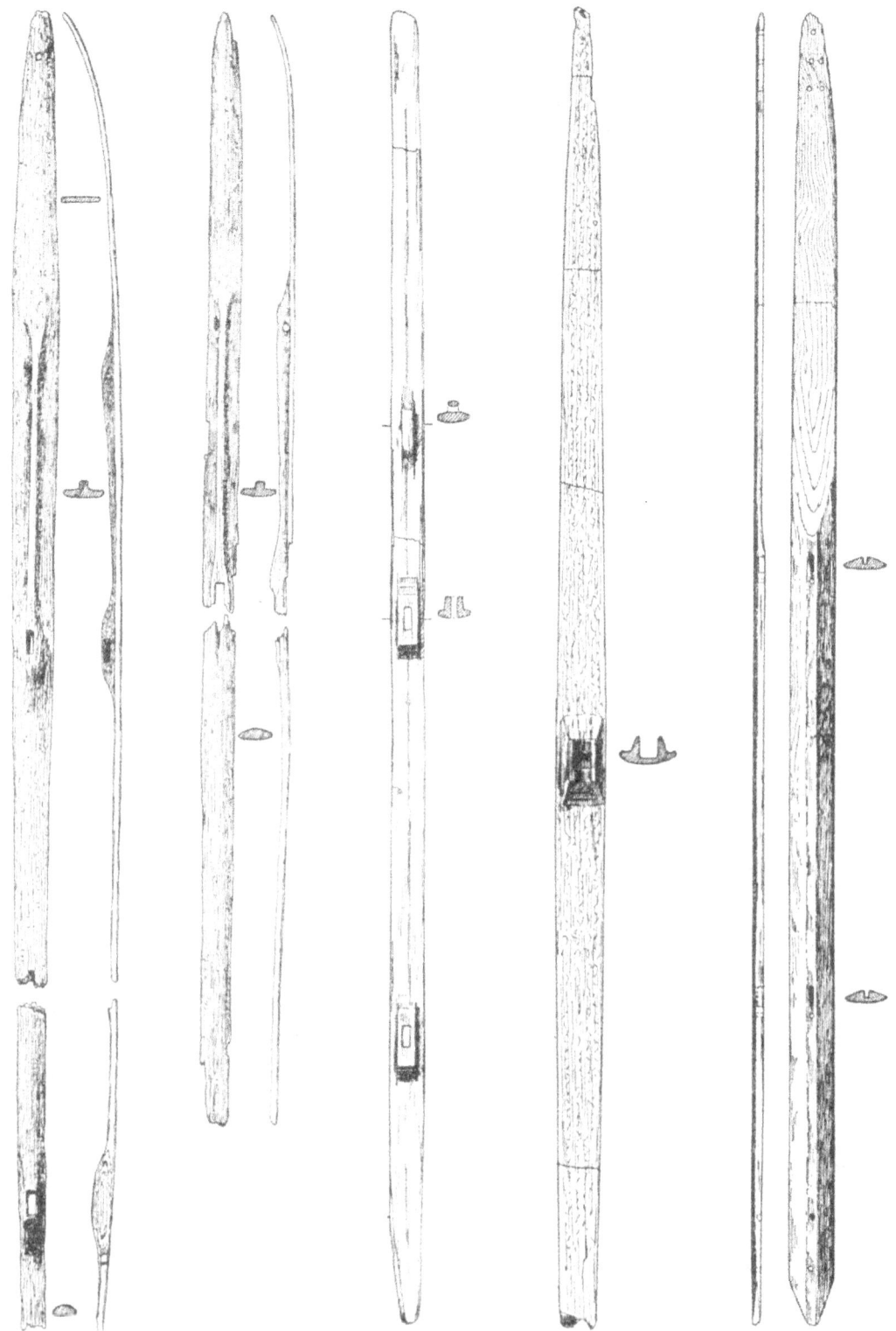

Fig. 21. A pair of sledge-runners. Bog-find from Hammerdal, Jämtland. — Fig. 22. Sledge-runner. Bog-find from Vilhelmina, Lappland. — Fig. 23. Sledge-runner. Bog-find from Björna, Ångermanland. — Fig. 24. Sledge-runner. Bog-find from Vilhelmina, Lappland.

The description of the first Finnish find by U. T. Sirelius was combined with a valuable indication as to how one should picture the sledge as complete. Sirelius rightly builds on the idea that the small holes lying by the side of the post-holes, are there to serve in connection with the lashing of the posts, and he refers to the Chukchee sledge, on which the posts are lashed to the runners, in such a manner as to remind one of the construction now under discussion, Fig. 25. According to his opinion "one should assume that a similar technique has been in use throughout vast areas of the North-Eurasian Continent."[1] Like methods, though deviating in detail, occur in many places, amongst for instance, both the Ostyak and the Zyryan.[2] The arrangement doubtless has to do with the relative thinness of the runner, which did not allow of a deep and firm mortising of the posts. The Rantasalmi and Viikinäis runners on Page 44, may have been constructed similarly to what we must presume as being the Morjärv type, although the runners are quite differently constituted.

The Swedish finds enrich our knowledge of the construction of sledges belonging to this category, in many respects. They vary very much from each other, yet they present such a similarity that one feels it is impossible to separate them. Very obviously one of the main elements of the construction is the horizontal side-rails, which connected the posts.[3] In comparison with these have the cross-bars played a rôle of lesser importance. As is known, this holds good concerning many types of sledges used by the North-Asiatic tribes. That the Morjärv type is of this construction may be gathered from several details. The only way of explaining the foremost hole, is by concluding that it contained the end of a post, which served as a support for the side-rail, which latter rested at the rear, on posts, fixed to the runner and, which, at the front, was mortised into the rectangular hole at the fore. Both the Botesflo runners afford examples of mortises for posts and penetrating holes, but they shew no lashing arrangements for the binding of the posts. I suppose they were wedged from the under-side. Here again, however, one meets with the vertical hole in the ridge, at the fore-part of the runner through

---

[1] Sirelius, 1928, p. 951. — A similar method of construction occurs also amongst the North-West Indians, Boas, 1909, p. 336.

[2] Sirelius, 1913 (a), p. 16.

[3] It is probable that, as Dr. Itkonen has pointed out to me, the two rectangular holes on the fore-end of the Morjärv runner served to support a forked side-rail, as seen on the Samoyed sledge (see, for instance, Sirelius, 1913 (a), Fig. 30). In this case, the form of the big hole would seem difficult to understand. I adopt the supposition, therefore, that they have served to hold auxiliary posts similar to those on Pl. V: 1. I know of the same construction elsewhere, for instance, in Czechoslovakia where a model is to be seen preserved in the Agricultural Museum, Prague. In other instances, these auxiliary posts are replaced by lashings as indicated by the Stensele, Botesflo, Malgonäs and the Finnish Sonkajärvi runners.

THE BUILT-UP SLEDGE

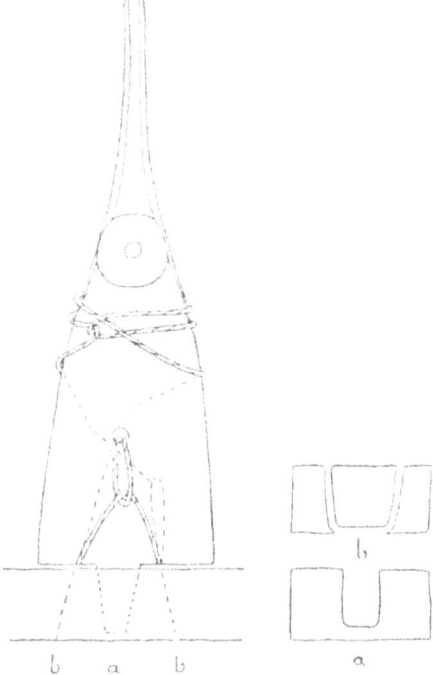

Fig. 25. The post-construction from a Chukchi sledge. After U. T. Sirelius.

which the lashings, which strengthened the rails, were threaded. The Malgonäs runner appears to me as demonstrating a still further step in the development. Here, both post-holes penetrate the runner as in the case of the Sonkajärvi, and are intended for wedged posts. It is obvious that the posts must have been considerably thicker than the holes themselves and that, like the posts on sledges of the Gråträsk-type, they were mortised into the holes. Unhappily at the moment we have no further details as to the construction of the Morjärv sledge. It is probable that, respecting the ski-sledges shortly to be treated, which should follow the same tradition, they may have been comparatively low. The slender erection affords an additional indication in favour of this assumption. Accordingly, in this respect, and as regards construction, they would seem to draw a clear line of distinction between themselves and the Gråträsk sledges. As stated, some of the runners of the Morjärv type which have been treated by pollen-analysis, have proved to be of relatively late date, that is to say, from about the time of the Birth of Christ. The closer connection which this type bears to later sledge forms in our country, and in Finland,[1] draws attention to the fact that we are dealing here with a younger product of the vehicle, from the extreme North.

---

[1] Itkonen, 1931—32, p. 63.

Though the material with which we are now familiar leads to no absolutely certain inference concerning the chronological and cultural position of the Morjärv sledges, it would seem that, due both to their appearance in general, and their technical treatment, one cannot avoid making still one more comparison. Characteristic for several of the runners is the convex under-side which should be technically explained as having been brought about in connection with the construction itself. As concerns the ski one has been able to shew how the resinous pine-tree was selected and also how it was sometimes treated. The wood from the upper side was hollowed out, the exterior was left in its natural condition and thus the ski acquired a convex under. I refer Readers in this connection especially to Torkel Tomasson's most instructive and detailed description.[1] The material for the sledge-runners has undoubtedly been treated in the same way.[2] The pre-historic skis of this kind I have grouped as the "Bothnian type" and estimated that, as a rule, they date from the time after the Birth of Christ.[3] From my point of view it is still not proved that the Lapps were the first who used this type of ski. As regards the Morjärv type of sledge, it is practically exclusive. On map, Fig. 15, I have marked all the known finds from Sweden, and also finds of skis of the Bothnian type. The Botesflo find, of all the sledge finds, for instance, could not under any circumstance whatever belong to Lapp culture. "It remains then, as the only conceivable possibility, that these sledges and skis have been the possession of traders who profitted by the Lapps and their articles of export. In more modern time traders in furs are well-known both through archeological research and through accounts in classical literature. I will only refer here to Erland Hjärne's investigation of the find from Storkåge in Västerbotten,[4] or Otto von Friesen's explanation of a passage, in Jordanes Scandia-description."[5] In other words, the finds shew according to my opinion, the beginning of a penetration into Lapp Territories on the part of the Finns (and Swedes).[6]

We do not either know with certainty whether the sledges of the Morjärv type were drawn by draught-animals or, if they more probably, and as later parallels seem to shew, were only hauled by man himself. It appears hardly likely that either the dog or the reindeer were made use of in this connection and obviously, the horse is quite out of the question as it was known in these parts at a later date, and brought with it sledges of other types. Taking a wide view of things, it would not seem difficult to verify how those types

---

[1] Wiklund, 1929, pp. 19, 21; cf. Norwegian Lapp Territory, K. Nissen, by Wiklund 1931, p. 32.
[2] v. Linné, 1732, p. 93 (Lule Lapp Territory); cf. the sledge of the Zyryan has convex runners, Ermans Archiv XI, 1852, p. 39.
[3] Berg, 1933 (a). [4] Hjärne, 1917. [5] von Friesen, 1922.
[6] Berg, 1933 (a), pp. 162—163. Cf. Tallgren, 1926, pp. 87—88, 1932, pp. 99—100.

with their relations and inter-relations once had obviously a vast expansion in North Asia and North Europe, and how they were pushed aside later by more technically developed and better carpentered forms which distributed themselves at various points, in Scandinavia, the Baltic Countries, and Finland, as well as North Russia etc. I shall return to this subject in the forthcoming.

In the foregoing, mention has been made of ski-sledges, by which term, I mean, sledges with the thin runners, more generally made of resinous pine. Ski-sledges are fairly low and are constructed in such a manner as to allow of their being as light as possible. From this definition it will be understood that I include the sledges of the Morjärv type. When Carl von Linné in 1734 visited Idre, in Dalarna, he wrote in his diary: "On the way stood a couple of simple runner-sledges with runners between 3 and 4 finger breadths wide, scarcely one in thickness, fairly light and simple, such as one uses in the mountains in the winter, to trail home shot reindeer."[1] This "ski-sledge" has been more nearly described, from the same district, by an investigator of later time. On the runners were fastened three pairs of pieces of wood with osiers, which were threaded through two holes on either side of each such piece. The holes were then wedged with wooden pegs. In the pieces of wood the real posts are fastened and into these the cross-bars were drilled. The sledge had side-rails almost as long as the runners themselves into which they were inserted at the front. These side-rails are strong and thus able to hold the runners in a curved position. To a cross-piece between the runner-ends was attached a cord of osiers or a rein as hauling-line, with a harness of elk-hide which is put over the left shoulder. On the left side of the sledge was a pole some meters long and fastened with osiers. This was held in the left hand whilst the ski-stick was held in the right.[2] The pole with which one steered, was used to prevent the sledge from going at a too great speed down inclines and mountain sides.[3]

The ski-sledge is common in greater parts of Northern Sweden as far southwards as west *Värmland*. It occurs here sometimes man-hauled as in S. Finnskoga (Nordiska Mus. 182,270, Pl. IV: 1) and sometimes drawn by the horse, for bringing in the hay from the meadows (according to Dr. N. Keyland, Nordiska Mus., Archives). From *Dalarna* I know ski-sledges both hand-drawn and drawn by the horse from Särna (there is also an example in the Ski Museum, Stockholm; here it has been used to transport timber in the forests, Geete, 1927; a younger and more developed form occurs here too, Nordiska Mus. 178,779; according to Dr. R. Jirlow), Älvdalen (Skansvakten, 13, 1928, p. 22; E. u. 4307), Transtrand (Jirlow, 1935, p. 41) and Malung (according to Herr O. Bannbers). The type occurs with fewer variations in *Härjedalen* (Älvros, Nordiska Mus. 125,180),

---

[1] von Linné, 1734, p. 290.
[2] E. u. according to Anna Arwidsson.
[3] Cf. Geete, 1927, p. 518.

Ångermanland (Tåsjö, Modin, 1916, p. 177; Bjurholm, E. u. 3307; Graninge, E. u. 4167) and *Lappland* (Tärna and Vilhelmina, E. u. 645).

Erik Modin relates that in Tåsjö, Ångermanland, the rye was brought home on the ski-sledge from the denshired land in the forests, after which it was threshed in the drying-house at home on the farm.[1] At a later date, it seems to have been most commonly employed for bringing home the hay in winter-time from the oft far-distant meadow lands. It was necessary to use the vegetation within the widely stretched areas around the settlements, for fodder. But to bring home fodder produced in the summer-time was a question of winter transport. We see, therefore, how, within the whole of North Sweden's culture zone, the sledge was of the greatest importance. In winter-time the greater part of the working-day was spent in bringing in fodder. The method of gathering bog-hay in the summer and bringing it home in the winter occurred in former times also in the south of Sweden. There are sporadic indications from a later date bearing on this.[2] Analogies are known from the other Northern Countries and from Russia.[3]

Before stock-raising had seriously gained ground in the North Swedish settlements and the transport of hay was a necessity, the employment of the sledge was certainly of another character. It was used for the transport of equipment and provisions as well as for bringing home the bag after the hunt. In this capacity it corresponds to the single-runner sledge, as it was used nearer our day, in most Northern Sweden, in Finland and in Carelia. Compared with this, progress is obvious by reason of its increased lightness, and above all for its greater freightage capacity. It must have been indispensable on the long hunting excursions, and the regular visits to the places where had been laid traps and snares and other contrivances for catching game. A near relation is the sledge which was used for seal-shooting, and which was used in various parts, on the long hunting-trips, over the ice in the Gulf of Bothnia.[4]

In reality stock-raising in the north of Sweden may in some ways be regarded as a descendant of the old hunting and fishing culture. From the half-nomadic manner of living so closely allied to the latter, even to rites of religious nature associated with the bag, one can trace its continuity.[5] A similar case is the hand-drawn ski-sledge which, later, and through influence from younger sledge-

---

[1] Modin, 1916, p. 177.

[2] Kullander, 1896, p. 31, Central Västergötland; Merwald, 1932, p. 28, Central Småland.

[3] See the Zyryan, Sidorov, 1932, pp. 8—9. — Cf. how in the mountainous districts of Central Europe, the procuring to the settled tracts and taking care of the fodder for the domestic animals is an important factor in the peasant's life, Goldstern, 1922, p. 41—45.

[4] Ekman, 1910, p. 233; Jirlow, 1930, p. 94; Brännström, 1934, p. 241; cf. Sirelius, 1919—21, 1, p. 139, 1933, p. 88.

[5] Cf. Berg, 1935, p. 226.

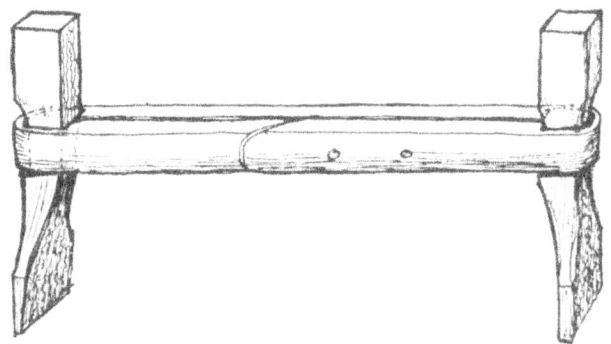

Fig. 26. The cross-bar construction on a sledge from Norsjö. Västerbotten. Nordiska Mus. 170,609.

types, came to be drawn by the horse. Viewed in this connection, the sledge has doubtless opened the way for man to exploit the vast stores of nature's infinite riches. As the sledge required no beaten way, it had the advantage over other means of transport in our snow and ice clad regions. Nothing other than ski and sledge was able to aid the exploitation of greater parts of Fennoskandia for permanent settlement. A first-rate expert on the nature and cultures of Norrland has written about this as follows: "Had it not been for the hay-marsh our topmost mountain settlements had still been void of permanent inhabitants. It was these natural hay-fields and good pasture and hunting-lands which induced the early settler to leave his old country-side for waste and solitude, far away from relations and friends, Church and fair."[1]

The ski-sledge akin to ours occurs exterior to Sweden. In *Norway* it was very common. According to answers received to my enquiry it occurred throughout the greater part of the country (there is information from every province). Besides the Swedish form there occur types even more developed (compare Plate IV: 2; excellent specimens are to be seen in the Norsk Folkemuseum, Bygdöy, Heiberg's Collection, Ambla, Ski Museum, Frognerseteren, Oslo, Museums in Hamar, Elverum, etc.). Information from Sör Tröndelag, Hordaland, Opland etc., states that some of the Norwegian man-hauled sledges also have a pole similar to that of the Swedish Idre-sledge. Excellent descriptions both as regards the appearance of the ski-sledge, and the uses it was put to, have been given by topographical Authors amongst whom may be mentioned, for Trysild, Smith 1796, pp. 15—18. Compare for Setesdalen, Skar, 1909, p. 158. There are times when the ski-sledge cannot be spoken of in a strict sense. This refers to the implement when constructed as a smaller sledge without ski-runners, but even here it is put to the same use, namely, to bring home the hay and fuel, when the horse was not available. My information is from enquiries, and comes mostly from Vestlandet.[2] From ancient west-Northern literature the ski-sledge is also familiar. The mention in the Olof Saga is the most interesting and important:[3] "Atli inn dælski à Vermlandi fór í vetr upp á markir med skí sin ok boga — — — Hann hafði fengit á fjelli svá mikla grávoru, at hann hafði fylt skiðsleða sinn, — — — Þá snøri hann heím af mǫrkinni — — —." Doubtless one may with safety apprehend the name

---

[1] Johansson, 1924—25, p. 78.

[2] A similar man-hauled, light sledge used by the poor who have no horse, for taking home wood, has occurred in many parts of Central Sweden (E. u. 4330, Västerlanda, Bohuslän).

[3] Heimskringla II, p. 184; cf. Flateyjarbók II, p. 1669, Fornmannasögur IV, p. 200.

ski-sledge as having originated from the ski-like runners[1] and there is no reason to assume the ski-sledge of the saga, other than fully coinciding with that of a later time more nearly approaching our day.[2]

In *Finland* the vehicle occurs and especially in the provinces of Österbotten and Lappland, that is to say, in the most northern parts of the country (according to Dr. T. Itkonen and Dr. K. Vilkuna). It has been indicated by many Scholars that there exist forms amongst the Eastern Peoples closely akin to the Scandinavian type (Nansen, 1898, p. 26). The *Zyryan* in Russia used long sledges on their hunting expeditions, with such thin runners that the vehicle bounded along in unison with the uneven ground (Hoffman, 1853—56, 1, p. xxxiii; cf. reproduction by Manninen, 1934, p. 227). Very nearly resembling these are certain types amongst the *Samoyed* and these also are drawn by hand (Lehtisalo, 1932, p. 133). The same form is used by the *Ostyak* (Lehtisalo, 1932, p. 133). Here we meet with the pole of the Scandinavian construction (Martin, 1897, Pl. 16). Finally, it occurs in the forest settlements of the Altai, with the steering pole, which is used in a manner similar to which we are accustomed in Sweden (photog. in På skidor, 1932, p. 335).

The forms found amongst the Siberian peoples are generally of a more advanced type, due undoubtedly to the dominating rôle played by the dog and the reindeer. It is asserted, however, by Berthold Laufer[3] and K. B. Wiklund[4] that this must be considered as a later stage. Highly probable does it seem that both in the Scandinavian man-hauled ski-sledge, and in the ancient sledge-runner finds, we are meeting with traces of an older ancestry, of a date prior to the dog and reindeer sledge. It is remarkable that never yet in Sweden has a find been made of ski-sledge runners of High Antiquity. It is not impossible that this may only be due to chance.

Should we more closely investigate the construction of the Scandinavian ski-sledge, certain characteristics would be observed which distinguish it from its Eastern analogies. As a rule, on the west-Swedish and Norwegian sledge, one finds on either side of the posts long tree-nails which pass through the side-rail down into the runner. Each nail has a knobby head. The work of the cross-bars is mainly to support the freight-platform and the freight, whilst the nails form the combining element, Fig. 27, Pl. IV: 1, VI: 4. I have mentioned previously that the Långtjärn-runner is of similar construction.[5] The same type appears again at a later date with the horse as draught-animal. It is employed mostly in connection with agriculture, and chiefly for the transport of fodder. In the following survey of its expansion, there will be no further details as to the varied employment of the vehicle.

The form appears in *Bohuslän* (Naverstad, Tjörn, sledge at the Gothenburg Exhibition, 1923, Pl. VIII: 2, E. u. 3388), *Dalsland* (Nössemark, Nordiska Mus. 180,707; Ärtemark, personal notes,

---

[1] Cf. Geete, 1927, p. 518.
[2] Cf. somewhat deviating, Sirelius, 1913 (a), p. 22.
[3] Laufer, 1917 (b), p. 138.
[4] Wiklund, 1918, pp. 258—259.
[5] To me it appears more probable that this sledge was of the nail construction than that the posts were fastened in a manner coinciding with the Zyryan, Sirelius, 1913 (a), Figs. 20—21.

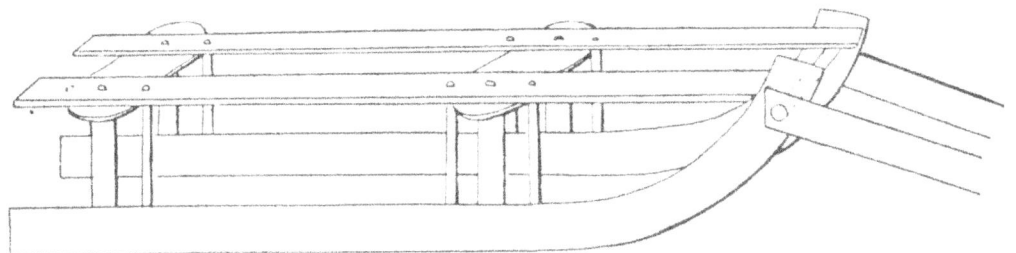

Fig. 27. Sledge with treenails on either side of the posts. Sogn, Norway. After Magnus Olsen.

E. u. drawing; Vårvik, according to Herr P. H. Nilsson; I have seen the same construction in other parts of the province too, cf. Pl. VI: 4 and Grieg 1928, p. 220), *Värmland* (Blomskog, according to Herr P. H. Nilsson; Köla, pers. notes; Silbodal, E. u. photog.; Södra Finnskoga, ski-sledge, Pl. IV: 1; cf. with notes in E. u. by Nils Keyland) and in *Härjedalen* (Granberg, 1927, p. 65).

From this brief survey one notices that the occurrence of the previously described nail-construction has close connection with the Norwegian boundary settlements. It has also its vastest distribution in this our neighbouring country, compare Fig. 27. From enquiries I made it seems that the nail construction is pretty well at home in most of the provinces, from Nordland in the north, to Vestagder in the south. It is met with in Östfold, Buskerud, and Sör Tröndelag but appears, from information received, to be missing in Hedmark, and this is interesting as I have no knowledge either of its occurrence in Dalarna, Sweden. Of course, this may be due to chance but it shews that the construction was not usual there in later time.

In this construction, as a rule, there is a nail on either side of each post but on some of the Norwegian examples there is, as on the Långtjärn runner, only one nail to each (in Vinje, Sör Tröndelag, Sand in Möre and Kvås in Vest-Agder).[1] As known, one of the sledges in the Oseberg find from the Viking Period is constructed in this way, namely "the simple sledge" which, in distinction to the other three, Grieg regards exclusively as an agricultural implement.[2] The sledge comprised in the Gokstad find is also constructed with these nails.[3] This fact indicates at least that this construction is not the result of any late evolution but must be viewed as a type having prehistoric ancestry.

The occurrence of the sledge in Esthonia substantiates this postulate. Judging from available material, its distribution here is restricted to the islands. Thus one meets with it on the sledges which are used at seal-shooting on Runö, Pl. V: 2,[4] and both here, and on Dagö and Ösel, one finds it on other

---

[1] As regards construction, cf. Grieg, 1928, pp. 41, 60.

[2] Grieg, 1928, pp. 212—220.

[3] Nicolaysen, 1882, pp. 39—40; Grieg, 1928, Pl. 5.

[4] Manninen, 1931—32, I, p. 85 (Runö); Russwurm, 1855, Pl. IX; photog. from Dagö in Nordiska Mus., Archives; information about sledges on Runö from Herr J. Österman; Manninen, 1928, p. 154 — sledge from Ösel with some nails.

types too. In these cases the treenails are not near the posts but are distributed between these and sometimes quite unsymmetrically.[1] Thus one cannot avoid certifying a direct connection between the appearance of the nail-construction in West Sweden, in Norway and in the districts east of the Baltic Sea. Should one assume, as indeed I have tried to make possible in the following, that the east-Finnish type of sledge, came to these parts as a younger form, of probable Russian origin, one might suppose that the construction with nails once had a comprehensive expansion throughout Finland. It must then be regarded in like manner as the push-runner which, in the foregoing Chapter, I essayed to assign to ancient ancestry, in Northern culture. Under such circumstances one must quite obviously incline to believe that the construction once was known also south of the Baltic Sea, and that it spread to either side of the Gulf of Bothnia. A noteworthy indication which supports this assumption is to be found in the analogies one meets with in Switzerland.[2] All these sledges have side-rails which are connected with the front-ends of the runners and which hold the cross-bars together.[3]

Characteristic for the recently described ski-sledges are the thin runners, which are either naturally curved or are made so by artificial means.[4] The shape of the runner varies according to the district. The thin artificially curved runner occurs also in another group of sledges which cannot be categorized as ski-sledges. A brief treatment is necessary here though their appearance in Sweden is restricted to the most northern provinces.

Finnish ethnographers have called this form the east-Finnish type, Pl. IV: 3, due to its occurrence in Finland. It is restricted to the eastern parts of the country, and the dividing line may be drawn approximately from the mouth of the Kymmene towards the north-west, to the neighbourhood of Gamla Karleby.[5] The type is characterized by its long up-turned runner-ends which are lashed to the first pair of posts. Thus the platform is not attached to the former.[6]

---

[1] It would not seem out of place to compare with certain Finnish sledges which appear to have auxiliary posts between the ordinary ones. See Vilkuna, 1930, p. 26 (sledge from Laturi, Österbotten).

[2] Huber, 1919, p. 25; Brockmann-Jerosch, 1929—31, 1, Figs. 264, 267.

[3] See the instructive illustrations by Huber, 1919. — A cord of some kind fastened to the runner and the platform, on a Siamese sledge in the Science Museum, London, serves the same purpose as the nail-construction. Illustration in Catalogue, 1926, Pl. I: 1.

[4] From Bjurholm in Ångermanland it is said that the hand-drawn ski-sledge had runners which were curved with hot water, E. u. 3307. — Otherwise the curved runner was constructed according to the illustration of the S. Finnskoga sledge, Pl. IV: 1.

[5] Atlas of Finland, 1925, p. 143.

[6] See Vilkuna, 1930; Grotenfelt, 1915, Figs. 17, 20.

THE BUILT-UP SLEDGE

Sledges of this east-Finnish type are met with in Sweden. We find them in the northern parts of Norrbotten. Another form of the same sledge, used as a conveyance, occurs in other parts of Norrbotten and in the Northern districts of Västerbotten, Pl. V: 3.[1] There is much evidence that the type was extensively used in more modern times. A form closely akin has become more and more popular amongst the Lapps. Gustaf Hallström writes: "This sledge is met with throughout the whole of the North of Finland, and in the northern part of the province of Norrbotten. It gains ground more and more at the expense of the 'akja' in tracts where the Lapps are making their settlements. In Enare such a sledge was never seen before, and the boat-sledge is still the common vehicle, but the reindeer sledge is making a great advance."[2]

Sledges with thin artificially up-turned runners of a similar type are also to be met with in Esthonia,[3] in Latvia,[4] Poland[5] and Russia.[6] It would be out of place here to give a lengthy survey as to how far east this type goes. It occurs amongst the Zyryan and Cheremiss[7] but seems to be unknown to the Siberian peoples.[8] The runners are curved by a steaming process in the bathhouse, or they are buried in fresh horse-manure. Later on they were fastened between plugs inserted in the wall.[9] Corresponding curving methods occur in other connections in certain parts of Sweden where the artificially bent runner is not known.[10]

The east-Finnish sledge is employed almost exclusively with the horse as draught-animal. It is seldom met with in connection with other and more primitive types. This implies at once that we are dealing with a younger form which won its expansion in connection with the introduction of the horse as draught-animal. Obviously this may have occurred at a relatively early stage,

---

[1] Notes in E. u., from Vilhelmina and other places, Västerbotten. — Petrus Magni Gyllenius tells from a journey, 1663, in Lekvattnet in Värmland that the "Finnish sledge" used there, was so light that it could easily be lifted over the uneven ground. See Gyllenius, 1880—82, p. 280. It is uncertain as to whether is meant here the east-Finnish type or possibly a ski-sledge. — Runners heated in water and curved in a corner of a building are mentioned from Gräsmark in the same province, E. u. 4362.

[2] Hallström, 1926, pp. 254—255.

[3] Manninen, 1928 (b), p. 153; Hupel, 1774—82, 2, Pl. 3 B.

[4] Bielenstein, 1907—18, 2, pp. 554—557.

[5] Pietkiewicz, 1928, pp. 209—214.

[6] Zelenin, 1932, pp. 134—135. — A conveyance of similar type is reproduced after a 16th century manuscript, des Noëttes, 1931, Fig. 163.

[7] Manninen, 1934, p. 224.

[8] Amongst the north-east Siberian peoples one meets occasionally with another system where the forepart of the runner is curved backward, forming at the same time the side-rail of the sledge. See e.g. Bogoras, 1904—09, pp. 90, 92; Mason, 1894—96, Fig. 241 etc.

[9] Rytkönen, 1931, pp. 102—126 gives an excellent description of the making of such a sledge. For the curving of the sledge see the literature of Bielenstein and Zelenin.

[10] Cf. the curving of the upstanding arched arrangement on the harness in Norrbotten, E. u., photog. and drawing. Cf. Paulaharju, 1932, p. 236; Manninen, 1928 (b), p. 110.

may be, so early, that sledge-types of another and more developed form were unknown within the expansion area in question. So much would seem certain, that the type must be explained as an innovation from the south and east, and doubtless from Russia especially.[1]

Of uncommon interest is the appearance of the type in the extreme north of Sweden. Obviously it coincides with other implements which are connected with the horse as draught-animal. Here, more especially I refer to an upstanding arched arrangement which took the place of the halter, and to which the shafts were attached.[2] It would seem evident from these facts that the horse came to these districts as a culture element from Finland. As far as artificially curved runners are concerned, it can rightly be said that they are particularly suitable for the ice and snow regions where they, more easily than their naturally curved fellows, could take themselves over the hard and frozen crust of the snow.[3]

There is a certain construction of cross-bar which occurs in connection with this type of sledge. It deviates to an essential degree from the form otherwise generally employed, but can be used in sledges of all kinds whether for conveyance or portage, Fig. 26. It is made of sallow or any other tree with a tough outer layer. As seen in the illustration, holes are made in the cross-bars for the posts, which former are bound round the latter and then nailed in the middle. I will call this construction in the following, the "bound cross-bar". One comes across it mostly in Västerbotten[4] and Norrbotten.[5] The construction occurs as an exception however in Ångermanland, where it is said to have been used chiefly by descendants of the Finns.[6] From Vilhelmina, Stensele and Tärna I have met with a somewhat varying type, where only short outer-ends of the cross-bar were bound to the posts and nailed fast.[7]

In Finland, the construction seems to have been rather common, especially in connection with the east-Finnish type, but even otherwise.[8] It occurs also

---

[1] Cf. how Manninen, 1932, p. 6 counts with a greater influence from Russia on the culture of the Finnish-Ugrian peoples, than has hitherto been assumed.

[2] This "upstanding arched arrangement" is a custom from Norrbotten and the northern half of Västerbotten. — Vilkuna, 1933, p. 11, faultily assumes that it only occurs in the Finnish-speaking Norrbotten. See Atlas of Finland, 1925, p. 140, and Vilkuna, 1933, pp. 11—12 for its expansion exterior to Sweden.

[3] Cf. with what Fale Burman says: "Finnish sledges with broad runners were often obviously needed in Jemtland", Burman, 1930, p. 87. — For the advantage of the thin runner, see v. Middendorff, 1874, pp. 1347—53.

[4] Notices from Norsjö by Dr. R. Jirlow; Nordiska Mus. 170,609, Fig. 26.

[5] E. u. photog.; pers. notes. — It appears almost regularly on the Västerbotten and Norrbotten conveyances. Examples in the Nordiska Museet.

[6] Ramsele, E. u. 5541.   [7] E. u. 911.

[8] Manninen, 1934, pp. 223—224; Vilkuna, 1930, pp. 30—34; cf. slide-car from Carelia, Sirelius, 1913 (a), p. 2.

in Esthonia[1] and Latvia,[2] as well as on the Kola Peninsula.[3] Other wood than sallow was used. Bielenstein tells that the people of Latvia employed the ash and the alm.[4] The cross-bars were fastened in various ways. Sometimes, as in Sweden, they were nailed together, sometimes they were lashed. The same construction occurs in Russia[5] and Poland,[6] and the Cheremiss avails himself of it too.[7]

There are countless numbers of parallels to this method in East Europe and Asia where the strong outer-layer of the tree plays such an important part. One might mention here that of the same wood a great many handles for hammers are made in the most northern part of Norrbotten.[8]

The normal type of sledge used for transportation in South and Central Sweden is built up in quite a different way. In this instance the platform is almost exclusively borne up by both the cross-bars which connect the posts. As a rule there are no side-rails. The manner in which the posts were fastened to the cross-bars varies considerably. Seldom is it so primitively done as on the sledges used for transporting wood to the kiln, which occurs in sundry parts of Sweden. Two sticks rest on small ledges in the sides of the posts and both are lashed together with osiers, Pl. VI: 1—2. Such sledges were put together quite temporarily for forest-work.

They occur in Sweden at the following places: *Dalarna* (Mora, photog. E. u. Sigurd Erixon; Leksand, pers. notes, Nordiska Mus. 161,320; Silvberg, pers. notes; Herr Ola Bannbers tells of their normal occurrence in the province; cf. Rietz, 1867, under Draga), *Västmanland*, pers. notes, from Grythyttan) and east *Värmland* (Brattfors, pers. notes; Ekshärad, photog. Nils Keyland in E. u.; Färnebo, photog. Nils Keyland, who positively asserts this to be an east-Värmland type). They appear to have been used also in *Jämtland* (cf. Rietz, 1867, under Draga) and *Småland* (Mörlunda, photog. in E. u., R. Odencrants). The latter may be due to later influence.

These sledges were very practical for their purpose especially by reason of their elasticity, which rendered it possible to use them on rugged ground. The method of lashing with osiers in one way or another, to aid in holding the

---

[1] Manninen, 1928, pp. 153—154; according to Herr J. Österman, on Runö seal-hunting sledges are constructed in this manner; 2 examples in the Nordiska Museet, Pl. V: 2.

[2] Bielenstein, 1906—18, 2, p. 556, Figs. 510, 512; Latvju Raksti XVI, p. 155, XXXXVI, p. 96.

[3] E. u., photog. D. Zolotarev.

[4] Bielenstein, 1906—18, 2, p. 556.

[5] Zelenin, 1927, pp. 134—135. Cf. from the Bashkir, Rudenko, 1925, p. 119.

[6] Pietkiewicz, 1928, pp. 211—215.

[7] Sirelius, 1913 (a), Fig. 23. — Cf. a Cheremiss chair constructed in the same manner, Heikel, 1888, p. 15.

[8] Specimens in the Nordiska Museet and in Torne Museum, from Norrbotten. Cf. Finland, Appelgren, 1882, p. 25; Paulaharju, 1932, p. 83 (cf. Sirelius, 1919—21, 1, p. 152). — Handles of pick-axes of the same construction as known from Assam in Further India, Heine-Geldern, 1923, p. 869 and from the Dené-Indians, Schmidt-Koppers, 1924, p. 659. — Cf. Chinese bambo chairs, Mason, 1894—96, pp. 540—541 Koeppen-Breuer, 1904, pp. 267—269, and also Boas, 1909, p. 331.

structure together is also known. Sometimes might a cord of osiers drawn across the sledge bind together both the uprights and posts which were in one piece. Such a construction Nils Keyland has described and reproduced from the Värmland Finn-forests, and I myself have seen them in Köla and Blomskog in the same province. In more modern time the osier-band which stretched across the sledge was replaced by an iron rod.[1] Similar constructions though more complicated were also usual in Medelpad,[2] Västerbotten[3] and Norrbotten.[4]

More usual is it, however, that the cross-bar overtakes the function of holding the sledge together. Thus the uprights and the posts are in one, run through holes in the cross-bars, a construction which has been very usual in most of the provinces of Central Sweden and South Norrland. It is also met with in other European Countries.[5] The sledge is not always equipped with uprights. The posts need only appear very slightly above the cross-bars. Sledges of this kind are employed for instance in the transport of charcoal and then the basket-body was used. But one found that the projecting cross-bars hindered a comfortable transport, as they so easily fastened in the trees etc. It is said in Västmanland that the type was abandoned at the time of the transition of the century.[6] In still another form the cross-bars are seen to have been inserted through the posts, as may be seen on Pl. VI: 3. This form is especially known in the various districts of Götaland.[7]

In addition to these very simple methods of construction there are others which should undoubtedly be brought forward in this connection. In the sledge which was used as a conveyance only, the posts were mostly inserted into the under-side of the cross-bars. This method, however, is of a certainty relatively young amongst the Swedish peasants, and rather is it contemporary with the appearance of the conveyance. Amongst the higher classes it can be assigned to the 17th century as several preserved sledges shew.[8] The posts and cross-bars on the sledges of the Oseberg find were fastened together in a very complicated fashion, and there are no Northern parallels from peasant culture.[9]

---

[1] Photog. for instance, N. Keyland from Mangskog, Värmland. Cf. Pl. VI: 3 from Ödsköld, Dalsland.
[2] E. u. photog. J. Granlund (Torp).
[3] E. u. 911, Vilhelmina, Stensele and Tärna. [4] E. u., a drawing, 1922.
[5] Bielenstein, 1906-18, 2, p. 556 (Latvia); Brüning, 1932, p. 103 and Leser, 1927, p. 40 (Germany); Huber, 1919, passim (Switzerland) etc.
[6] According to Dr. S. T. Kjellberg.
[7] Also in Värmland, E. u. photog. from V. Fågelvik. — Very usual in many places, in old-time sledges with standards, which were drawn and managed by hand, and used both for shorter transport and as toys.
[8] See for example "Axel Oxenstierna's sledge" and "Queen Kristina's sledge" in the Royal Armoury, both from the early half of the 17th century. The former reproduced Kreisel, 1927, Pl. 39 B.
[9] Cf. strengthening arrangements on two of the sledges, Boëthius, 1922, p. 38.

The constitutive elements here are the runners in their rough, natural state, into which the posts are fixed, and wedged fast. Sometimes also a horizontal plug is inserted through runner and post to stabilize the latter. The method of shoeing the cross-bar sledge with wood is often met with.[1] Similar shoeing occurs on two of the sledges in the Oseberg find,[2] and is also to be seen on the Oxenstierna sledge, in the Royal Armoury, previously mentioned. Not only did the shoe serve to protect the runner from wear and tear but, as regards the summer-sledge, it contributed towards an easier movement on rugged ground. Later, the wooden shoe was replaced by an iron-bar but the former was still considered to be the better, on bad roads.[3] As a rule, in our country, the wood mostly used is birch but, juniper, yew (taxus), oak and the apple-tree are mentioned, as also are fir or spruce and the resinous pine.[4] The shoes are fastened to the runners by means of plugs which are inserted into holes specially drilled for the purpose.

A short survey of the European expansion of the sledge should not be deemed unsuitable here. The material for such a collation is still very inadequate and especially on behalf of Central Europe it craves completion. It must be understood how exceedingly important is the European material for the putting forward of an intelligible and concise survey of the culture history of the sledge on the whole.

Apart from its use as a conveyance, the built-up sledge also occurs as a means of transport exterior to Sweden, Norway and Finland. It is known in *Denmark* (see Ingvorsen, 1918, p. 132; a Zealand sledge in Landbrugsmuseet, Lyngby, Copenhagen; used for transporting rape, see specimens in Landbrugsmuseet, Lyngby and compare Kristensen, 1900, p. 155; from Schleswig-Holstein, Krieg, 1931, p. 50). It seems to have been much less used here. The same applies to *Germany*, where it is met with in the north-west (Brüning, 1932, p. 103), in the Rhine Countries (Leser, 1927, p. 40), in Oberhessen and elsewhere (Mitzka, 1935, pp. 11, 15, Leser, 1927, p. 40). The form used here is exclusively the sledge with cross-bars and two pairs of posts. The normal type one finds also further southwards. For example in *Switzerland* (Huber, 1919, Stebler, 1903, pp. 302—303; Brockmann-Jerosch, 1929—31, 1, Figs. 264, 267), in *France* (Goldstern, 1922, pp. 40, 44, Savoy; Giese, 1932, pp. 93—96, Dauphiné; Brunhes, 1926, pp. 205—208; Zéliqzon, 1922—24, p. 353, Lorraine; Fahrholz, 1931, p. 143, Ariège in the Pyrenees) and in North *Italy* (Rehsener, 1891, pp. 429—31, the Tyrol; Phieler, 1934, pp. 72—73, Marche). The built-up sledge is found as far south as *Spain*, and is met with in Valencia (Thede, 1933, p. 256/257). It seems to be missing in the countries of the Mediterranean. It occurs in *Austria* (Mitzka, 1935, p. 15, Moravia, Styria; Agricola, 1556, p. 168, reproductions of sledges from the Tyrol), *Czecho-Slovakia* (Moszynski, 1929,

---

[1] More as an exception it seems to occur on the east-Finnish type, Rytkönen, 1931, pp. 114, 123.

[2] Grieg, 1928, pp. 42, 48.

[3] See, for example, Säve, 1873, p. 43; notes in E. u. from Värmland, by N. Keyland and others. — Iron-shod sledges are known from the early 18th century, Berg, 1925 (b), p. 8. Cf. from Norway, Bull, 1916—19, p. 156; Essendrop, 1761, p. 204.

[4] Special information may be obtained in E. u. — Cf. Säve, 1873, p. 43 and Hyltén-Cavallius, 1864—68, 2, p. 96; cf. for Norway, Hersoug, 1932, p. 59; for Finland, Hermans, 1918, p. 92, Petterson, 1917, p. 150; for Denmark, Grundtvig, 1909, p. 120; for Latvia, Bielenstein, 1907—18, 2, p. 557.

p. 631; Schramek, 1915, pp. 104—106, 229, Bohemia; its occurrence amongst the Huzuls in the Carpathians is well-known, Wiener Zeitschrift 8, 1902, p. 217) and *Yugoslavia* (Patsch, 1909, p. 113, 1912, p. 138; western Bosnia; Moszynski, 1929, p. 631; Nopsca, 1925, p. 137 and Grothe, 1913, p. 34, Montenegro). It is very usual in *Roumania*, in the Balkan Peninsula (Papahagi, 1928—30, 2, pp. 75—76; Pamfile, 1910, pp. 153—154), and is found in *Bulgaria* (Marinov, 1901, pp. 126—127; according to Mr. R. K. Trichkov, Vratza). The occurrence of the built-up sledge in *Russia* is well-known (cf. Zelenin, 1927, pp. 134—137) and it is also usual in *Poland* (Moszynski, 1929, pp. 630—632), as well as in the Baltic Countries. — In addition, attention must be drawn to the expansion of the sledge as a conveyance. It has occurred in this capacity in many European Countries, especially in Germany, Holland, Switzerland and Austria (see, for instance, Kreisel, 1927, pp. 131—171). Only in places where snow and ice are very frequent has the vehicle in this capacity become popular.

From this much too summary account, one is able to gather that the built-up sledge has a sporadic though remarkable distribution in Europe. Its appearance beyond the snowy areas is associated with its employment on bare ground. In connection with hay-making and harvesting it was put to a more comprehensive use in the Scandinavian lands. The summer-sledge has also been used as a vehicle of transport in Finland, the Baltic Countries and in Russia.[1] Natural conditions themselves have put no great obstacles in the way of its expansion, but this must be explained purely historically. One can scarcely venture to believe that the vehicle once had a more comprehensive distribution over greater parts of North Europe.[2] One of the most contributing factors to its migration from the many settlements would seem due to the more general employment of the waggon in Central Europe. The sledge has maintained its position where the terrain conditions considerably hampered or rendered impossible the use of wheeled vehicles.[3]

It is also worthy of note that, in spite of certain diversity of detail, the sledge shews a remarkable consistency of construction over the greater part of its European expansion-area. As previously indicated, it is only in the east of Europe that any great independence is manifested. In addition, as regards the harnessing arrangements, close analogies appear in widely separated parts of its expansion. I shall bring forward here just such a detail. On the reproduction of the Zealand simple runner-sledge, Fig. 33, one meets with a cylindrical piece of wood which is fixed in holes at the fore-end of the runners. This object is movable.[4]

---

[1] A number of statements by Anučin, 1899. — Anučin treated the curious custom which was kept up into later time, of using the sledge in summer for transporting the dead, at burials. Known in Russia, Poland, Servia, Slovakia and Croatia. Cf. Gavazzi, 1929 and 1934.

[2] A comparison should be made with such objects as osier-made snow-shoes which, as known, occur both in the North and in the mountain districts of Central Europe. Perhaps also the ski which appeared early in Carniola, Zettersten, 1933.

[3] Cf. Phieler, 1934, p. 72. Gielleböl, 1771, p. 94, gives a Norwegian evidence.

[4] Cf. Ingvorsen, 1918, p. 131.

1. Dung-sledge from Aurland, Sogn-Fjordane, Norway. Heiberg's collection, Ambla.

2. Dung-sledge from Ore, Dalarna. Nordiska Mus. 156,717.

3. Sledge from Lillerupsholm, Jutland, Denmark. The open-air museum at Lyngby, Copenhagen.

PLATE VIII

1. Sledge with semi-cylindrical body, used for hay-transport. Venjan, Dalarna.
Photog. A. Nilsson.

2. Hay-sledge from Tjörn, Bohuslän. Photog. T. Lenk.

PLATE IX

1. Conveyance from Bredared, Västergötland. Skara Museum.

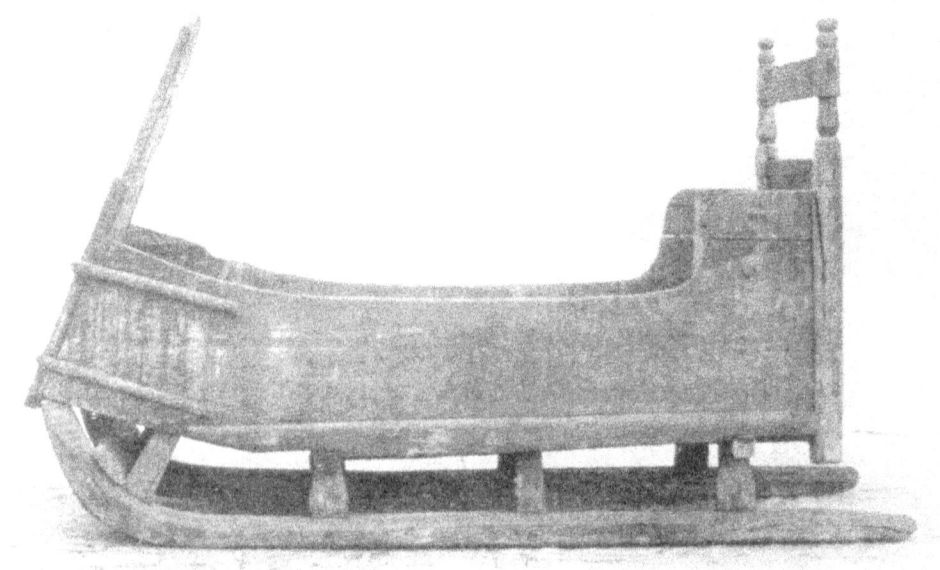

2. Conveyance from Orsa, Dalarna. Nordiska Mus. 89,225.

3. Conveyance from Oppmanna, Scania. Photog. S. Svensson.

PLATE X

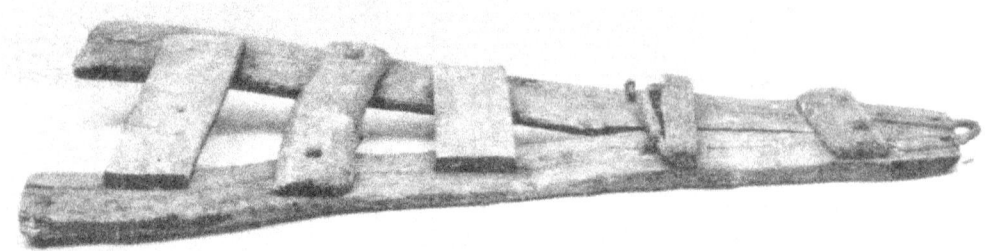

1. Sledge for carting stones, from Kullerstad, Östergötland. Nordiska Mus. 187,761.

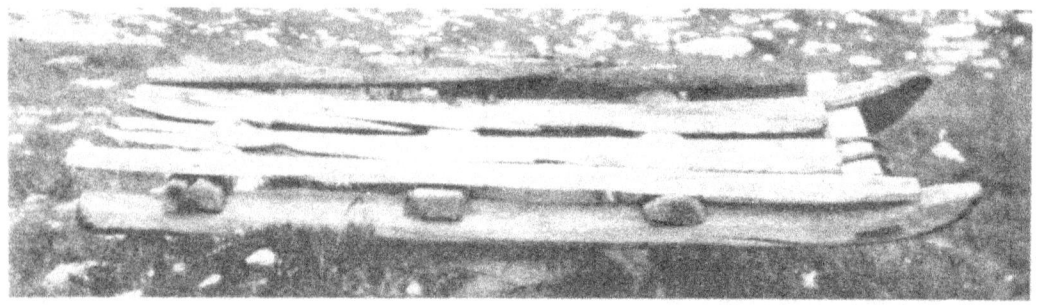

2. Sledge for carting stones, from N. Ny, Värmland. Photog. Alma Nordqvist.

3. Simple runner-sledge, used for water-transport. Sorunda, Södermanland. Photog. G. Berg.

The method occurs in Sweden in the following provinces, for instance: *Östergötland* (Sund, photog. E. u.), *Gotland* (Fårö, E. u. 3241), *Småland* (Mörlunda, photog. E. u.; Linneryd, E. u. 5588), *Västergötland* (Sundén, 1903, p. 36) and *Dalsland* (Nössemark, according to Herr P. H. Nilsson). I know such a harnessing arrangement from *Finland* (Vilkuna, 1931 (b), p. 57), *Italy* (Phieler, 1934, p. 72), *Bosnia* (Patsch, 1912, p. 138) and *Hungary* (model in the Hungarian National Museum, Budapest). It has doubtless occurred in other parts of Europe where oxen in pairs have been employed as draught-animals for the sledge.[1]

"The simple sledge" in the Oseberg find is equipped with harnessing arrangements of this kind. Noteworthy is it that the more complicated harnessing arrangements of the three other sledges in this find, as well as the Gokstad example, may also be attributed to this method.[2] Doubtless could other observations of a high degree of similarity be made throughout the sledge-area in respect to other harnessing equipments. For instance, may be mentioned the form, with its shafts attached to the outer-side of the runners, as it appears on the east-Finnish sledge. This is the most common form in Central Europe.[3] Many of these harnessing methods are so very correlative to those of other transport vehicles[4] that it would be advisable to treat them collectively. Such a task would entail pleasurable and profitable, though onerous labour.

It has now been seen that the normal type of Swedish sledge with carpentered cross-bars has affinity with Central European forms and that these collectively comprise a relatively uniform group of vehicles. As far as Sweden is concerned, the explanation lies in the fact that this type came into the country in company with the employment of the horse and the ox as draught-animal for the vehicle. The new type has had to combat with older forms such as, for instance, the ski-sledge treated earlier in the Chapter. From this contrast, have evolved such concessional forms as the horse-drawn ski-sledge.

Quite another question is the connection assumed to exist between the European cross-bar sledge and the more primitive east-European and Siberian forms. This is still uncertain ground, and there remain so many unsolved problems that the greatest caution seems necessary. At the same time it would seem impossible to isolate these two main groups. An original relationship must exist and it appears all the more urgent to pay attention to European

---

[1] The illustration from Switzerland is not clear, Huber, 1919, p. 11. It is not impossible that the fork-shaped "waggon-pole" found in Saalburg, mentioned by Grieg, may be a sledge-pole instead (Grieg, 1928, p. 28).

[2] Grieg, 1929, passim.

[3] For the Alp Countries see Huber, 1919, passim and Zeissler, 1922, p. 25. The method was also usual in Vestlandet in Norway. See Anda, 1881, p. 37, Hasund, 1932, p. 134 and specimens in Heiberg's Collection, Ambla. — For Finland, for example, see Vilkuna 1930, pp. 30—32. Cf. this method is usual also amongst the Buryat, Jochelson, 1933, pp. 143, 186—187.

[4] Such has doubtless been the case with us regarding the loose shafts which are fastened in various ways to a ring, attached to the cross-piece at the ends of the runners. The method of fastening two loose shafts to iron hooks at the fore-part of the runner is almost exclusively used for conveyances.

material. The probability that an investigation yield forms which might have to be regarded as younger than the Asiatic, should not be allowed to daunt. Circumstances exist which indicate an expansion, and this must obviously have had an Eastern basis. This expansion doubtless occurred at a very ancient date and the vast and profound difference between the groups serves to corroborate this assumption.

The construction of the platform of the two main types presents also some remarkable variations. The ski-sledge has a very light platform, as a rule, composed of thin boards pieced together, but a similar construction may also be met with on the fairly well-developed cross-bar sledge of Central Sweden. The method is particularly common in regard to the sledge where posts and uprights are in one. But this kind of platform has never been entirely absent. By degrees a body of rails or basket-work was built upon it, and in time a regular and normal body was brought into effect.[1] Of interest in this connection should be certain forms of a more precisioned, and as far as expansion goes, to some extent, restricted types.

One of these is the sledge with the concave platform nailed fast to a frame of curved rails. In later times, this vehicle was employed to transport manure out to the fields, but earlier it seems to have been put to a much more all-round use, Pl. VII: 2. Nowadays, the platform is shaped so that it is wider at the back but, from here and there, still appear platforms which are of uniform width. Reference to Sam Schultze, 1747, for instance, corroborates this statement.[2] Tradition maintains to this day that these concave platforms were specially suitable on account of the stability they ensured the implement.

Especially from the districts neighbouring Norway, see Map, Fig. 28, are these concave platforms known to me and amongst these may be mentioned, *Jämtland* (Laxsjö, E. u. photog.; Ström, E. u. photog.), *Dalarna* (Orsa, pers. notes; Ore, Nordiska Mus. 156,717; Rättvik, E. u. photog. and notes, S. Erixon; Boda, pers. notes; Våmhus, pers. notes; Venjan, photog. E. u., drawing by N. E. Hammarstedt; Leksand, pers. notes; Bingsjö, photog. E. u.; Lima, E. u. 4142; Malung, E. u. 5168; Nås, E. u. photog., Sigfrid Svensson; cf. Schultze 1747, Fig. 10, mentioned here as hay-sledge), *Värmland* (Dalby, E. u. photog.; Blomskog, according to Herr P. H. Nilsson), *Dalsland* (Vårvik and Nössemark, according to Herr P. H. Nilsson) and *Bohuslän* (Orust and Tjörn, Kalm, 1746, p. 242).

In Norway these platforms are very well-known. According to answers to my enquiries they occur in the following provinces: Möre, Sogn-Fjordane, Hardanger, Rogaland, Vest-Agder, Aust-Agder, Buskerud, Hedmark and Akershus (cf. they are mentioned from Spydeberg in Östfold by Wilse, 1779, pp. 391—392 and from Höland in Akershus by Gielleböl, 1771, p. 312).[3]

---

[1] "The simple sledge" in the Oseberg find from 900 A. D. had already then, such a loose box-shaped body, Grieg, 1928, Pl. XVI.
[2] Schultze, 1747, Fig. 10.
[3] Examples in the museum at Bygdöy; Grieg, 1928, p. 220.

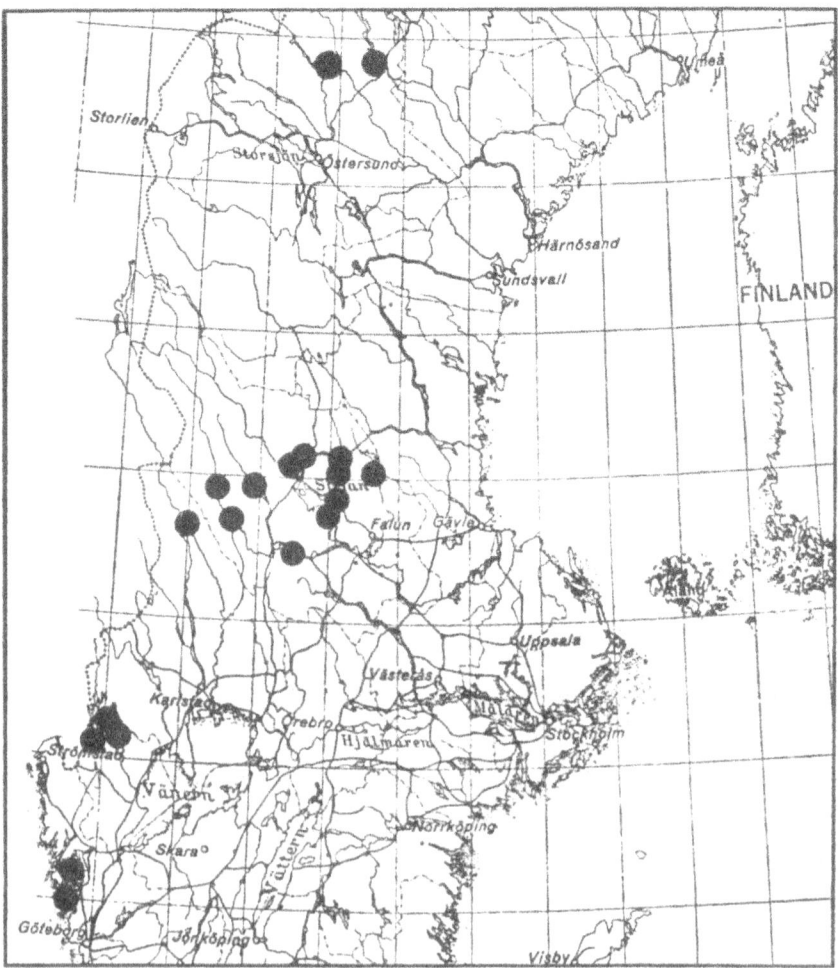

Fig. 28. The distribution of sledges with semi-cylindrical body, in Sweden.

As we have seen, the sledge with the concave platform is a development characteristic rather of the west of Norway, but it occurs also in the two provinces Hedmark and Akershus which neighbour Sweden. It seems to have been put to a more varied use there than in our country. It would doubtless seem that the Swedish and Norwegian expansions cohere, and that we are touching upon a culture phenomenon which, in certain respects, may be compared, for instance, with the disc-wheel in Chapter V. It is more than probable that the element is of ancient extraction. To a certain degree is this assumption supported by the affinity of the type with forms in other areas. There are analogies in Finland,[1] in the East Baltic Countries[2] and in Russia.[3] A relation-

---

[1] Vilkuna, 1930, p. 34. [2] Russwurm, 1855, Pl. XI; Bielenstein, 1907—18, 2, p. 356.
[3] Zelenin p. 1927, Fig. 80. — Cf. sledges with the concave, platform were in use in England, Seebohm, 1927, p. 304.

ship in some way may also be noted with the conveyance type which has a concave platform and is met with in the most northern parts of Finland and Sweden. The resemblance is especially striking when a comparison is made between the Norwegian sledges and these latter. Certain details of the construction are very akin. One particularly notices that in some cases the wood of the platform is plaited together with osiers.[1]

A somewhat dominating type of superstructure is that of the hay-sledge which either comprises side-rails and plaited screens at the fore and rear, or is made of rails with vertical laths. This form was common throughout great parts of Northern and the whole of Central Sweden. It was used especially for transporting hay, and was also extensively employed as a summer vehicle at harvesting times. Through the pen of J. Rhezelius the form was known in the early half of the 17th century.[2] On the reproduction which Rhezelius described there were arched superstructures at the ends, a form not known to me from later time. Olof Broman states that, in Hälsingland, in the early half of the 18th century, a superstructure as described in the foregoing, without the arched attachments, might easily be used on a sledge or a cart.[3] Some time later, Magnus Crælius told of forms from the Kalmar district, Småland, which were comprised of five railed pieces, and which could be used on the waggon as well.[4] An intimate interaction between the body of the sledge and that of the cart and the waggon can easily be understood, and instances, here and there, make their appearance. There is in the west of Sweden a type of sledge-body, where the laths forming the framework are weaved into the bottom, Pl. XI: 1. Carl von Linné describes this body as having been seen on a cart in the surroundings of Alingsås.[5]

Similarly common was the square, box-shaped body type. In its primitive form, sewn together with osiers, it still appears today, here and there in North Sweden but, as a rule, only incidentally.[6] Of a more developed construction, with a body of regular carpentered formation, and built in one with the sledge, it became extensively employed in porterage.[7] Variations of this type, which I am unable to treat here, have made their appearance, especially in connection

---

[1] Examples in the Museum at Bygdøy and Heiberg's Collection, Ambla. — The barrow in the Oseberg find is of similar construction, Grieg, 1928, pp. 228—230.

[2] Rhezelius, 1634, p. 20.   [3] Broman, 1911—, 3, p. 43.

[4] Crælius, 1774, p. 366.

[5] E. u. 4296, Erikstad, Dalsland. — Linné, 1746, p. 145.

[6] E. u. 541, Ljusdal, Hälsingland; Arenander, 1906, p. 10, Angermanland; Nordiska Mus. 183,469, Vilhelmina, Lappland.

[7] For porterage in general and its connection with the vehicle, see Erixon, 1934, pp. 32, 62. On the general importance of porterage previous to the railway, see, especially, Heckscher, 1907, pp. 86—90 and compare Furuskog, 1924, pp. 89—92.

with the transport of iron-ore and the shipping of iron-bars.[1] To this group belongs the sledge which is known from Jämtland,[2] and which was used on the long trading excursions in Norrland. Specific types for the transport of charcoal, which the peasants of Central Sweden burned in their kilns for the use of the iron-foundaries, also developed. Of these there exists a rich subject-matter in the form of notices and older literature, but these belong to such comparatively late and specific stages in the development, that they scarcely need to be described further in this connection.[3]

Amongst the forms included in the "box" type, we meet with the conveyance in contradistinction to the transport vehicle, with its rectangular shaped body. The body is always attached to the under-carriage.

Thanks to the Oseberg find, we know three sledges from the Viking Age, which are generally assumed to be conveyances. It must be emphasized, however, that, as in the case of the waggon, there is no absolute guarantee for such an assumption. The exceedingly rich and artistic decoration with which they are embellished, need not necessarily be regarded as a criterion. At any rate, in its main features, the type corresponds more to the porterage sledge than to the conveyance used for persons. From a somewhat later date, however, evidence is forthcoming which indicates that the vehicle was also used as a conveyance. There is a sledge on the remarkable 12th century wall-hanging from Övre Hogdal, in Härjedalen, which is harnessed to a horse, and evidently on the way to Church, which latter is also pictured on the weaving. In the sledge are two persons.[4] It is of interest to note the high front and rear ends of the body of the sledge as being a characteristic feature which recurs in the oldest of the Swedish provinces, Pl. IX: 2.

This type of conveyance was in use up to the 19th century under the characteristic name of "barkslade," in many of the Upper Dalarna districts. If

---

[1] Especially noteworthy is the type which was common in the mining districts of Värmland, Västmanland and Nerike. It has a high back by means of which the vehicle is steered. The runners are high and placed close together. Examples in the Nordiska Mus.; Hofberg, 1878, p. 43; Bore, 1891, p. 15; pers. notes. — A sledge for the transport of bars of iron, which has holes at the front and rear is in Västmanland's Museum, Västerås.

[2] See Larsson, 1912, pp. 78—81; Johansson, 1924—25, pp. 87—91; Granberg, 1927 and Arbman, 1932. — A similar box-shaped sledge for transport from Gothenburg is known from Åsenhöga, Småland, Nordiska Mus. 140,619.

[3] Charcoal sledges were mentioned as early as the 16th century, for example, from Husby, Dalarna, 1545 (State Archives). From Hälsingland were similar sledges described by Broman, 1911—, 3, p. 85, in the early half of the 18th century.

[4] Lindblom, 1932, Pl. 6, pp. 11—13. — A journey by sledge in the year 1332 was made by the Bishop of Västerås to the Norwegian boundary, in connection with an inspection in Dalarna, see Boëthius, 1922, p. 109.

one should venture to believe, and it is not unlikely, that the term really was connected with just this type of sledge, one might follow the ancestry of the same by means of archival testimony, back to the 15th century.[1] About this time, and during the next century, it seems to have spread throughout the Mälar Provinces. Typical of Upper Dalarna is the conservation of various cultural specialities which, in older times, were characteristic of the districts round the inland seas of Central Sweden.

The sledge was oft-times the product of very skilled carpentry. In its later form there are obvious traces of the cabinet-maker's art with its inserted mirrors and painted decoration, Fig. 30. How one was placed in these comparatively narrow sledges may be seen from a picture executed by a peasant painter from Mora in Dalarna and reproduced here, Fig. 29.

About the middle of the last century these narrow sledges (called "bredslädar" after the breadth between the runners), were replaced by more spacious and comfortable forms.[2] We know of another type of sledge which was used as a conveyance in the 16th and 17th centuries by foreigners, who visited our land. The traveller lay in the body of the sledge and was completely covered with skins. Samuel Kiechel, a Dutch merchant, tells how in the year 1586 he travelled from Stockholm in the company of a Netherland woman: "It is strange to see how women are conveyed in the winter-time. The sledges are specially made so that the women can lie down and be completely covered over, with the exception of the face. The sledges are then covered with sheepskins which are tied down, and the traveller lies like a child in its cradle."[3] It is probable that the oldest known Swedish sledge in preservation, the so-called Axel Oxenstierna's sledge, in the Royal Armoury, was used in a similar manner.[4] The type must have occurred at an early date, as there is no special mention of it in later time. However, it coincides in certain respects with the conveyance which is in use at the present day in most Northern Sweden under the name of the "åkrissla," Pl. V: 3.[5] It is conceivable that these later sledges are preserved relics from very early and more general ancestry.

---

[1] Bergström, 1892—95, I, p. 156; several evidences in Svenska Akademiens Ordbok, under Barkslade; from Skara in Västergötland, 1554, Västergötlands fornminnesförenings tidskrift, 8—9, 1897, p. 91; from Uppland, 1631, Edling, 1925, p. 83.

[2] The development was rather uniform in Central Sweden, cf. Hälsingland, Hillgren, 1925, p. 36.

[3] Kiechel, 1586, pp. 17—18. Cf. Ogier, 1634—35, p. 58.

[4] Cf. Gödecke, 1885, col. 11. — Sheep-skins and feather-beds ("slädbolstrar") were mentioned in 16th century inventories, for instance, 1554 at Benhammar in Västergötland, Lundberg, 1931, pp. 226, 229.

[5] In 1674, a rector on leaving his home in Härnösand for Piteå received as a gift "a feather-bed for a sledge, with harness and bear-skins", Nordlander, 1914, p. 63. I am indebted to Dr. N. L. Rasmusson for this information. — It is not improbable that by the expression "rusken," Russian, sledge, mentioned from the 15th century, from Vadstena, Östergötland, reference is made to this type. Stockholms Stads Skotte-

Fig. 29. Detail from a painting 1874 from Mora, Dalarna. Nordiska Mus. 3,941.

The vehicles of the peasantry of the central and south Swedish provinces in later time bore traces of much influence from the culture of the higher classes. The conveyance became shorter and many different types presented themselves in connection with the varying styles. One more clearly defined than the rest played an important part in the development of the vehicle on the whole. This was the real narrow-sledge ("kappsläde"), Pl. IX: 3. A. Mitzka says summarily that in Sweden it is not "volkskundlich."[1]

Circumstances connected with this development varied according to the different parts of the land, and obvious is that the type came into use amongst officials, public functionaries and the gentry but, before long, it was an important element in peasant culture too, where its influences soon was brought to bear on other types. In Sweden it was not until towards the end of the 18th century that these sledges gained a more general expansion.[2] On the other hand, they seem to have made victorious progress in Norway as early as the middle of the 18th century. Here, it has become nationalized to a far greater extent than in Sweden, and one can trace its reaction in some of the Swedish neighbouring districts, though due to purchase.[3]

Sledges of a type which, in some respects, resemble the foregoing and, which, doubtless, have paved the way for its introduction, exist as a national culture-element in our land. Under the name of "troll-hopper" ("trollhoppa") it was chiefly used on bad roads, Pl. IX: 1. One sat astride with one's feet on the runners. In some places it is said to be the oldest form of conveyance.[4] I can mention examples from Västergötland,[5] Halland,[6] Scania,[7] Dals-

bok, pp. 12, 366 (Dr. S. O. Jansson has drawn my attention to this notice). — It is noteworthy that this long, low and broad sledge of Finnish type was still in use during the last century in the Swedish Finn Territories, for instance Gästrikland, Gottlund, 1817, p. 106.

[1] Mitzka, 1934, p. 15.

[2] Prof. S. Erixon has informed me that the narrow sledge was mentioned before the middle of the 18th century in an inventory after the decease of a peasant, in Skultuna, Västmanland.

[3] Examples in Arvika Museum, Värmland, and in Jämtland's Museum, Östersund; pers. notes from Värmland: Erixon, 1933, p. 278.

[4] E. u. 240, Central Småland.

[5] Many examples in the Skara Museum; Ljunggren, 1913, p. 6.

[6] Example in Varberg Museum.

[7] According to Herr A. Cronquist, from Skarhult.

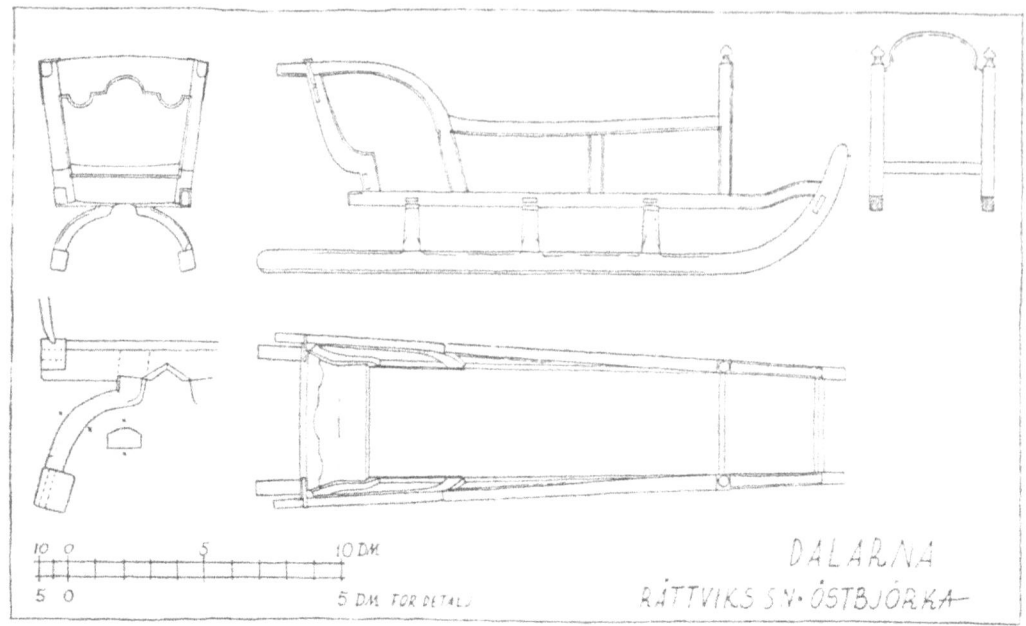

Fig. 30. Conveyance from Rättvik, Dalarna. After a drawing by G. Gustafsson.

land,[1] and also from Denmark[2]. From the middle of the 17th century mention is made of the type by a foreign traveller. He writes: "They are shaped like high stools on which the men ride, with their feet on either side, sometimes two or three on each, just as they would sit on the same horse."[3]

The main point of interest in connection with the real narrow-sledge lies in the fact that it is an imported culture-element which in some natural way associated itself with that of the Country's own. It is a difficult matter to acquire closer knowledge as to the manner in which the vehicle found its way to the North, but evident it seems, that the land of its origin is Germany. From the early half of the 17th century have similar forms been used, some magnificently garnished, as an equipage for entertainment and merry-making at the courts of princes. Mention should not either be omitted as to the part they played in the merry-go-round, an amusement indulged in on certain occasions when the cavalier took the little back seat and drove, whilst his lady sat in the front with the lance.[4]

---

[1] Hembygden, 1928, p. 8.
[2] Example in Dansk Folkemuseum, Copenhagen.
[3] Ogier, 1634—35, p. 58. — A sledge closely akin was used by forest-surveyors in the 19th century in Värmland and in Österdalen in Norway (according to Prof. H. Geijer; Bull, 1916—19, 2, p. 158).
[4] See Kreisel, 1927, pp. 132—166.

In an earlier treatise the author has expressed his opinion that these German narrow-sledges were related to the Hornschlitten or traineaux à cornes which were in use in the Swiss and south-German alpine districts.[1] It seems that only due to this assumption can one give a natural explanation of the long upward curving runners. On the horn-sledge, as known, they serve as handles for the man who hauls, and as brakes on the mountain sides.[2] The so-called Bockschlitten are transition types. The runners are coupled together at the front, doubtless due to the inconvenience caused by the points of the runners, when the sledge is being hauled by draught-animals.[3]

---

[1] Berg, 1929, pp. 57—61. It is worthy of note that from Uppsala in 1657, is mention of the purchase of a sledge "upon which 'horns' were erected," Bottiger, 1891—92, p. 8.

[2] See Huber, 1919, pp. 5—7; Schramek, 1908, pp. 105—106, 314; Friedli, 1905—28, 2, pp. 85—87.

[3] For Bockschlitten see, for instance, Huber, 1919, pp. 18—19 and Zell, 1902—03, Fig. 76 b.

CHAPTER III

THE SIMPLE RUNNER-SLEDGE AND THE ORIGIN OF THE BUILT-UP SLEDGE

The theory more nearly approaching the scientific concerning the origin of the built-up sledge has been expounded by U. T. Sirelius. He endeavoured to trace the evolution of this vehicle from the sled which has a single-runner of the type described in Chapter I in connection with the finds from Gråträsk, Delsbo and Laukaa. Sirelius arrived at his conclusion by means of actual experiment with a number of runners having double pairs of traces and which were found in bogs (see foregoing Chapter). He inserted sticks within the trace-holes and discovered that, as regards the foremost pair, these remained vertical, whilst those at the rear tended to diverge. On the other hand, the intervening space between the staves was not sufficient to raise the question of a real single-runner sled. Sirelius came to the conclusion, however, that the finds referred to double-runner sledges, but that typological development had left behind a certain affinity with the construction of the single-runner sled.[1] As a result of careful investigation on the part of Toivo Itkonen and myself, it has been proved that Sirelius' conclusion was solely based on the worn condition of the trace-holes, whilst it was found that unquestionably the holes had formerly been parallel.[2] This discovery deprives Sirelius' theory of its main support and one is obliged to seek for enlightenment in another direction.

A certain group of vehicles which has not yet been touched upon, might be considered of evidential value here. Both in Sweden and throughout a vast expansion area in foreign countries, there is a simple runner-sledge, the platform of which lies directly upon the runners. Undoubtedly there should be some connection between these two types, i. e., the simple runner-sledge and the built-up sledge, but in order to facilitate investigation, they must be kept distinct. Much confusion has ensued within the field of scientific research, owing to an extensive use of the term sledge, void of any closer definition.

---

[1] Sirelius, 1913 (a), 1916, p. 14. [2] Itkonen, 1930, p. 87.

In our country, as well as in northern Europe and northern Asia, the simple runner-sledge has been employed mostly in summer-time. It may not have been so earlier. And should this be the case, its predecessor must have been almost entirely crowded out by the built-up sledge which, even in the capacity of summer-sledge within enormous parts of its expansion area, also invaded the territory of the simple runner-sledge on bare ground. This is due, of course, to the greater practicability which the built-up sledge affords by reason of its lightness, and the protection it gives to its load from damp and from contact with the ground.

The simple runner-sledge is principally used in Sweden as an implement of agriculture for carting stones from pasture-lands and for transporting the plough to and from the field. In the central districts, amongst the dwellers on the plains, it is also used for the daily cartage of water in barrels and tubs. It generally consists of two roughly-hewn runners held together by means of cross-bars of wood which, in most cases, are nailed to the upper sides of the runners. On older examples treenails have been used. In the foremost crossbar which is generally mortised into the runners, there are staples to which the traces are fastened. Sometimes placed horizontally are planks which form a kind of platform, Pl. X: 2—3.

The simple form is met with all over Sweden from Lappland to Scania. In the latter province, the forked type to which we shall return appears to have been more commonly used, undoubtedly and mostly, because it was an economical way of using up this more easily accessible kind of wood. The simple-runner sledge however, as already mentioned, is closely associated with agriculture and was therefore principally used on the plains.[1] It can only have gained ground at a later date, in certain parts. There are evidences only in the south-west part of the country that it was put to a more all-round use and, even also to some extent, may-be, in winter-time. We have three rather vague and hazy indications from Scaina,[2] Halland[3] and Bohuslän[4] which in some way are supported by a couple of Danish parallels, Fig. 33.[5]

A forked sled has already been mentioned as appearing in south Sweden in variation with the simple two-runner sledge, which is mostly contrived

---

[1] This is apart from its more incidental employment for transport of heavy objects, even in modern times. A simple-runner sledge loaded with a mill-stone from about 1700, is reproduced by Dahlberg, 1716, Pl. 124 (Rosersberg).
[2] Munka-Ljungby: "gumpaslädе", E. u. 236.
[3] Kalén 1923, under "Slädsveg".
[4] Lindberg, 1921, p. 47.
[5] Gruntvig, 1909, p. 120 (Falster); Ingvorsen, 1918, p. 131 (Själland).

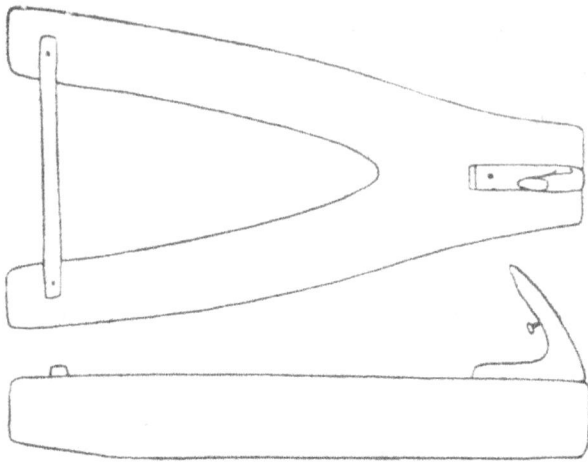

Fig. 31. A fork-shaped sledge from Fågeltofta, Skåne. After a sketch by G. Gustafsson.

from a forked tree-trunk, Fig. 31. The hook for the traces is at the fore, and the two branches are often connected by means of one or two crossbars, Pl. X: 1. In Central Sweden there are instances where this type was supplanted by another model, formed of two branches nailed together at the fore. Cf. map, Fig. 32.

I know of the forked simple runner-sledge from *Scania* (Fågeltofta, according to Dr. G. Gustafsson, Fig. 31; Brandstad, E. u. 4041; St. Herrestad, E. u. 612; Harjager, E. u. 193; Jonstorp, E. u. 428; Dagstorp, E. u. 193; Munka-Ljungby, E. u. 236; cf. Karutz, 1925—26, 2, p. 45 and Leser, 1927, p. 42, note 5[1]); *Småland* (Linneryd, E. u. 5588, Fryele and Hogshult, E. u. 5260; Lommaryd, E. u. 3315; Mörlunda, photog. S. Erixon in E. u.), *Gotland* (Fårö, E. u. 3241), *Västergötland* (Sjuhärad, E. u. 436; Tidavad, photog. E. u.; according to Dr. Gösta Montell there is such a sledge in the Fristad Museum, which has served for bringing home the hay), *Dalsland* (Frändefors, pers. notes; Eriksstad, E. u. 4296), *Nerike* (Snavlunda, according to Herr G. Persson, used for transporting the plough), *Östergötland* (Kullerstad, Nordiska Mus. 187,761, Pl. X: 1; Kimstad, E. u. 203; Horn, photog. in E. u.; cf. E. u. 65) and *Uppland* (Tensta, E. u. 5402; Vaksala, according to Dr. S. Drakenberg, Västerås). A closely related vehicle is from *Småland*, which was used for collecting timber. It was known as "hammel" or "vagel." There are examples from Sjösås, according to Herr J. A. Göth, Torsås (E. u. 223), Linneryd (E. u. 5588), Öja (E. u. 4301) and Urshult (E. u. 5623; cf. Virdestam, 1923, p. 28).

Exterior to Sweden we meet with the normal as well as the fork-shaped simple-runner sledge, throughout a widely-stretched area. I know of the latter from *Norway* (Olsen, 1914—24, p. 126, Sogn), *Denmark* (Grundtvig, 1909, p. 236), *England* (Seebohm, 1927, p. 304), *Spain* and *Portugal* (Krüger, 1927, p. 72; Ebeling, 1932, pp. 52—54; Messerschmidt, 1931, pp. 142—143; Bergmann, 1934, pp. 46—48; cf. from the French frontier districts, Fahrholz, 1931, pp. 141—142). The type formed of two runners joined together at the fore occurs also in *Poland* (Moszynski, 1929, p. 629). Noteworthy is its occurrence in Assam, in *Further India*, where it is of enormous size and fitted with cross-bars. It is employed here for transporting huge stone monuments (Hutton, 1929, pp. 336—337; a model from Naga Hills in Pitt-Rivers Collection, Oxford).

The fork-shaped runner-sledge appears nowadays as a by-form of the normal type. It is not unlikely that it may have connections one way or another with

---

[1] The implement is used in certain places also for transport of the plough.

SIMPLE RUNNER-SLEDGE AND ORIGIN OF THE BUILT-UP SLEDGE 77

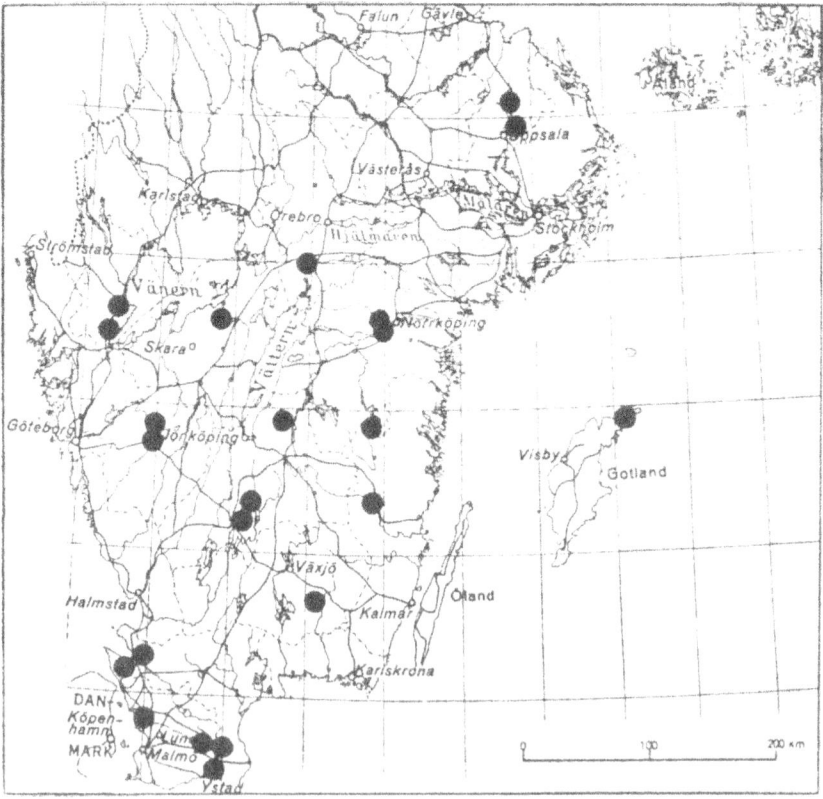

Fig. 32. The distribution of the fork-shaped simple runner-sledge in Sweden.

the forked slide-car as we shall learn to know it in Chapter VI. The beam-like harnessing arrangement should in this case have been exchanged for a new form having a loose pole or traces.[1]

In the European culture-area, the normal two-runner sledge very often resembles the one in Sweden, but it occurs in a more elaborated form and with the cross-bars mortised into the runners. This is especially the case in Germany and further southwards. Most likely this is partly because the vehicle was not only used for the transport of stone and other heavy loads but also for carting hay and meal-sacks etc. Not infrequently does one find the cross-bars projecting outside the runners, and in the bars are holes containing upright staves between which the load is placed.

This runner-sledge has had a somewhat comprehensive expansion in our part of the world. It occurs in *Denmark* (Ingvorsen, 1918, p. 131; Olsen, 1914, p. 31), the *Faroe Islands* (Jirlow, 1931 (a), p. 130), *Finland* (Pettersson, 1917, p. 149; Suomen suku, 1928, 1, p. 279), *Esthonia* (according to Herr J. Österman from Runö), *Latvia* (Hupel, 1774—82, 2, p. 42, tells of its employment in Riga), *Germany* (Hamburgs Vergangenheit, 1896—97, p. 618; Almgren, 1932, p. 184, the figure of Roland in Lübeck;

---

[1] Strangely enough it is stated from Urshult that the fork-shaped sledge was sometimes made so that the beam and the sled were in one (E. u. 5588).

Fig. 33. Simple runner-sledge from Falster, Denmark. After Fr. L. Grundtvig.

Palmstedt, 1780, p. 180, Stralsund; Mielke, 1912, p. 144; Daehne, 1930, p. 265, Leipzig; Leser, 1927, p. 479, Hunsrück; Heyne, 1901, p. 34, Bavaria; cf. Florinus, 1722, p. 554; Boerner, 1930, Pl. XXXVIII, 1505; Gröber, 1928, p. 60), *Holland* (Blok, 1897, 1, pp. 74, about 1570, 24, 1610, 71, 1618, 46, 1694, and passim; Granberg, 1929—31, 1, Pl. 11, 1632; Romdahl, 1905, Pl. 20; Schotel, 1905, p. 409, used at a burial in Amsterdam; Schück, 1923, p. 33, 1729; Hirth, 1882, 5, Pl. 1556; Palmstedt, 1780, p. 169; Tersmeden, 1912—19, 2, p. 21, 1734; cf. a runner-sledge for the transport of casks in a town, reproduced about 1505 in Flämisches Fest-Kalender, reproduced, for example, by Zoepfl, 1928, p. 464), *England* (Pulbrook, 1922, p. 234; Traill-Mann, 1903, p. 184; Fox, 1931, Pl. II—III), *France* (Chauvet, 1921, pp. 33—35, 130, Normandy; Krüger, 1928, p. 199, the north-east and west of France; Giese, 1931, p. 365; Flagge, 1935, pp. 152—154, the Alpine district of Provence; Fahrholz, 1931, pp. 142—143; Kruse, 1934, pp. 73—74, the two latter for the Pyrenees; cf. Ogier, 1634—35, p. 58), *Switzerland* (Huber, 1919, pp. 8—9; Freuler, 1906, pp. 6—7; Stebler, 1903, p. 303), *Italy* (Phieler, 1934, pp. 72—73; Krüger, 1928, p. 199, the mainland and Sicily; Wagner, 1921, p. 72, Sardinia; Palmstedt, 1780, p. 146, Genoa), *Spain* (de Aranzadi, 1894, p. 222, Calabria; Karutz, 1898, p. 335, the Basques; Huber, 1919, p. 56, the Basques; Krüger, 1927, p. 73, Asturia, Galicia; Krüger, 1928, p. 199, Santander etc.; Ebeling, 1932, pp. 52—53) and *Portugal* (Krüger, 1927, p. 73).

The occurrence of the runner-sledge in Madeira should be included within the European expansion area, both as regards rural districts and the town.[1] A well-known fact is that it occurs here also as a pleasure vehicle. Sometimes it is drawn, and often it is used for sliding down mountain sides.[2] There is said to be a similar conveyance in North Africa, probably due to European influence. R. Karutz assumes Portuguese influence for Madeira,[3] and the same may most probably refer to the sledge in Porto Rico, in the West Indies. It is stated that at the great excavations in Egypt, "the runner sledge after the old method" was employed to transport the greater finds.[4]

The clearly defined westerly expansion of this sledge is indeed remarkable. From what is known it seems to be in direct opposition to that of the built-up sledge, which appears to have spread distinctly eastwards. It is uncertain however, as to whether the runner-sledge had such a widely-stretched expansion in olden times, as the one recently referred to. That the cult of agriculture may have been an important factor in its expansion in ancient days, would

---

[1] Hartnack, 1930, pp. 150—151.
[2] See, for example, Mason, 1894, p. 546.
[3] Karutz, 1898, p. 335 [4] Borchardt, 1907, p. 165.

seem obvious, when it is remembered that the vehicle was chiefly used in this connection.

Moreover, the simple-runner sledge has spread to a certain extent with town-culture. In many towns in the central and western parts of Europe, it was used far into later times, as the foregoing evidences have shewn. The idea was to spare the roads as much as possible, and the use of the sledge was supported to the extent that high charges were made to the owners of wheeled-vehicles.[1] It is said that only certain streets were open to wheeled-traffic, whilst all others were available to the "simple runner-sledge, drawn by oxen."[2] The fact is well-known that the Amsterdam livery-stables carried on their activities in the 18th century and the early part of the 19th, with a kind of sled of a closely related type.[3] It is quite possible, but not absolutely certain, that the Stockholm carters, in olden times, used this sledge for the transport of goods. In 1622, the "släpa" — in all probability the simple runner-sledge — was mentioned amongst their vehicles, in addition to the cart and waggon.[4] The transportation of water-casks, in cases of fire, was specially charged to the Stockholm carters.[5]

In connection with the employment of the sledge in towns have certain methods been brought about to improve the glide of the runners, and probably also as A. Wiedemann avers, to prevent ignition through friction.[6] Most common was it to splash water on to the roadways. According to Erik Palmstedt's description from Amsterdam, 1780, "the sledge is shod with wood, and at the front of the vehicle is a vessel which splashes out water to facilitate the driving, or else there is a wet swab with which the driver can water the road before the runners."[7] From what Tersmeden writes in 1734, grease seems to have been used for the same purpose. He states that "the driver walks beside the sledge with a long kind of mop dipped in (whale) oil which he slings under both runners."[8] The same method occurs in Spain.[9] As known, there are ancient Egyptian pictures portraying in like manner a man going before the sledge and watering the ground beneath the runners, from an earthenware vessel.[10] Quite recently an investigator has endeavoured to point out that this watering

---

[1] Schück, 1923, p. 33, Amsterdam, 1729; Hamburgs Vergangenheit, 1896—97, p. 618.
[2] Palmstedt, 1780, p. 146, Genoa.
[3] Kreisel, 1927, p. 95. Fig. 40, the middle of the 18th century; example in Amsterdamsch Historisch Museum, the early half of the 19th century.
[4] Lundin-Strindberg, 1882, p. 511.
[5] For example, Stockholmsbilder, 1924, Pl. 74, the fire at the Royal Palace, 1697; Feldhaus, 1914, Figs. 207—209, 371, Nuremberg, etc.
[6] Wiedemann, 1920, p. 210.   [7] Palmstedt, 1780, p. 169.
[8] Tersmeden, 1912—19, 2, p. 21.   [9] de Aranzadi, 1897, p. 222.
[10] Wilkinson, 1878, 3, pp. 448/49, 451.

of the ground is indicative of no rational purpose but is, on the contrary, only connected with religious cults and ceremonies.[1] The utter impossibility of this theory should have been brought to light through the foregoing European evidences to the contrary. This watering before the runners has more in common with the ice-tiring system known almost everywhere within the radius of the Northern Climate. In Åsele, in Västerbotten, the under-sides of the runners were wiped three or four times before use, with a cloth dipped in warm water.[2] Russians from the Amur districts employed the same method. They wiped the under-sides with a wet cloth, or piece of skin, to produce a thin coating of ice before starting off on their expeditions.[3] The custom of the Central Eskimos is not unknown. They shoed their runners with peat, and moistened the peat every morning with warm water. On long journeys they often had with them a bag of pulverised peat for repairs.[4]

To what extent the simple-runner sledge was employed in Central Europe may be gathered from its occurrence in another connection. For example, its appearance in the form of the sledge for children, in which function it is also known in Sweden. G. A. Aldén, from Småland, writes "Papa thought that I should do as he did when he was a boy, make a kind of vehicle for myself known as the 'sugga' (sow). Two broad boards were given to me which were hewn at the one end, in such a manner that they, from the side view, roughly resembled the figure of a sow. The boards were held together by means of a couple of cross-bars, and a third board was nailed into place, to sit upon."[5] This kind of child's sledge has been very common in many parts of Sweden.[6] In other Northern Countries as well as in Central Europe it has also been popular.[7]

Small, low sledges, which are used on the ice, and pushed along by means of spiked staves, sometimes one, sometimes a pair, belong to the foregoing type. I have met with them from the south-east of Scania, where they are much favoured by the youth.[8] In Husby, in Södermanland, they seem to have

---

[1] Horwitz, 1931. Cf. Horwitz, 1934, p. 847.
[2] According to Dr. Ragnar Jirlow, Västeras.
[3] v. Schrenck, 1891, p. 484. [4] Birket-Smith, 1927, p. 78. [5] Aldén, 1927, pp. 22—23.
[6] I have noted its occurrence in *Småland*, Östra härad, according to Dr. S. Erixon, Lommaryd, E. u. 3315; *Västergötland*, Sundén, 1903, p. 44; *Östergötland* according to Dr. S. Erixon; *Värmland*, according to Herr P. H. Nilsson; *Dalarna*, painting by O. Arborelius, reproduced Cederblom, 1923, Pl. 12 and *Stockholm*, drawing by Jacob Silvan, Nordiska Mus., Archives.
[7] See, for *Finland*, Paulaharju, 1932, p. 112; *Germany*, Florinus, 1722, p. 523; Howitt, 1842, p. 183; v. Bode, 1930, 1, p. 11, Hartzburg, about 1850; Wiklund, 1928 (b), p. 54, Weimar; *Switzerland*, Huber, 1919, p. 15 Friedli, 1905—28, 2, p. 85; *Austria*, examples in Museum für deutsche Volkskunde, Berlin, and in Volkskunde Museum, Salzburg; *Hungary*, Bátky, 1906, Pl. 112.
[8] According to Dr. S. Svensson.

PLATE XI

1. Sledge, used at wolf-hunting. Västergötland. Detail from a drawing 1849 by Fr. v. Dardel.

2. Timber-sledge from Åsele, Västerbotten. Nordiska Mus. 177,040.

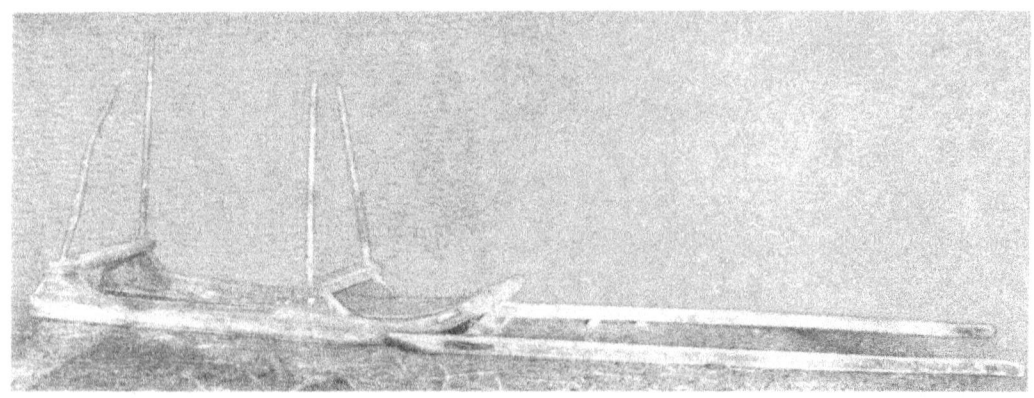

3. Sledge from Frändefors, Dalsland. Photog. G. Berg.

PLATE XII

1. Timber-trailing without runners. Ytre Rendal, Sör-Tröndelag, Norway. Photog. S. Erixon–O. Ekberg.

2. Timber-transport with a short-sledge only. Häggenås, Jämtland. Photog. O. Ekberg.

3. Timber-transport (the man is wearing snow-shoes). Frostviken, Jämtland. Photog. G. Modin.

PLATE XIII

1. Short-sledge for timber-transport. Kisa, Östergötland. Photog. T. Heimer.
2. Short-sledge for timber-transport. Idala, Halland. Varberg Museum.
3. Short-sledge for timber-transport. Venjan, Dalarna. Photog. O. Bannbers.
4. A pair of sledges, for timber-transport. Norrbotten. Nordiska Museet.

PLATE XIV

1. Double-sledge. After a drawing by Fr. v. Dardel.

2. Double-sledge for hay-transport. Silvberg, Dalarna. Photog. J. Lindros.

3. Double-sledge for timber-transport. Central Småland. After a sculpture by C. A. Rolander.

been employed in connection with winter-fishing,[1] and in this instance one seems to have sat or stood on them. Vehicles used in this way, but not always of the simple runner-sledge type are also known from Norway,[2] Denmark[3] and especially in Holland. German and Dutch sledges often used in connection with skating parties, on the ice, are generally of this type, but they are equipped with a handle at the back for the pusher.[4]

There is a certain affinity in appearance between the sledges pushed along by staves and the sledge with bone runners, which, latter, is in reality, merely a seat fixed upon bone skates. They are also similarly employed. Relatively imposing evidences of such sledges are forthcoming from many Central European Countries, sometimes in the form of more or less authenticated ancient finds and often as traditional discoveries.[5] In the North they seem to be quite missing, but as Henry Balfour says "one might reasonably expect them to have occurred there."[6]

The simple runner-sledge appears, however, to be just as much at home in other branches of Swedish peasant-culture. In Central Sweden it was the custom to transport the harrow to and from the field in an upside-down position, and for this purpose a couple of runners were attached to the back of the vehicle which, together with the harrow itself formed a kind of sledge or trailer, if one may so say. I know this type from several places in Östergötland,[7] Nerike,[8] Västmanland,[9] Uppland,[10] Dalarna[11] and Ångermanland.[12] An implement for crushing clods of earth was often conveyed in the same manner.[13]

According to Gudmund Hatt, it was not seldom that in later years the Lapps of Västerbotten equipped the under-sides of their sledges with runners.[14] This reinforcement may be viewed as an attempt to ensure a more satisfactory balance.[15] It is quite obvious that we meet here with influence from the Northern sledge. Hatt is of the same opinion, but Kai Donner, on the other hand, has tried to shew that it is the emerging of the double-runner idea in connection

---

[1] E. u. 5343. — Cf. v. Wright-Fries-Ekström, 1836, appendix, pp. 18—19.
[2] Bogeng, 1926, p. 552.
[3] Grundtvig, 1909, p. 200, Falster; Reimer, 1910—19, pp. 381—382, Funen; painting by Peter Hansen in Statens Museum för Kunst, Copenhagen.
[4] Howitt, 1842, pp. 179 ff.; Bogeng, 1926, pp. 531—556; v. der Ven, 1920, p. 82.
[5] Virchow, 1887, pp. 361—362; Balfour, 1898; Herman, 1902, pp. 226—232; Goldstern, 1922, pp. 107—110.
[6] Balfour, 1898, p. 11.
[7] From numerous districts, see E. u. 1930; E. u. 6005, 4622 etc.
[8] Personal notes. [9] E. u. 4097; 3275. [10] E. u. 3137; 3911.
[11] Personal notes (Gustafs and Mora); E. u. 4307.
[12] Boding, 1747, p. 68; E. u. 5541.
[13] Arenander, 1906, p. 9 (Ångermanland); E. u. 4622 (Östergötland).
[14] Hatt, 1913, pp. 140—141.
[15] Elgström, 1922, pp. 150, 153.

with the Lapp-sledge.[1] Closely related is the equipping of ice-boats used on long seal-hunting expeditions in the Golf of Bothnia, with runners. J. Bureus wrote at the beginning of the 17th century, that the people from the coastal-districts of Norrland, "sail with ice-boats, fitted with runners covered with seal-skin, between the lanes in the ice."[2] In olden times it seems that even quite large boats had runners, but nowadays the practise seems to be relegated to smaller skiffs.[3]

Some implements should be brought forward here as having parts which in some way or other bear more or less resemblance to parts included in the structure of the simple runner-sledge and, which, whilst seldom serving any transport purpose, aid in stabilizing the implement in question. In the vernacular here and elsewhere, no doubt, terminology often hints at the resemblance between the simple runner-sledge and the built-up sledge, and it is not at all unlikely that even the construction itself has been influenced by the same. To this group of implements belongs the sledge on which is placed the eel-buck, out in the water. It is used in the eastern parts of Sweden and is common in Småland, Östergötland, Södermanland and as far north as Uppland.[4] As far as form goes, the sledge, on which the cylindrical bee-hives of Thuringia are laid to prevent them from rolling, may also be said to have kinship.[5] A sledge should not be omitted which, laden with stones, not rarely serves as a counter-weight in the ropery and similar works. From the East Baltic Countries and Russia a similar sledge-like contrivance is known in connection with the "runner-net."[6]

Only in exceptional cases has it happened in Sweden that whole buildings have been methodically erected on runners or on the platform of a runner-sledge to facilitate removal from place to place. Dr. Sigurd Erixon has given me information as to a fishing-hut in the neighbourhood of Söderköping, which is moved about on runners, and used for winter-fishing. J. M. Lund tells of a shepherd's hut on runners from Telemarken in Norway which is "just large enough to accommodate one person, and is used as a resting place at night for the shepherd or whoever tends the cattle. It is used especially in places where there are no dairy farms."[7] Similar to the hut in Östergötland, and

---

[1] Donner, 1915, p. 103. [2] Bureus, 1886, p. 201.
[3] Ekman, 1910, pp. 219—220; cf. Jirlow, 1930, pp. 81—82. Nordenskiöld has reproduced a boat with runners from a Fuegian tribe in South America which was used for transport from one water-course to another. He considers it to be an example of autochthonal invention. (Nordenskiöld, 1930, pp. 73—74).
[4] Olsson, 1914, p. 41; Ekman, 1910, p. 363; cf. Modéer, 1933, p. 190.
[5] Armbruster, 1926, p. 103. [6] Manninen, 1931—32, I, pp. 151—152.
[7] Lund, 1785, p. 107. The Norwegian building by Phleps, 1934, pp. 26—27, is most certainly not a movable dwelling. — The Swedish Lapps in Arjeplog have a movable store-house on runners (Nordiska Mus. 192,580).

its purpose, is the one on runners used by the Ingrians for winter-fishing, round the inner parts of the Gulf of Finland.[1] A movable hut on runners is said also to occur amongst the Latvians.[2] Throughout great parts of Europe there is the well-known shepherd's cart on two wheels, which serves the same purpose as the little structure from Telemarken mentioned above.[3] To me it seems highly probable, though Franz Oelmann suggests only possible, that these "Schäferkarren," at least in some instances, are a later development of the sledge-hut which, at a later date, was more likely supplanted by the newer form.[4] In the south-west of Europe however, the sledge-hut still survives, and plays an important rôle still, in our day. R. Meringer has closely investigated this "Schlittenhaus" and shewn its intimate connection with the tending of cattle and the subsequent necessary removals. The sledge-hut serves as a dwelling-place for the shepherds, and as a dairy for the milk.[5] The purposes to which it is put, vary according to the different places, for instance, in Hungary. In olden times, from what is known, it was also used by certain nomadic tribes as a dwelling.[6] In his treatise Meringer drew attention to the very interesting fact that the Lykian tomb-stones portray buildings on runners, that is to say, sledge-huts of the type dealt with here.

After these observations regarding the occurrence of the simple runner-sledge in Europe, in more modern times, it remains to make a few statements as to its appearance in the Old Culture Countries of the Mediterranean. Strange to say its usage seems difficult to trace in Greek and Roman culture.[7] None the less, as Hugo Mötefindt also asserts, the sledge should of antiquity, have had a vast expansion in Central Europe.[8] Moreover, the sledge is believed to occur on Spanish sculptured stones from the Copper and Bronze Ages. It appears both in its normal and its forked type.[9] Most likely are the sledges seen on the Ligurian stones drawn by pair-yokes of oxen, and these are presumably contemporaries of our Northern rock-carvings. Leopold Rütimeyer has indeed interpreted them as harrows, but this construction is less probable.[10]

---

[1] Manninen, 1932, p. 105.   [2] Oelmann, 1927, p. 15.

[3] Similar shepherd's carts, probably through foreign influence, have been used by shepherds in Västergötland; Linné, 1746, p. 79; Hamilton, 1928, p. 19.

[4] Oelmann, 1927, p. 15.   [5] Meringer, 1906, 1907.   [6] Bellosics, 1913.

[7] Huber, 1919, pp. 1—2, undoubtedly and rightly regards H. Hottenroth's representations, 1893—96, Pls. 56, 104 as reconstructions. Concerning the meaning of "traha" and the support hereby gained for the occurrence of the sledge, see Meyer-Lübke, 1909, p. 217.

[8] Mötefindt, 1927—28.

[9] Breuil, 1933—35, 2, pp. 63—64.

[10] Rütimeyer, 1924, pp. 286—288. Burkitt also, 1929, p. 158 assumes these representations to be possible sledges.

In the Egypt of Antiquity the simple runner-sledge was extensively employed, generally drawn by oxen, but sometimes by man. Due to its usage in festive processions for the conveying of idols, at burials for the transport of coffins and inventarium of the tomb, and for the removal of greater and lesser sculptures, have a great number of representations been preserved.[1] However, the sledge is known to have served other purposes and inclusively should be mentioned two sledges of smaller size employed in the transport of corn-sacks.[2]

The Assyrians used the simple runner-sledge for the transport of stone monuments. Several instructive pictures have been preserved to our day in the form of reliefs. On many of these can one trace the method of decreasing the friction by throwing wood under the runners.[3]

On the other hand unfortunately, there are only scanty accounts of the Asiatic occurrence of the sledge in later times. J. G. Ginzrot, who reproduces a typical simple runner-sledge, closely boarded with cylindrical pieces of wood and loaded, states that "these are in use throughout the whole of Asia, especially in the coastal-towns," but he gives no further details to support his statement.[4] There is an interesting reproduction by Ellsworth Huntington of a sledge harnessed to a pair-yoke of oxen, and used for the transport of hay, in a village, inhabited by half-nomadic Kirghiz.[5] It is well-known that the sledge is used to a great extent in the Turkestan mountain regions. In such places as East-Buchara, Karategin etc., it is regularly employed for bringing in the harvest, and transporting goods which cannot be carried by the pack-horse. The runners are unshod, and the sledge is used winter and summer, equipped when need be, with a basket of plaited osiers.[6] Paul Leser reproduces, after Bitschurin, an example, short in structure, and unique in type from China, used for carrying seed to the field.[7] Sledges which, as regards their construction belong to the category of the simple runner-sledge, but which are equipped with a kind of structure built upon the runners, seem not to be unusual in China.[8] At times may be seen the sledge acting as conveyance on the ice, and it is then manipulated in the same manner as here in Europe. We are informed by Leopold von Schrenck that, in this capacity, it served the Dutch Embassy at

---

[1] Wiedemann, 1922, pp. 209—210; Huber, 1919, p. 1, concerning two sledges in preservation; reproductions by des Noëttes, 1931.

[2] Schäfer, 1908, p. 172.

[3] Meissner, 1920, p. 328; reproductions by des Noëttes, 1931.

[4] Ginzrot, 1817, 1, p. 4, Pl. 3, 5.

[5] Huntington, 1907, p. 130/131.

[6] v. Schwartz, 1900, pp. 336—338, 440; Olufsen, 1911, p. 125.

[7] Leser, 1927, p. 42 and 1928, p. 479.

[8] See Mallory, 1926, Fig. 20, for Central China.

the Court of Peking 1794—95.[1] At Luzon, in the Phillipines, sledges very much resembling those found in Central Asia are used for the transport of agricultural implements, and for bringing home the rice at harvest times. The harnessing is done by means of traces which are attached to the ends of the runners.[2]

The simple runner-sledge is seldom seen amongst the peoples of Northern Asia whilst, on the other hand, the built-up sledge with which we have recently become more nearly acquainted, has an important part to play. Apart from a few more uncertain instances amongst the Gilyak and the Ainu,[3] I am not in a position to mention more than the Chukchee, amongst whom, as a winter vehicle, one meets with the form in which the cross-bars are fastened on the runners, and the type having the cross-bars mortised into the runners.[4] These Chukchee sledges, so to say, bridge over to the cultures of the most northerly parts of America. According to Kaj Birket-Smith, the sledge is in all-round use amongst the Central and Labrador Eskimos. They are shorter and lighter in Baffin Land and Greenland. The more westerly Eskimos, on the other hand, only use the sledge for the transport of boats and the hunter's bag. As a conveyance, one finds here only the sledge of north-Asiatic type.[5]

The simple-runner sledge appears, as we have seen, in the garb of a summer as well as a winter vehicle, and undoubtedly there lies behind it a stage when it was able to serve both purposes. Unquestionably, as far as concerns this sledge, and as Gustave Huber has already put forth, is an expansion from north to south highly improbable, and this precludes the idea of a winter vehicle being put to summer uses.[6] It would seem reasonable to suppose instead that, when the vehicle reached a certain climate, it served also under winter conditions. Whichever way it was, however, it was supplanted in this function at an early date by the built-up sledge.

Its vast expansion classifies the simple-runner sledge as a culture-element of High Antiquity. Birket-Smith has assigned the vehicle to the archaic, which he characterizes as the "ice-hunting culture."[7] North American and North Asiatic cultural conditions have primarily been taken into consideration here,

---

[1] Horniman Museum, 1925, p. 22. Cf. with an indistinct picture in Globus 78, p. 27; v. Schrenk, 1891, p. 498.
[2] Cole, 1922, pp. 390—392.
[3] Birket-Smith, 1929, 2, p. 167.
[4] Bogoras, 1904—09, p. 107; Nordenskiöld, 1880—81, 2, pp. 98—99.
[5] Birket-Smith, 1927, pp. 78—79, 1929, 2, p. 72.
[6] Huber, 1919, p. 2.
[7] Birket-Smith, 1929, 2, p. 214.

and from what is understood, the European occurrence does not oppose the conclusion. Birket-Smith is also most emphatically of the opinion that the Eskimo sledge and the European simple runner-sledge are "genetically related."[1] This doubtless coincides with his view that the earliest Eskimo culture may, to some extent, be compared with the Period of Paleolithic culture of our part of the world.[2] Obvious is it that the simple runner-sledge is an older culture-element than the built-up sledge. It would seem that the latter's marked occurrence amongst the North Asiatic peoples — where the simple runner-sledge is rarely to be seen — is mostly due to its sturdy expansion. One is able to compare the expansion of the built-up sledge with that of reindeer-breeding within the same area. Fritz Flor's[3] statement may especially be referred to,[4] and Birket-Smith, it is interesting to note, also regards the two as coincident. It is impossible however, to share Birket-Smith's opinion, as far as Europe is concerned, that the built-up sledge "in the main, corresponds to that of reindeer nomadism, although it passes a little beyond the boundaries of the latter."[5] But this need not exclude the probability that, in North Asia, it may have spread in connection with the tame reindeer. A preponderancy of reasons would thus seem to insinuate that the built-up sledge is a later form than the simple runner type and this leads one to wonder whether the former should not be accepted as an evolution of the latter. Birket-Smith appears to consider both forms as varying developments of the "guide runner" or single runner-sledge.[6] Flor states that he views the simple runner-sledge as the prototype of the built-up sledge.[7] In another connection, however, he has spoken in favour of U. T. Sirelius' theory, though indeed not fully convinced, that the built-up sledge had its origin in the vehicle comprised of two runners and their upper-framework.[8]

Gudmund Hatt refers to experience precursory to the built-up sledge, in that he draws attention to the fact that the object in view was to raise the body of the vehicle out of reach of the loose snow, "above the puddles and pools of the spring."[9] In doing so he inclines towards A. Th. v. Middendorff, who so excellently describes the obvious and very natural form of the high Samoyed sledge, suited as it was for crossing the numerous shallow waters between the mountains, during the hot summer time.[10] We find A. G. Schrenk entertaining the same point of view. He writes: "The tundra often heavy and swampy, always uneven, and without ways or roads, allows of no other vehicle, not

---

[1] Birket-Smith, 1929, 2, p. 168.
[2] Birket-Smith, 1929, 2, pp. 216—219.
[3] Flor, 1930 (a), pp. 88, 98, 144.
[4] Cf. also Hatt, 1919, p. 179.
[5] Birket-Smith, 1929, 2, p. 166.
[6] Birket-Smith, 1929, 2, p. 165.
[7] Flor, 1930 (a), p. 98.
[8] Flor, 1930 (a), p. 88.
[9] Hatt, 1916 (b), p. 287.
[10] v. Middendorff, 1874, p. 1271.

even in the summer, than the ordinary little sledge."[1] The carts of Central Asia with their high wheels should undoubtedly not be omitted in this connection. Quite obviously they are constructed for the crossing of marshy land and water-course.[2]

The attempt to raise platform and load from the ground-surface has not always resulted as in the case of the Samoyed sledge. There are other solutions to the problem known from the North. For instance, sometimes the posts or uprights and the runners themselves are hewn in one piece, as exemplified in the Västerbotten wooden sledge, Pl. XI: 2. Such raised platforms are not uncommon on wooden sleds. Odd and interesting is it that Otis Mason publishes a parallel so far distanced as Labrador.[3] In Sweden, sledges of a similar type, and put to various uses as a winter vehicle, Pl. XI: 3, seem to have been specially common in the provinces of West Sweden.

I can mention such sledges from *Dalsland* (Frändefors, pers. notes; Erikstad, E. u. 4296; Ör, E. u. photog N. I. Svensson; Töftedal, E. u. 977; Vårvik, pers. notes), *Bohuslän* (Västerlanda, E. u. 4330) and *Dalarna* (St. Tuna, E. u. 4137).

With reference to this type's expansion, it would be well to seek some connection with those sledge-like sled forms, in the foregoing, from South-West Sweden and Denmark.[4] Evidences are much too uncertain to warrant any absolute opinion. The post-like pieces of wood on the wooden sleds were general in many places, see, for example, Plate XIII: 2—3.

In North Asia as well as in Alaska there are certain sledges which should be called built-up sledges, but which have no posts. Instead, the cross-bars are curved, and they support the platform. This applies from all accounts to the Kamchadal, Koryak-Chukchee and Yukaghir sleds.[5] One might with considerable right assume here, as well as in respect to the Swedish form, influence from the built-up sledge of an original simple runner type. Flor has unmistakably drawn attention to the Samoyed sturdy, cultural influence obvious throughout the whole of North Asia.[6]

A stage in the development previous to the mortised posts is probably met with in the Rantasalmi-runner[7] and the newly-found Viikinäis-runner.[8] In each case the posts are bound in one way or another to the runners through bored holes. However, it remains very uncertain as to whether these runners are parallel with younger sledge types with mortised posts.

[1] Schrenk, 1848—54, 2, p. 392.
[2] See, for ex., v. Schwarz, 1900, p. 334.
[3] Mason, 1894—96, p. 573.   [4] Page 75.
[5] Flor, 1930 (a), p. 294.   [6] Flor, 1930 (b), pp. 138—140.
[7] Sirelius, 1916, p. 14, 1928, Plate.   [8] Itkonen, 1935.

The question may arise as to whence came the idea of raising the platform with its load above the runners, and one's attention is drawn to other culture-elements, where is found the same aim and tendency to elevate above the surface of the ground. Birket-Smith, in referring to the dwelling-house platform, gives certain reasons for the possibility that it should not be archaic amongst the Eskimos and, as is known, it is not the custom amongst the North-Asiatic hunting peoples.[1] The history of store-houses built on piles, within the North Eurasian culture-area is not yet unravelled, and it can in any case, scarcely have had any connection here.[2] One is therefore probably obliged to come to the conclusion that the sledge affords traces of an independent evolution which took form according to its definite purpose and undoubtedly also to its more comprehensive all-round usage. The employment of the reindeer as draught-animal may have had not a little to do with this development.

Hatt has endeavoured to shew that the older simple runner-sledge may have originated quite independently in a kind of toboggan, amongst the Eskimos north of the forest boundaries. He says "If one, due to scarcity of material, constructs a toboggan out of tree-stumps, one can scarcely avoid developing a form like the simplest Eskimo sledges."[3] Birket-Smith, however, and rightly too, has raised objections to this point of view.[4] Considering, for instance, the expansion of the vehicle in the Old World, the theory would seem highly improbable. With hesitancy has Birket-Smith himself coupled the slide-car together with the simple runner-sledge, and opined that the latter, in its long form as used by the Eskimos might probably have arisen out of the former.[5] The same idea has earlier been put forward also by the author of this Work.[6] But the wider perspective in which one is obliged to view the subject in hand, renders further justification of the point impossible. Finally, there remains Sirelius' opinion that the simple runner-sledge and the built-up sledge have evolved from the mechanical coupling together of two runners.[7] The evidence he brought forward was seen in the foregoing to be untenable.[8] His line of thought would seem to maintain itself, however, all the same, and Birket-Smith has taken up the hypothesis in a modified form, as already mentioned, by crediting both the simple runner-sledge and the built-up sledge as a development from the simple tree-trunk sledge.[9] The parallel with which Sirelius supports his postulate, namely, the coupling to-

---

[1] Birket-Smith, 1929, 2, p. 138.　[2] Cf. Oelmann, 1927, pp. 13—15.
[3] Hatt, 1916 (b), p. 287.　[4] Birket-Smith, 1929, 2, p. 165.
[5] Birket-Smith, 1929, 2, p. 168.　[6] Berg, 1926, pp. 1—2.
[7] Sirelius, 1913, pp. 24—25.　[8] Pp. 40 and 74.　[9] Birket-Smith, 1929, 2, p. 165.

gether of two boats, which is well-known from many places including the North[1], serves as an indication, but in a manner other than he had thought. In each case there lies behind, an attempt to stabilize, a problem which is similarly solved and, which, scarcely in itself, needs the assumption of the simple tree-trunk as prototype. Kai Donner tells of still another interesting parallel from the Tungus where, he says "that they transport heavy and big objects on a platform carried between two reindeer, harnessed side by side."[2] Judging from everything concerned, the simple runner-sledge should thus be regarded as a prehistoric culture-element of a primary nature. Rather should it be considered as contemporary with the primitive forms touched upon in Chapter I.

[1] I have annotated the method from Norway, Grude, 1891, pp. 78—79, and Carniola, Valvasor, 1689, 1, p. 200; from the Cheremiss and Votyak, Manninen, 1932, pp. 221, 251, and from the Koryak, Jochelson, 1908, p. 541.

[2] Donner, 1915, p. 101.

CHAPTER IV

THE DOUBLE-SLEDGE FOR TIMBER AND OTHER TRANSPORT

Methods and implements which are employed in the transportation of timber have obviously, and in Northern Countries especially, accumulated to a rich variety. The greatest development in this direction occurred at a comparatively late date, and there scarcely seems sufficient reason to go into the subject further. On the other hand, fundamentals in the evolution must be briefly defined, more especially as there is cause to suspect interaction between the timber-vehicle and other groups of vehicles.

The most evident and primitive way of transporting a log of timber is obviously to trail it along the ground. This method has also been considerably employed both in Sweden and elsewhere for collecting timber, felled in the summer-time. I have made note of a number of central Swedish provinces which used this method, but at the same time it may have occurred throughout the whole of the country. In Hjersås, Scania, a strong iron chain was fastened to one end of the log, which was then trailed by the horse from the forest to an open space, to be transported further by means of the short-sledge.[1] In Sjösås, Småland, this only occurred when one could not get at the timber or remove it in any other way.[2] In various places a similar method was employed for transport on greater distances, Pl. XII: 1. In this case a hole was made at the upper end of the log with an axe specially used for the purpose, and to this the chain was attached. Not seldom was the log pointed at the thinnest end to facilitate the trailing. Traces of this method of transport are still sometimes seen in old buildings where a log here and there has been so placed that the holes appear in view.[3]

---

[1] E. u. 232. [2] E. u. 240.

[3] The author has personally met with occurrences in Värmland and Dalarna. Similar holes were also used in float-making for fastening the timber together, but more especially in olden times (Västergötland, Jubileumsutställningen in Gothenburg, 1923, p. 108; Malung in Dalarna, according to Herr O. Bannbers; cf. with Buskerud, Norway, Ström 1784, pp. 202—203). They have also come into use in the transport of timber with the simple built-up sledge, when the length of the logs rendered attachment to the vehicle impossible. There are accounts from Orsa in Dalarna, E. u. 3906; cf. from Norway, Östberg, 1926, p. 79.

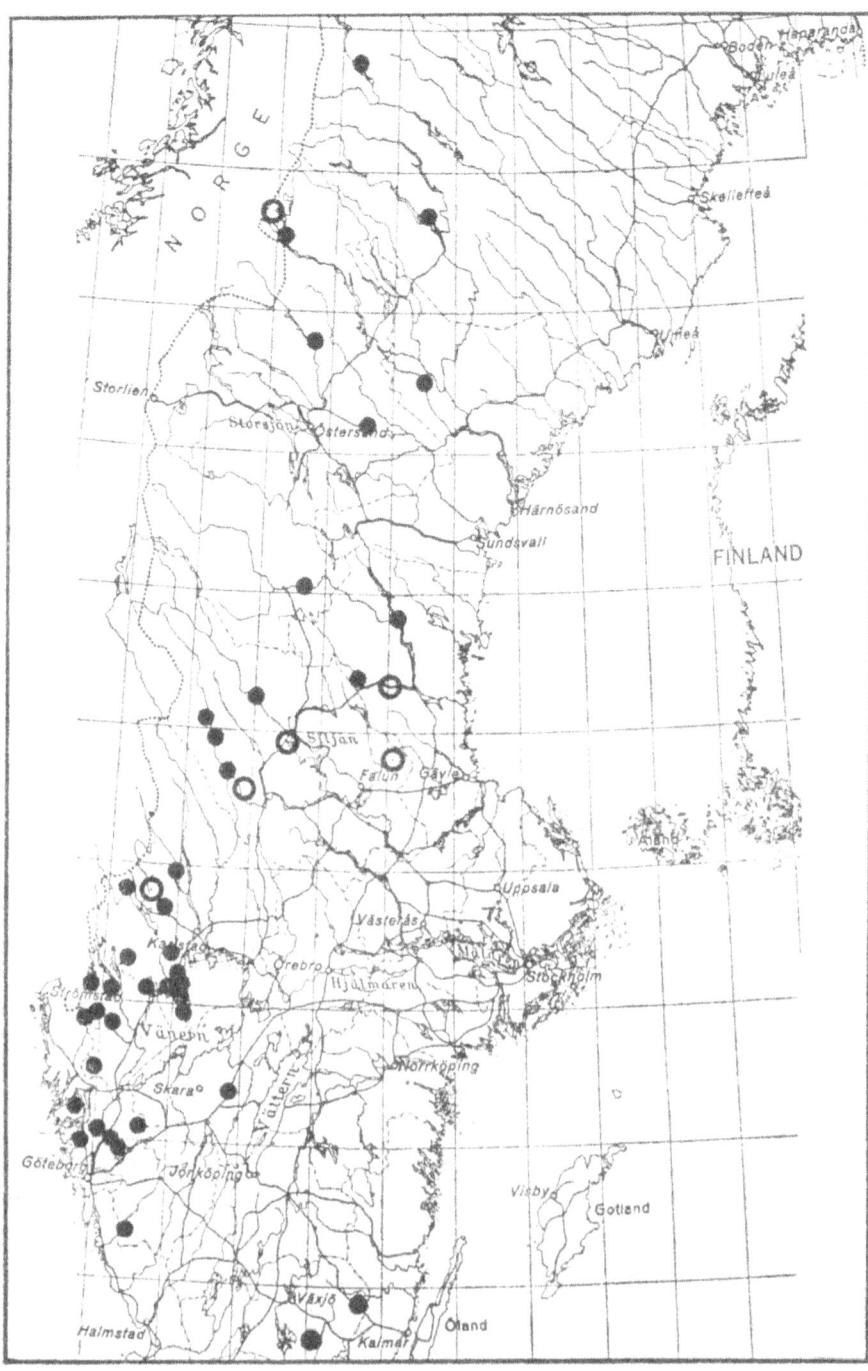

Fig. 34. The distribution of the transport method of trailing the timber on the ground. The open circles are after Erixon, 1933.

This method is known to me from *Småland* (Linneryd, E. u. 5588; Hälleberga, E. u. 3254, at the latter place for the transport of tree-trunks for masts), *Västergötland* (Istorp, E. u. 2780; Erska, E. u. 2601; Skepplanda, E. u. 1573; Östad, E. u. 3048; Skövde, E. u. 2432, in the latter it is used on the ice), *Bohuslän* (Solberga, E. u. 2906; Torp, E. u. 3879; Västerlanda, E. u. 1580, 4330), *Dalsland* (Ödsköld, E. u. 1427, Linder-Berg, 1923, p. 40; Torp, E. u. 1807; Ärtemark, E. u. 925; Dals Ed, Töftedal and Nössemark according to Dr. Nils Ivan Svensson), *Värmland* (S. Ny, Huggenäs and By, E. u. 429; Botilsäter, E. u. 837; Olserud, E. u. 3042; Borgvik, E. u. 1435; Eskilsäter, E. u. 477; Bro, E. u. 3943; Brunskog, E. u. 1436; Köla, E. u. 863, 2457; Gräsmark, E. u. 826; Mo and Sillerud, E. u., N. I. Svensson), *Dalarna* (Malung och Transtrand, according to Herr O. Bannbers, E. u. 5168; Lima, E. u. 764, 1610, 2888, 4143; Älvdalen, E. u. 2964, 4307), *Härjedalen* (Älvros, according to Dr. Ragnar Jirlow), *Hälsingland* (Ljusdal, E. u. 860; Voxna, E. u. 4446), *Jämtland* (Laxsjö, E. u. 691; Stugun, E. u. 1528; Frostviken, E. u. 3185), *Ångermanland* (Ramsele, E. u. 5541) and from the Lapps in *Västerbotten* (Wiklund, 1929, pp. 254—255; cf. for the Swedes, illustration in Uppfinningarnas bok, 4, Pl. III and E. u. 645 from Tärna and Vilhelmina).

In some of these places, seven or eight logs, or even more, were often bound together with birch-osiers and trailed on the ground in a long row, one behind the other. This method was specially employed on transport down steep country, where the logs acted on each other as brakes. It was known in Dalsland, (Ödsköld, Töftedal, Dals-Ed, Ärtemark, Nössemark), Värmland (Köla, Gräsmark), Dalarna (Transtrand, Malung, Lima, Älvdalen), Härjedalen (Älvros), Jämtland (Laxsjö, Klövsjö; here the fore-end of the foremost log was drawn up on the sledge[1]) and Västerbotten (Tärna and Vilhelmina). In the latter places it is said that this means of transportation came from the inhabitants of Värmland who exercised much influence in general on the timber-transport methods of North Sweden. The same is said as regards Ljusdal in Hälsingland and Klövsjö in Jämtland. From Ramsele it is stated that this kind of transport was introduced from Norway about the year 1850. Sigurd Erixon took up the question for investigation and has suggested the possibility that, in Sweden, the method may be due to Norwegian influence. He refers also to its employment in connection with the more developed lumbering carried on in Östlandet.[2]

As may be seen from the map, Fig. 34, the method of trailing timber as described above is rather clearly outlined geographically within our country, and it would therefore not seem unreasonable to interpret the facts of the case in favour of this suggestion. The occurrence of the method in Västergötland and Småland may also be due to a Värmland mediation as corroborated by the Norrland statements mentioned above. On the other hand, the trailing of timber itself cannot possibly be referred to such a culture-influence. As I have already indicated a similar trailing method of transport occurs in various parts of our country, and it is to be met with in many other places in Europe.[3]

[1] E. u. 691, 4115.
[2] Erixon, 1933, pp. 266—268, with map; a good description is given by Bull, 1916, 1, p. 232.
[3] Similar timber-trailing has occurred at saw-mills. An aquarelle from Trollhättan from 1833 is a good illustration. Photog. in Nordiska Museet, Archives; cf. Norsk kultur, 1931, Plate 65, 1763.

As Sigurd Erixon has indicated, it is employed in *Norway*, especially in Östlandet and Österdalen. But one meets with it as far north as S. Tröndelag, and a photograph from Ytre Rendal gives an excellent illustration, Pl. XII: 1. Here three logs are fastened together side by side by means of an iron-chain which is threaded through holes, thus forming a hold for the hauling shafts. For Norway, see Östberg, 1926, pp. 76—77; Bull, 1916, p. 232; Essendrop, 1761, p. 202, 203; cf. Gielleböl, 1771, p. 313 and illustration, p. 354/355. The latter is a copy after Essendrop. It occurs also on the plain of Lüneburg and elsewhere in *Germany* (Bomann, 1929, p. 9; Mitzka, 1934, p. 2, from the surroundings of Marburg), in *Switzerland* (Freuler, 1906, p. 6; Friedli, 1905—28, 2, p. 180, 8, p. 414), in *Spain* (Krüger, 1929, pp. 228—229) and *Hungary* (Pacala, 1916, p. 135). From Europe the method spread to North America. Henry C. Mercer describes an implement from Pennsylvania which goes by the name of "spandogs". It is comprised of two short iron chains, with a hook at each end, attached to a ring, to which the horse is harnessed. The iron hooks in their turn were driven into the ends of the logs, for transport from the forest. It is probable that the implement was also known as the "spanshackle" which was in use in the middle of the 17th century (Mercer, 1925, pp. 19—21).[1] The arrangement closely resembles the one from Switzerland described by Freuler.

Dr. D. Hummel has informed me that in the north of Tibet a hole is made in the timber for the hauling-chain, by means of an axe. The same method is met with in Further India.[2] But the chain was not always attached to the logs by means of a hole. The method is so obvious and so simple that one has no reason to reflect on any direct connection.

More common in Sweden than the trailing of timber on the ground is its transport with the aid of a short sledge, on which, as a rule, the thick ends of the timber are laid whilst the thinner ends trail along the ground, Pl. XII: 2. This method has been employed in later times throughout the whole of the central and southern part of our land. Even further north such a means of transport seems to be the older form which lies behind the later development and which, with the advance of lumbering during the 19th century, vanished into the back-ground. The short-sledge had posts and a cross-bar as an ordinary sledge, but there was only one post to each runner. Sometimes a sledge of the type illustrated on Pl. XIII: 3 made its appearance and quite a number of variations developed in the different districts. The short-sledge came into use mostly for removing the felled timber to a passable road, or to the places from which the wood could be cast down into the water and set afloat. It should be mentioned in this connection that the axle-tree is not only used abroad, but also in Sweden for such shorter transportations.[3]

This short-sledge is used in other European Countries for the same purpose, for example, *Norway* (see Olsen, 1914—24, p. 120; specimen from Feios, Sogn-Fjordane in Heiberg's Collection, Ambla), *Finland* (Österbotten, Petterson, 1917, pp. 149—151), *Esthonia* (Runö, according to Herr J. Öster-

---

[1] The trailing of logs as a modern custom in the forests of Canada is described by Ekman, 1922, pp. 284—285.
[2] Thay, Bourlet, 1907, p. 814/815; Laos, Globus, 49, p. 133.
[3] Personal notes from south Dalsland; E. u. 4330, Västerlanda, Bohuslän. — Freuler, 1906, p. 21, Switzerland; Zelenin, 1927, p. 138, Russia; Mercer, 1925, p. 32, North America, etc.

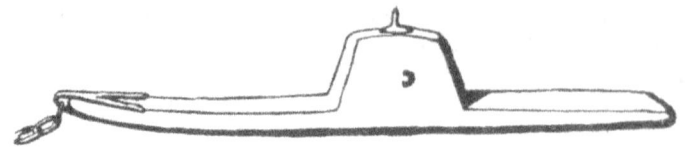

Fig. 35. A guide-runner, used as trailer for timber-transport. Ångermanland.

man), *Latvia* (Bielenstein, 1907—1918, 2, p. 558) and from the *Austrian* and *Swiss* forest-tracts from which places is a description of the method by v. Schulenberg (v. Schulenberg, 1896, p. 75; cf. Zeissler, 1922, p. 25) and by G. Huber (Huber, 1919, p. 10; Friedli, 1906—28, 7, p. 414 with short sledge having two cross-bars).[1] In the eastern States of North America we find the short-sledge again assisting in the transport of timber, and strangely enough the types here closely resemble our Swedish forms. Henry Mercer states that "employed since the settlement of Pennsylvania, this ancient transport apparatus fell gradually out of use after about 1885."[2]

From out of the use of the short sledge many newer transport methods appear to have developed. Albert Viksten has rightly described the development in its connection with the north Swedish provinces in the following manner: "By degrees there began to be a greater demand for wood and for this reason lumbering was also carried on in further distant forest tracts. In these districts the beams were mainly cut to a good size and the question of transport began to give trouble. Then arose the idea to use a trailer in the form of a runner. The first type used was called 'latmede.' It consisted of a single piece of wood 12—13 inches wide and about 1.5 ell long. If possible, resinous pine was chosen and the outer-side was turned downwards. A piece of chain was rivetted at the fore-end and when chain was not available, osiers were sometimes used instead. A pin or nail of iron was fastened in the middle. When freighting was in process the runner was placed under the beam and fastened to this with the iron-nail. To prevent the runner from slipping away from the timber when trailing along more or less uneven ground, the runner and timber were lashed together. The chain was fastened with iron pins to the beams, to keep the runner from turning sideways."[3]

I know such runners from *Härjedalen* (Älvros, according to Dr. Ragnar Jirlow), *Medelpad* (Borgsjö, Nordiska Mus. 171,548—171,549, the former with a movable cross-bar; E. u., photog.) and from *Ångermanland* (Ramsele, E.u.4268; a similar runner is preserved in the Kulturhistoriska Museet, Härnösand, but there are no details as to its origin, Fig. 35). Exterior to Sweden I only know of this runner from *Finland*, where it occurred in Österbotten and in the western part of Tavastland, (Vilkuna, 1930, p. 6, 1935, p. 250). U. T. Sirelius published a similar object some time ago, dated as early as 1641. It is preserved in the National Museum, Hälsingfors. It originates from Haukipudas in Österbotten and according to Sirelius was used up to the 19th century quite alone for the transport of timber logs, which latter were attached to a piece of wood and this was fastened to the iron nail in the runner.[4] Dr. T. Itkonen corroborates that an implement very similar to the push-runner dealt with in Chapter I, was common in the north of Österbotten and especially in the river-valley of the Ule.

---

[1] Cf. also Rehsener, 1891, pp. 429—431. [2] Mercer, 1925, p. 22.
[3] Viksten, 1916, pp. 48—49. [4] Sirelius, 1913 (a), pp. 21—22.

In Norrland the trailer is substituted by a really well-made though primitive short-sledge. In Central Sweden it is obvious how one has had recourse to this lighter and lesser implement. Afterwards, as Viksten has intimated, the development was discontinued by the introduction of a sledge comprised of several cross-bars. Tradition tells that it was the Värmland forest labourers who brought in this wholly divergent type. Viksten is of the opinion that in Värmland this vehicle evolved from a sledge of more common type.[1]

In the North of Sweden a sledge was used for transporting timber which was devoid of any sledge-like attachment, either at the fore or the rear and which, at the same time, did not permit of the timber trailing along the ground, Pl. XII: 3. As the picture illustrates, it was handled in such a manner that the one who hauled by means of a rope or trace drawn over the shoulder, simultaneously took hold of the log which lay balanced on the top of the sledge. In this manner could both log and sledge be steered.

I have noted the employment of this type from *Jämtland* (Frostviken, to which place it was introduced at a comparatively later time, probably from Norrbotten, — according to Herr Gunnar Modin), from *Västerbotten's* Lapp Territory (Dorotea, according to Herr Modin; Åsele, according to Dr. Ragnar Jirlow; Vilhelmina and Tärna, E. u. 645; Risbäck, according to Herr Modin) and from *Norrbotten* (according to Herr A. E. Sucksdorff, verderer, through Herr Modin).

It is not my intention to go into a detailed description of this forest implement in all its phases and newer types found in the various parts of Scandinavia. It should primarily be of more local interest as the influx of culture-influences from all directions, in later times, render a closer unravelling of this question very difficult. On the whole it occurred during the latter half of the 19th century, and closely coincides with the extensive development brought about by the utilization of forest productions, due mostly to increased demand on the part of the export market. It was first noticeable on the west of Sweden but afterwards exerted its influence in the north Swedish provinces. It is from such a basis that one must consider the influence in connection with methods and implements which so obviously came from Värmland. As a supporting circumstance it might be mentioned that the peasant inhabitants of Värmland, to some great extent, migrated to other districts to seek work, just in connection with the busy timber-transport season.[2]

The large sledge, "bordsläde" or "bogsläde," which was comprised of several —often four to five—cross-bars, spread from about 1860 and onwards to most

---

[1] Viksten, 1916, pp. 49—53.

[2] There are accounts in E. u. of such summer migration to various Swedish rural districts, especially in Norrland and Västergötland, but the subject requires special investigation.

of the north-Swedish forest districts.[1] I have made a traditional discovery of such a sledge, or trailer from N. Ny and from Köla in Värmland, comprised of several cross-bars dating from about 1860, which often went by the name of "bogsläde" as in Norrland. It is possible that one should regard this sledge in its turn, as being due to influence from Norway, where similar forms were undoubtedly in use.[2] It seems impossible, however, to arrive at any further conclusions as long as the subject-matter is so little investigated.[3]

The appearance of the double-sledge in connection with the transport of timber can be dated in many parts of Sweden, as far back as to the early half of the 18th century. Carl v. Linné describes this vehicle from Kalix in Norrbotten, and gives an illustration of one.[4] A detail in the construction points to the existance of a connection between these double-sledges in their extensive distribution throughout the country, namely, the two struts which extend to the cross-bars from the fore-part of the runner, Pl. XIII: 1, 4. This construction is not only known from Norrbotten,[5] but also from the central Swedish provinces as far south as Östergötland and Västergötland.[6] Sigurd Erixon has drawn my attention to "the forest sledges" in pairs, which, during the 18th century were not so seldom seen on peasant inventories, in Skultuna, Västmanland. On the other hand it seems that the double-sledge was introduced into the various districts at a later date, very often not before the end of the 19th century. Not rarely does tradition give excellent information in connection with its introduction. In many districts, especially in the east of Sweden, the double-sledge appears to have been put to an all-round use, to the extent that it almost became the universal vehicle employed in conjunction with the "box-sledge" and the railed sledge etc. We have evidence from the beginning of the 18th century that such

---

[1] According to Viksten, 1916, pp. 51—52 it is still used in some parts of Medelpad and Ångermanland. For the latter province cf. Östergren, Nusvensk ordbok, under Bordsläde. There are notes in Svenska Akademiens ordbok, under Bordsläde, referring to Jämtland and Härjedalen. Concerning the former province I have received further information from Prof. H. Geijer; also cf. E. u. 5520, Mörsil. E. u. 645 gives statements from Vilhelmina, Lappland; cf. also Ekman, 1922, p. 254.

[2] In the Norsk Folkemuseum, Bygdöy, there is a similar sledge from Österdalen with not less than six cross-bars; cf. Östberg, 1926, p. 79.

[3] Labourers from Värmland seeking season-work have also been employed in lumbering in the forests of the east of Norway, Scheel, 1921, p. 137; Erixon, 1933, p. 296. There has also been influence of later years in the opposite direction, that is to say, from Värmland to Norway. See Bull, 1916—19, 1, p. 233.

[4] Linné, 1732, p. 184.

[5] Cf. illustration, Linné, 1732, p. 184 and Nordström, 1925, p. 108.

[6] For instance, Härjedalen, Nordiska Mus. 125,258; Uppland, Eriksson, 1925, p. 107; west Nerike, Hofberg, 1861, under Stjärt; south-west Värmland, according to Herr P. H. Nilsson; Västergötland, Dr. J. Götlind has informed me of its occurrence in Falbygden; Östergötland, also Nordiska Mus. 185,111. — Cf. Österbotten, Petterson, 1917, pp. 149—151, and from south-west Finland, Grotenfelt, 1915, pp. 19—20. — The construction occurs also on sledges comprising several boards, but not so frequently in Sweden, cf. for Finland Vilkuna, 1930, p. 54.

PLATE XV

1. A pair-drawn ox-cart, as seen on an engraving in Svecia Antiqua.

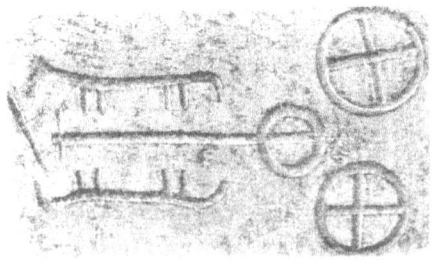

2. Cart from a rock-sculpture at Rished, Askum, Bohuslän. After G. A. Gustafson.

3. Cart from a rock-sculpture at Rished, Askum, Bohuslän. After G. A. Gustafson.

4. Wheel, bog-find from Lilla Mellösa, Södermanland.

PLATE XVI

1. Cart with disc-wheels. Älvdalen, Dalarna. Nordiska Mus. 71,630.

2. Cart with disc-wheels. Röros, Tröndelag, Norway. After a drawing by J. F. L. Dreier.

3. Dung-cart with disc-wheels. Älvros, Härjedalen. Photog. R. Jirlow.

PLATE XVII

1. Corn-cart with wheel-guards. Svärdsjö, Dalarna. Photog. S. Erixon-O. Ekman.

2. Corn-cart with wheel-guards. Järvsö, Hälsingland. Photog. S. Erixon.

3. Hay-cart. The surroundings of Falun, Dalarna. Nordiska Museet 155,664.

PLATE XVIII

1. Hay-cart. Norum, Bohuslän. Photog. T. Lenk.

2. Hay-cart. Söderbärke, Dalarna. Photog. S. Erixon-O. Ekberg.

3. Hay-cart. Narunga, Västergötland. Nordiska Mus. 174,501.

was the case in Södermanland.[1] From what is known, the use of the double-sledge in Östergötland is from remote time. Like Linné's specimen from Norrbotten they are often linked together by a chain. When drawn without freight they could be placed one above the other, with the body part uppermost.[2] Inclusive of the two recently mentioned provinces, the implement, as regards this form and its more all-round manner of usage, seems to have gained expansion relatively early[3] in Scania and certain north Swedish provinces, not omitting Jämtland.[4]

Still more ancient does another form seem to be where both sledges are joined together by means of a beam, corresponding to that of the waggon, which is fastened to a ring in the cross-bar of the rear sledge and placed on a hook under the foremost one, Pl. XIV: 3.

Double-sledges of this type are known from *Småland* (Väckelsång, E. u. 4557; Lommaryd, E. u. 3315; Kråksmåla, E. u. 6559; Fryele and Hogshult, E. u. 5260; N. Hestra, E. u. 3891; S. Vi, according to Herr Hjalmar Johansson), *Gotland* (Fårö, E. u. 3241; Burs and Sproge, E. u. 576), *Östergötland* (Heda, E. u. 4622; Hycklinge, see account in E. u.), *Västergötland* (Solberga, Sundén, 1903, p. 36), *Dalsland* (Mo, E. u. 492, where the double-sledge was first introduced about 1870).

The fact that this vehicle occurs abroad would seem to support the opinion that it is an older form, but I am sorry to say, that I am only able to bring forward a very few instances, and these do not make the culture-connection fully evident. Its occurrence in Österbotten is worthy of note, and K. P. Peterson gives a good description of the construction of the beam and its uses.[5] From Switzerland there is an illustration of a similar double-sledge with a forked-beam, by G. Huber,[6] and in the Museum für Volkskunde in Vienna there is another, originating from Hallstadt. In each case the sledge has two pairs of posts. Double-sledges without the beam are unknown to me from Central Europe.[7]

One seems uncertain as to whether the double-sledge is in reality the result of an independent development which had its origin in the simple sledge and was employed as a trailer attached to a larger sledge. Neither is it easy to discern to what extent one may be face to face with influence from the waggon with its two pairs of wheels, back and front. The ancient construction lately described

---

[1] Drawing with motive from Stockholm by J. Sevenbom, Wrangel, 1899, Pl. 1; for dating cf. Hazelius, 1913, p. 12. — Compare a drawing from later times by N. Anderson 1817—65, depicting peasants on their way from Sorunda to Stockholm, Cederblom, 1923, Pl. 60.
[2] Personal notes from Sorunda, Södermanland, E. u. 978.
[3] According to E. u.
[4] Cf. Vörå, Österbotten, Finland, Wegelius, 1825, p. 20.
[5] Petterson, 1917, pp. 151—152.
[6] Huber, 1919, pp. 11—12.
[7] Cf., however, for timber-transport in Bohemia, Blau, 1917, p. 52.

would just seem to add importance to the latter factor. In many places the beam goes by the same name both as regards the waggon and the double-sledge. Quite obviously is this the case concerning the nave-sledge which came into use as a conveyance at the close of the 18th century, in our land. The waggon-body was often directly mounted on to the nave-sledge.[1]

However, one should not fail to see that the occurrence of the double-sledge so far north as Norrbotten (cf. foregoing, Linné) can scarcely be explained in this way. It is not improbable that both factors have played their part. One must call to mind that a coupling together of sledges occurs elsewhere than in the North and Alpine Countries. Fritjof Nansen tells how the Samoyed of Jamal occasionally coupled their sledges one after the other. He noticed how on one occasion they linked three sledges together in order to transport boat-planks from Obdorsk.[2] In Central Europe there is a similar coupling method closely related to the "Wagenzug" which is met with in the modern transport technique.[3] I know of cases from Switzerland where as many as five sledges have been coupled together, freighted with hay, and drawn by the horse.[4] This tendency to connect several sledges, together with that older usage of the short sledge as a trailer, may have led to the independent origin of the double-sledge in various places.

---

[1] There were such vehicles in Sweden in the latter half of the 18th century. See, Berg, 1926, p. 8. Several examples are in the collections of the Nordiska Museet.

[2] Nansen, 1914, p. 24.

[4] "Wagenzug," see for ex. Oudemans, 1926, Fig. 32.

[3] Friedli, 1905—28, 7, p. 136.

CHAPTER V
THE CART

On many of the Swedish rock-carvings there are figures of two-wheeled carts and, in most cases, it can be quite clearly discerned that these are harnessed to draught-animals. The most familiar are those of Bohuslän. We meet with them on carvings at Backa, in Brastad, at Björneröd, Kalleby, Lilla Arendal, Lilla Gerum, Tegneby and Vitlycke in Tanum, and at Rished, in Askum, Pl. XV: 2—3. Similar representations may also be met with elsewhere, for instance, on the carvings at Vadebacka, in Skepplanda, Västergötland, at Hjulatorp, in Berg, Småland and Frännarp, in Gryt, Scania. Oscar Almgren has reproduced the greater number of them, though partly from older and not altogether reliable copies.[1] At Begby in Borge in south-eastern Norway there is also a rock-carving with a cart of similar type.[2]

On these carts quite frequently the spoke-wheels and the pole are easily discernible. The body of the cart is often there too, but this is sometimes very faintly outlined. Often they are depicted in a sort of "diffuse" perspective, like that in earlier Sumerian art.[3] Other examples shew the cart and its draught-animal in profile, and one might suppose the cart is being drawn by a single animal.[4] On closer examination, however, it becomes evident that only a simplification in perspective has taken place. The Kalleby picture is a good example of this. Here one can only see the end of the yoke with which the draught-animals are harnessed to the pole.

Gabriel Gustafsson has made a most noteworthy observation concerning the reproductions from Rished, Pl. XV: 3. He states "that the double or threefold beam is singularly constructed, and that there appear to be three rings at the front end which probably correspond to those in use today for the bridle; the carts are quite evidently drawn by horses."[5]

---

[1] Almgren, 1934, Fig. 61—65, 75, 159, 163. For rock-carvings from Tegneby see Baltzer, 1881, Pl. 23—26. For rock-carvings from Björneröd see Baltzer, 1881, Pl. 47—48. Details with a cart from this carving are reproduced "with certain corrections," by Almgren, 1912, Fig. 200.
[2] Coll, 1902, pp. 120—122.
[3] Cf. the interesting representation of corresponding objects given by Dedekam, 1920.
[4] Almgren, 1934, cf. the Kalleby picture with harness on the well-known Trundholm sculpture (p. 100).
[5] Gustafsson, 1886, p. 492.

It is not unlikely that we meet with the same rings, from a later period, on a picture of a waggon seen on the wall-hangings of the Norwegian Oseberg-find, from the early half of the 9th century,[1] but it is impossible to discern any details of the harness in these pictures. Max Hilzheimer has verified the same idea on a mosaic in the Royal Capital of Ur, dated 3000 B. C., and he has also recognized it on a Sumerian seal from about the same time. He points out that, as regards these examples, it is a kind of "Kappzaum" that is to say, a bridle without the bit. On later Assyrian pictures the bridle is entirely absent, and horses are always found harnessed with the bit. The rings were attached to a cross-piece which was not fastened to the pole, but which served only to hold the draught-animals together.[2] It seems, as a matter of fact particularly suitable for a harness with two poles. In this connection it should be remembered that on the Oseberg-waggon, the two poles are held together at their outer ends with an iron chain, evidently for the same purpose (cf. p. 155). Hilzheimer is unable to give a detailed explanation of the function of the rings. An indication has been given, however, of the intimate connection existing between the widely separated parts of the pair-carts' area of expansion, in a most convincing manner.

Draught-animals pictured on carvings with carts have generally (for inst. by Almgren) been accepted as horses, and comparison with oxen appearing on the same carvings in connection with the plough and four-wheeled waggon would seem to verify such an assumption.[3] But regarding this, as well as other details, the exceedingly simple nature of the carving renders interpretation difficult, and it must also be remembered that, as above seen, the copies of these interesting and ancient relics of bygone days is far from satisfactory. It is quite clear, however, that the cart is driven by yoked animals attached to a pole.

Carts on rock-carvings are firstly of importance in that they provide us with possibilities of verifying the idea that carts were drawn by pairs of animals, here in the North, in pre-historic times. How this time will be more nearly approximated is a problem not yet solved. Research seems inclined to believe, nowadays, that rock carvings of this kind were executed in the period between the Early Bronze and Early Iron Age.[4] A cart from a tomb in Kivik, in Scania,

---

[1] See for illustration Salvén, 1923, Fig. 3.

[2] Hilzheimer, 1931, especially pp. 7—10.

[3] Carts on the older carvings from Hessen-Cassel mentioned later are drawn by oxen (p. 104). It is possible that the horse is a later element in this connection, in Sweden. Hilzheimer, 1931, states that the horse superseded the ox in Ur (pp. 12—13), a development which had even then taken place or at least has been repeated in Europe.

[4] See, for example, Almgren, 1934, pp. 221—228, 350—351; Sarauw, 1922, p. 278; cf. Nordén, 1932, p. 68.

THE CART

Fig. 36. Pair-drawn ox-cart from Karinainen, Finland. After K. Vilkuna.

dates from the middle of the Bronze Age,[1] and another, carved on the "Villfare"-stone in the same district, may be dated to the same time.[2]

Oscar Almgren has endeavoured to point out that representations on rock carvings from the middle and south of Sweden, should be interpreted as pictures illustrating religious rites. With a wealth of idea and untold energy, he has collected significant material with which to substantiate his views, but not even his latest treatise on the subject seems to have succeeded in convincing his readers. The opinion that certain carts seen on rock-carvings may be regarded as implements of cult is held by others, amongst whom may be mentioned, Hugo Mötefindt and Robert Forrer.[3] Other representations have been interpreted as war-chariots (Renn- und Streitwagen)[4] by many investigators, and quite lately Jörg Lechler[5] has expressed himself as being entirely of this opinion. But this explanation seems not to be convincing either. The problem cannot be solved by isolating it. It must be handled in connection with the interpretation of rock-carvings as a whole.

Enlightenment as to the *purpose* of these carts should be considered of relatively less importance in this connection. As in the case of the plough — whether or not it was used as an implement of cult — which is represented in a way we know more nearly coincided with reality, must the artist have got his ideas for the wheeled-vehicle, from objects of every-day life. Though nowadays obsolete in our country, this type of cart, with its forked pole fitting into the axle-tree and its yoked animals, has been common in Sweden, quite up to later times.

At one place in the North, in the most south-western part of Finland the cart and pair may be seen today, Fig. 36. Kustaa Vilkuna has pointed out that such carts drawn by oxen were still generally employed in the eighth decade of the 19th century in some parts of Finland[6] and from the end of

---

[1] Reproduced by Almgren, 1934, Fig. 118.
[2] Reproduced, for example, Kossinna, 1915, Fig. 205 (after photograph, Nordén, 1926, p. 20).
[3] Mötefindt, 1917, p. 230; Forrer, 1932. — Heyne, 1901, p. 27, regards rock-carving pictures as quite ordinary carts. It should be observed that a round body of the kind seen on the Rished sculpture would not be considered unreasonable if found on a lorry. Cf. for ex. Haddon, 1908, p. 175 and on a wheeled vehicle, Peasant Art in Italy, 1913, Fig. 35.
[4] Mötefindt, 1917, pp. 210—217.
[5] Lechler, 1933.   [6] Vilkuna, 1931 (a).

the 17th century a pair-draught cart is figured in Suecia Antiqua, Pl. XV: 1. Within the greater parts of those districts in the Northern Countries where was the custom to use oxen in pairs (the use of the ox singly appears to be of less early origin, cf. p. 112) the four-wheeled waggon prevailed in later times. But also in our country we have a couple of instances from Småland where oxen were yoked in pairs. In his unpublished notes on travels in Småland, 1775, (in the University library, Uppsala) A. G. Barchæus states that carts for a pair of oxen were used in Gemserum, whilst in Misterhult the "waggon was preferred to the cart, as the latter threw to much weight on the necks of the oxen." Not far from here, in the central parts of the Kalmar district is a cart for two oxen, indicated by M. Crælius, who mentions it in contrast to the one-horse cart, or as he says, carts which "could be drawn by a yoke of oxen, or comfortably by a single horse."[1]

As it is obviously impossible to accurately judge from a find of a single wheel, or even of a pair of wheels, as to whether or not these have belonged to a cart, and much less conclude as to whether the cart was drawn by a single, or pair of animals, it might not be considered out of place here to investigate finds of the kind in our possession from the Northern Countries. Most of those now known are from Denmark, and there is one each from Norway and Sweden.

Two of the Danish finds differ in type from the others. They are in the form of discs pierced through the centre and fitted with tubular hubs, in which the axle revolved. Both are from Jutland. The one, which, through much usage is in a bad state of preservation, is from the Dystrup Bog, Fig. 35, the other, from Tindbæk. The former, as can be seen, is made of three pieces of plank (originally), the latter of a single block of wood, whilst both have semi-circular perforations in the middle. Sophus Müller, who has published these finds, refers partly to a corresponding find in Germany, on the boundary between Hanover and Oldenburg, and partly to one of the well-known wheels from Mercurago, on Lake Maggiore, in North Italy. Guided by the latter, he dates them to the transition period of the Stone and Bronze Age.[2]

All other wheel-finds which might, with any degree of certainty, be assigned to prehistoric times, are spoke-wheels. One example is the Swedish find from Lilla Mellösa, in Södermanland, Pl. XV: 4, which can probably be

---

[1] Crælius, 1774, p. 365.
[2] Müller, 1907, pp. 75—79, 1920, p. 90. It is to be regretted that these and other Danish bog finds of wooden objects have not been subjected to pollen-analytical investigation.

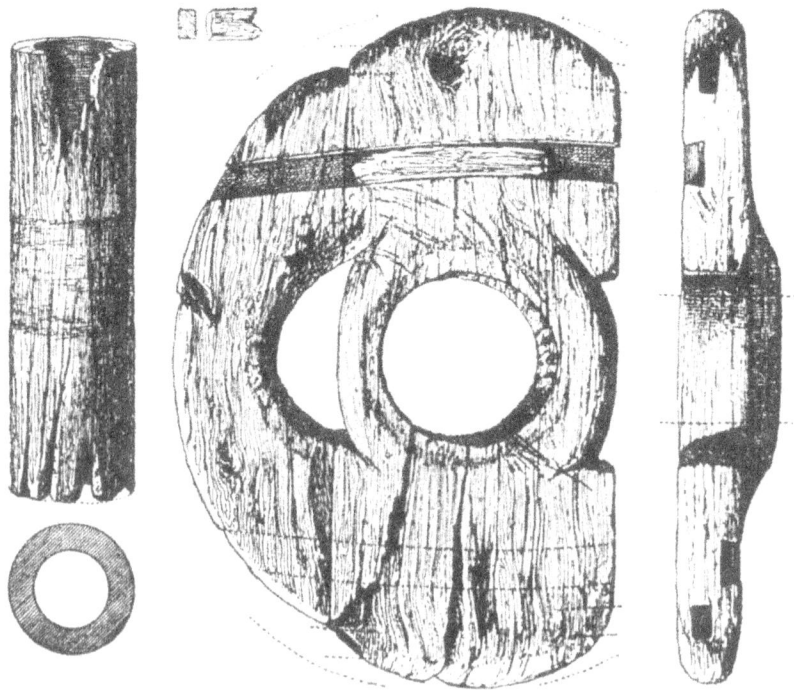

Fig. 37. The Dystrup wheel. Bog-find from Örum, Jutland, Denmark. After Sophus Müller.

dated to the Iron Age. The hub is turned, as in later times, and into it are fitted the ten spokes. It has also five broad felloes.[1]

Two similar wheels from Jutland have turned hubs, and these are to be found in the Danish National Museum. One is from Ölgad in the district of Ribe, the other from Torning in the district of Viborg (from the latter place, there are also parts made for felloes and hubs). They have each six felloes and twelve spokes. Five finds of wheels, very similar in character to these, are to be found in the same museum. *Three* of them were found at the same place in a bog at Skjærup, in West Jutland. In this find, other parts of carts or waggons are included, amongst which is a complete axle with a three-forked attachment fitting into the beam, a fragment of which is still in preservation; and there are parts of the body of a waggon clearly shewing the holes where the rails have been. In the present existing state of these relics, it is difficult to fix, with certainty, any opinion as to the original character of the vehicle.[2] The two remaining finds are contained in

---

[1] For information concerning this find I have had the opportunity of seeing the unprinted treatise of Dr. Andreas Oldeberg, Stockholm. I found valuable items regarding similar finds, which I have made use of here. The Danish finds I have studied myself in the National Museum, Copenhagen.

[2] In the Danish National Museum are solitary finds of parts of carts or waggons from Danevirke, from Vibbestrup and from Taarup (from the latter place there is a rough axle).

the well-known bog finds of the 3rd century, at Vimose on the island of Funen[1] and at Thorsbjærg in South Jutland.[2]

To complete the subject, mention of a find of a wheel, in all probability from the Middle-Ages, should not be omitted. It was found within the old city area of Oslo (now in the University collection). The wheel has had five felloes and ten spokes, but is now somewhat defective.

Similar finds have occurred on various occasions, beyond the Northern Countries. A disc-wheel from Hanover has already been mentioned above. Another such wheel has been discovered in East Prussia, at Schönsee, Braunsberg (now in the Prussia Museum, Königsberg). This wheel is in one piece.[3] Felloes like those of the Mellösa wheel have been found during investigations in fortress-like places at Stellenburg, in Holstein. Two wheel-finds have been made in the Dutch Province of Friesland. One consists of two felloes, the other is a rather complete spoke-wheel.[4] Of finds further south are especially the wheels from Mercurago in North Italy familiar. As already pointed out, one is a solid wheel, the other, a kind of spoke-wheel.[5] Finds quoted here are exclusive of war-chariots belonging to "Celtic" culture centres.

These are not all necessarily cart-wheels, but it is exceedingly probable that the majority of them have served in this capacity. At the same time, it is to be deplored, that other parts of vehicles have neither been found, nor preserved, as the case may be.

For enlightenment as to the earlier history of the cart in more southern countries, there exist, as is known, valuable, and in many cases ancient illustrations of various kinds. These are exceedingly heterogenous however, and have not been investigated on modern lines.[6] Closely connected with our rock-carvings are a number of figures of carts engraved on North-East-German urns,[7] on a tomb-stone in Züschen, in Hessen-Cassel,[8] and on Ligurian rock-carvings.[9]

---

[1] Engelhardt, 1869, Pl. 15:28. The reconstruction is faulty as the nave is greatly out of proportion. — For a couple of other finds, known only through tradition, for example from the bogs of Kragehul and Nydam, see Engelhardt, 1869, p. 28, note, and Engelhardt, 1863, p. 56, note.

[2] Engelhardt, 1863, p. 56, Pl. 16:2. — Wooden parts found in Thorsbjærg are believed by Engelhardt to belong in all probability to the body of a waggon and harness.

[3] An uncertain find of a solid wheel from Waldsee-Aulendorff in Wurtemburg, see Mötefindt, 1918, p. 42 (with illustration).

[4] Pleyte, 1877, Pl. IV: 3—5; XXVII: 10. — I am grateful to Dr. Oldeberg for these references.

[5] Déchelette, 1908—14, 2, p. 289. For a disc-wheel of wood from Castione in Parma, Italy, see Mötefindt, 1918, p. 51.

[6] Of special interest are the illustrations collected and published by Lefebvre des Noëttes, 1931.

[7] La Baume, 1924, pp. 19—21.   [8] See, for example, Lechler, 1933.

[9] Déchelette, 1908—14, 2, p. 494.

The pair-driven cart is obviously not used in our day nor in our part of the world to any great extent, but in other places than the North its displacement may have taken place comparatively late. As an example, the pair-draught cart was still in common use at the end of the 18th century in parts of Wales, whilst in our day it seems to be obsolete in the British Isles.[1]

<small>The pair-draught cart was first met with in the Landes in south-west *France* (Laloy, 1902; photog. of a cart and mule, des Noëttes, 1931, Fig. 182). The French Basques also used it (Laloy, 1904, p. 189), and it was employed in those parts of the Pyrenees bordering on Spain (Fahrholz, 1931, pp. 144—147). It is widely spread over the greater parts of the *Pyrenean Peninsula* (see Krüger, 1925, pp. 195—227 and 1927, pp. 74—78; Ebeling, 1932, pp. 54—94; for the Basques, see de Aranzadi, 1897, p. 216 and Karutz, 1898, p. 336; for Portugal, see Messerschmidt, 1931, pp. 143—153; for Mallorca, Rokseth, 1923, pp. 124—126). In north-east Spain it seems to have been superseded nowadays, however, by the one-horse cart (Thede, 1933, pp. 264—265). The appearance of the pair-draught cart in Portugal and *Madeira* must undoubtedly be connected (Krüger, 1927, p. 75). Its occurrence in the greater parts of *North Africa* should be assigned as coincident (Stuhlmann, 1914, p. 26). Parallel with the advance of Spanish and Portuguese culture the pair-draught cart has become more extensively used in *South and Central America* (cf. Krüger, 1927, p. 75). In *Italy* it is customary throughout the country, though here and there it may be seen alternating with the one-horse cart, which is specially used for mules (see Bottiglioni for N. Italy, 1914—15, p. 95; for central Italy, Phieler, 1934, pp. 73—75; for Sardinia and Calabria, Wagner, 1921, pp. 66—72, p. 67 note 3; for Sicily, Pitré, 1913, p. 356). The pair-draught cart occurs also on the coastal districts of *Albania* in the Balkans (Haberlandt, 1917, p. 48; for Montenegro, see Durham, 1904, pp. 22/23, 342/343), and it is to be commonly met with throughout the coastal area of the Ægean Sea (Nopsca, 1925, p. 138; cf. for *Cyprus*, Ohnefalsch-Richter, 1913, pp. 285—287) as well as in *Thessaly* and *Macedonia*. *Ukraine* is the last place to mention as far as Europe is concerned (see Zelenin, 1927, p. 138). In *Caucasus* and *Asia Minor* the pair-draught cart is in general use (Nopsca, 1925, p. 138; see also, for instance, a reproduction from Georgia in Findeisen, 1934, p. 340, from the Abkhas-Cherkess, Matériaux pour l'ethnographie de la Russie, 1, 1910, p. 73, from Armenia, Rohrbach, 1919, Fig. 38; cf. Endres, 1916, p. 41), and this is the case as regards *Syria* and *Palestine* (Dalman, 1932, Fig. 40—42). It is quite the ordinary vehicle in *Persia* (Montandon, 1934, p. 571), *Afghanistan* (Markowski, 1932, p. 111) and *India* (Grierson gives an excellent description, 1885, pp. 27—42). We find it also in *Further India* and one notes here that it belongs to those elements of culture which have been acquired from the West (Heine-Geldern, 1923, pp. 959, 965).</small>

Amongst the nomadic tribes of the interior of Asia and even in China, the pair-draught cart is a rarity, but as we shall see, the one-horse cart is frequently to be met with. Thus it is obvious that the expansion of the pair-draught cart coincides with the old districts of the pair-drawn plough. Similarly as the yoking of the ox to the plough is technically related to the harnessing of draught-animals to the cart, have these elements of culture both advanced and spread together. The cart has from the beginning, and in many places still has its primal function as a farm implement, for carrying manure or bringing in the harvest. In comparison with this original type, the war-chariot must take a back-seat, though it is more often met with on reproductions

---

[1] Peate, 1929, pp. 40, 68. For England, see Forde, 1934, p. 454, and Seebohm, 1927, p. 305.

from olden times. The cart, at an early stage, was brought into use for another purpose, in which capacity it also became widely-spread.[1]

The comparisons alluded to regarding the plough may be looked further into as far as Europe is concerned. As a basis for the history of the plough, Paul Leser has set apart a group, which he calls "Pflüge mit Krümel."[2] He considers the simplest explanation of the expansion of this type is, that it radiated north-east from the Mediterranean Sea[3] (in southern Asia it occurs, but is rarely seen in China[4]). He compares this expansion with that of other cultural developments (threshing-carts and sowing ploughs), but it is obvious that the spreading of these has no connection with that of this type of plough. The latter is more widely spread in Scandinavia than Leser imagines.[5] It may be questionable as to whether the distinction between the type "Pflug mit Krümel" and some of his "older forms" always holds good.[6] From these surmises it may be gathered, that this type of plough probably was spread in olden times still further over Europe, the eastern and north-eastern parts excepted. Leser's "four-sided plough" which over the greater part of its European expansion is found typically enough equipped with wheels, must be regarded as a younger form of the plough. It corresponds in its peculiar way to the four-wheeled waggon as we should conceive of it. "Pflug mit Krümel," eventually including some of its older forms, corresponds on the other hand to the pair-draught cart, and the European distribution of remoter time thus is comparable with that of Asia.

The main point is, however, that here too, in Europe, the pair-cart once expanded over almost the entire area where the pair-yoked plough had already been in use. Occurrences in Sweden, Finland and Wales may be regarded as survivals. From all parts of Central Europe it became supplanted by the four-wheeled waggon, pair-drawn, and usually by oxen. In the West of Europe, in the British Isles, in parts of Holland and Belgium, in France and Switzerland, the one-horse cart was spread, though probably later. This development, as will shortly be seen, took place in connection with the transition from ox to horse as draught-animal. In parts of Central Sweden a similar development may have taken place but here, as in Central Europe, in Denmark, in South-West Finland etc. it was the four-wheeled vehicle above all, which dominated in the long run.

---

[1] The distinction between the cart and "war-chariot" appears vague and confused. According to Wahle, 1929, p. 237, it seems mainly to depend as to whether the draught-animals are "schnellaufende Tiere."

[2] Leser, 1931, pp. 471—499.   [3] Leser, 1931, p. 483.
[4] Leser, 1931, p. 472.   [5] Cf. Stigum, 1933.
[6] Leser, 1931, pp. 531—550.

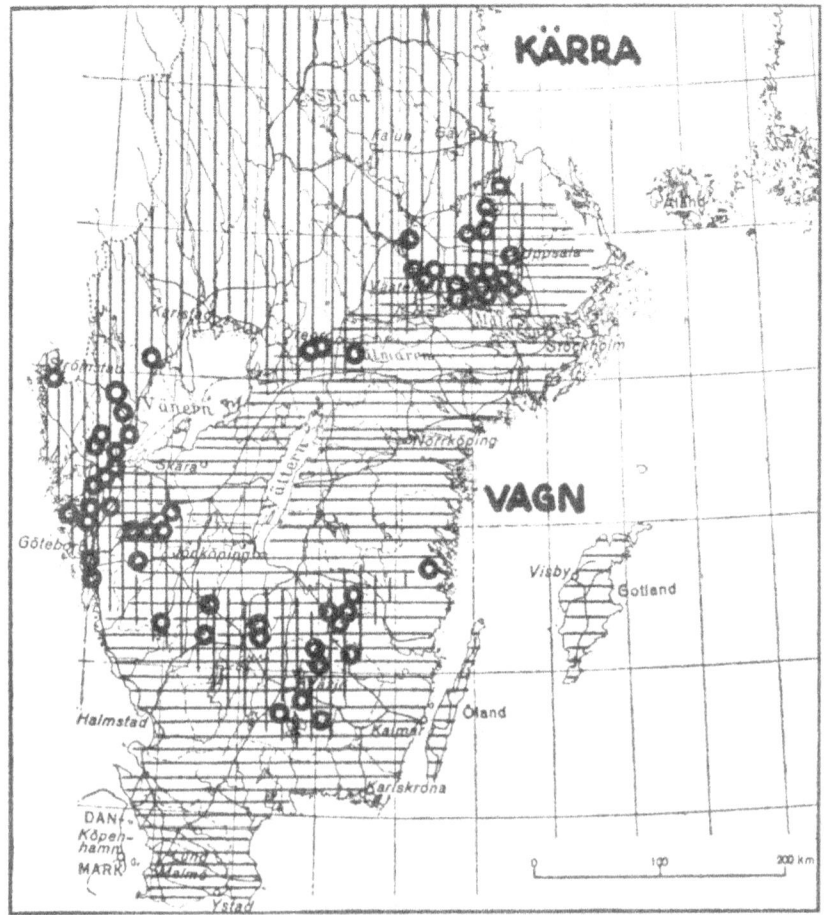

Fig. 38. The most southern distribution of carts in Sweden. 'Kärra' = cart, 'Vagn' = waggon.

The cart commonly used in Sweden is a single-draught vehicle, mostly drawn by the horse. It has been chiefly used for agricultural purposes in comparison with which its use as a conveyance is of little significance from an ethnological point of view. Its restricted expansion, on the other hand, is of greater importance on the whole, and this is quite clear and distinct in the Northern (and greater) parts of the country, but it scarcely occurs in the South of Sweden. Some account is rendered here of the boundaries themselves, and a comparison should be made with the appearance into the country of four-wheeled vehicles, as seen on the map, Fig. 38. Only such information is included which gives concise accounts of the all-round manner in which carts have been used. Of preserved specimens hay and corn carts are retained.

It may be said that the one-horse cart is almost predominant in *Bohuslän* (Ske, Lindberg, 1921, p. 46; Forshälla, Nordiska Mus. 96,733; Resteröd, photograph E. u.; Västerlanda, E. u. 4330;

Valla, photograph E. u.; Norum and Solberga, photograph E. u.). It is said to occur in the North of *Halland* (Erixon, 1933, p. 187). In *Dalsland* it was commonly used (Mo, E. u. 492; Ödsköld, E. u. 1427; Dalskog, Nordiska Mus. 180,710, E. u., Svensson 1928; Färgelanda, E. u., Jirlow 1919; Ödeborg, private notes; Erikstad, E. u. 4296, 3817; Frändefors, private notes). In close connection with this expansion, occurrences should be mentioned as having taken place in certain parts of *Västergötland*, including the Väne-district, in the north-west of the province (Linné, 1747, p. 230; a similar cart, now in the Gothenburg Museum, cf. annual publication 1933, p. 106). It should be stated, however, that the cart otherwise occurs for the most part in the central and most southerly districts bordering on Bohuslän (Askim, Barchæus, 1773, p. 8; a fine reproduction from Gothenburg 1787 (?), Kjellberg-Clemensson, 1933, p. 118; Horla, photog. E. u.; the surroundings of Alingsås, Linné, 1747, pp. 145—147; Hudene, photog. E. u.; Nårunga, Nordiska Mus. 174,501; Bollebygd, personal notes; Mjöbäck, E. u. 5259). It was commonly used in the mining district in *Nerike* (Kvistbro and Knista, personal notes). It occurs as a hay-cart on a painting by J. V. Wallander of Stora Mellösa (in the Nordiska Museet). It spread in *Västmanland* over the mining district and over the greater part of the plains (for mining district, see Bore, 1891, p. 14, personal notes; Karbenning, E. u. 4865; Ramnäs, notified by Dr. S. T. Kjellberg; Haraker, photog. E. u.; Harbo, Barchæus, 1772, p. 17; Skultuna, according to Prof. S. Erixon; Björksta, photog. E. u.; Kungsåra, E. u. 2817). In *Uppland* it seems to have gained considerable ground (Biskopskulla, according to A. Rylander; Övergran, E. u. 3907; Lillkyrka, E. u. 4066; Litslena, Grau 1748, pp. 28, 30; Härnevi, ex. in the Rectory at Härkeberga; in the neighbourhood of Enköping, Kalm, 1742, p. 4; Harbo, Barchæus, 1772, p. 17; Östervåla and Tierp, Eriksson, 1925, p. 106; Huddunge, E. u. 3911; Läby, according to Dr. N. Ålenius).

In *Småland* the cart found a home, which, later on, became of an isolated character. It seems to have been specially in use in the central and north-eastern parts of the district (Villstad, Haraldsson, 1893—94, p. 47; N. Hestra, E. u. 3891; S. Solberga, E. u. 3602; Fryele and Haghult, E. u. 5260; Alsheda, Korsberga and Vetlanda, according to Dr. J. Svennung; for Östra-härad cf. Gadd, 1871, p. 52 and Nordiska Mus. 183,516; V. Torsås, according to Dr. E. Elgqvist; Tävelsås, Barchæus manus. in UUB.; Linneryd, E. u. 5588; Sjösås, according to Herr J. A. Göth; Åsheda, Lannér, 1765, p. 191; Kråkshult, E. u. 5573; Gladhammar, Barchæus manus.; cf. for Tunalän, Sevede and Aspeland, Cræilius, 1774, pp. 369—370).

From the above is seen that here in Sweden, the southern boundary for the one-horse cart runs approximately through the north of Halland, over Västergötland, through Nerike and Central Uppland. Extraordinary, however, is the extent of its appearance in the various parts of Västergötland, and especially its occurrence as a survival in great parts of Småland. One may undoubtedly and rightly assume, that a distribution of a more coherent nature over the greater part of the country took place, in remoter times. The cart gave place to the four-wheeled waggon which had long been undergoing a process of sturdy expansion. This does not infer the absence of the waggon from the great agricultural plains, in ancient times. Its early occurrence there will be fully substantiated in a later Chapter. It is striking how deliberately the expansion made its way straight to the agricultural districts. In Västmanland, it penetrated, for instance, as far as the district of Fellingsbro, and a similar advance had taken place in Uppland, already in the 18th century (in olden times it had not spread north of Lake Vänern). In the history of its evolution, the appearance of the cart in a survival sense, is undoubtedly of a more comprehensive nature the further we recede in time, and the expansion in Småland consequently less isolated. An indication as to this may be obtained from the fact, that the one-horse cart appears to have been used in the north-east of Östergötland, in the 18th century.[1]

North of the outlined boundaries, the one-horse cart was common in our country, to the extent that specific restraining influences had to be reckoned with. Outside these areas, the cart has obviously proved itself, in such specific functions as the carrying of manure, and as a conveyance etc., to be of practical value, and has undoubtedly been used to much good purpose. But it never became a normal vehicle, so to say indispensable, especially as regards agriculture. One restraining feature of the kind indicated above was a particularly rough and rugged country, but one should not over-estimate such geographical conditions. They have played a significant rôle in cases where the cart was used for transport of goods or as a conveyance, and the latter, it should be mentioned, is of later date here in Sweden.[2] It craved a maintenance of roads or at any rate, some kind of constructed ways.[3] At a much earlier date, however, it may have been used in dairy-farm work. In those districts where the employment of carts for purposes of transport was thus rendered difficult, the summer sledge and slide-car were put into comprehensive use.

It is not inconceivable that the extensive employment of the summer-sledge, in certain of Sweden's west country districts, prevented the cart from coming into more general use until a much later period. A. E. Holmberg tells that at Tjörn, in Bohuslän, the cart dates no further back than to the beginning of the 19th century.[4] With reference to districts in North Sweden, possibilities of acquiring some idea of the age of the cart, when dealing with remoter times, are very limited. Reliable documents from the 16th century tell of carts in Dalarna, and from these we are able to gather that the late expansion into Bohuslän, is of a more local and incidental nature. In the year 1520, for example, a vicar in the parish of Mora received a cart amongst goods noted in the vicarage inventory.[5] In Stora Tuna, 1571, a wheel-wright is recorded on the

---

[1] Broocman, 1736, 2, p. 78.

[2] One notices, for instance, how von Lassota, the political prisoner who, during winter-time in the 9th decade of the 16th century, was always conveyed to his various residences by sledge, was, in summer-time, allowed to ride. — v. Lassota, 1590—91, passim. The evolution varied in different parts of the country. In Vislanda in Småland, the first conveyance on wheels came into use about 1790 — Hyltén-Cavallius, 1863—68, 2, p. 154. In 1717, E. von Hofsten from Grava, in Värmland mentions driving in a cart. — v. Hoffsten, 1717, p. 56. In 1798 Fale Burman found carts only in solitary villages in Ragunda, Jämtland — Diary, in manus. Government Archives, Östersund. The first cart was driven to Råvmarken, in Dalsland, during the war with Norway 1813—14, E. u., N. I. Svensson.

[3] The history of Swedish road-ways was excellently investigated by Schück in brief, 1933.

[4] Holmberg, 1842—45, 2, p. 78.

[5] Dalarnas hembygdsförbunds tidskr. 1, 1921, p. 15.

list of craftsmen.[1] Carts with and without fittings of various kinds are found mentioned in inventories of estates in the mining districts, from the latter half of the 16th century.[2]

Amongst his investigations, Sigurd Erixon has ethnologically estimated the boundary between the cart province and that of the waggon which, as indicated, stretches across Central Sweden.[3] Even here one must not omit to point out a marked difference as regards Northern Sweden and the more southern parts of the country. It is just the same with the occurrence of mountain dairy-farms, store-houses on piles, chairs hollowed out of trunks etc. There is obviously no genetic connection between the cart boundary and other boundaries. The boundary in this case is due to retrogression and it separates the more conservative parts of Sweden from those in which innovations had gained a footing, and been accepted, before older ideas were abandoned. This becomes so much more evident, when one considers the earlier expansion of the cart, as already shewn. In like manner, other culture-elements having a similar expansion can be proved to have existed in remoter times, further south. As an example, one may mention store-houses on piles which, up to the 18th century, still existed in Central Småland.[4] Whether, and to what extent, mountain dairy-farms occurred further south than we were able to ascertain in the 19th century, is still an open question.[5] It is possible, nevertheless, that a general regression, at least to some extent, has taken place during the last centuries.

Exterior to Sweden the one-horse cart is common, especially in North and West Europe. In *Norway*, it has practically been the only wheeled-vehicle in use, though in many parts of the country one has got on tolerably well, somehow, without it. Full and interesting accounts have been given by especially 18th century topographical writers. In *Iceland*, carts are used on the farms today (Bruun, 1928, pp. 266, 269). In those parts of *Finland* where, during the last century, wheeled vehicles were employed, the cart was everywhere in use, with the exception of Åland, in certain districts in south west parts of the country, and in a rather concentrated region in the south-east, principally including Carelia (Atlas of Finland 1925, p. 140, map 23: 10). In east Baltic Countries it is the contrary. The four-wheeled waggon is almost prevalent whilst the cart is only known in *Esthonian* Ingria and there, nowadays, it serves only to carry manure (Manninen, 1928 (a), p. 54; cf. picture from Narva, Olearius, 1656, p. 115). In *Great-Russia*, the cart again is quite common (Zelenin, 1927, p. 138; Manninen, 1934, p. 232. Such carts are also used by the Zyryan and the Votyak (Manninen, 1934, p. 233). South of this North European cart area, lies a comparatively wide tract where the waggon, so to say, reigns supreme. The cart is rarely to be seen in Denmark, but

---

[1] Forssell, 1872—83, p. 78.

[2] State Archive. — By means of such inventories, one should be able, by thorough systematic search, to discriminate between cart and waggon in the various Swedish provinces. For example, on the Liljestad estate, Östergötland, year 1590, 4 waggons and 2 hay-carts were notified. Great care is necessary, however, as the terms are not always clearly defined.

[3] Erixon, 1933, pp. 187, 196.

[4] Gaslander, 1774, p. 85; cf. Erixon, 1933, p. 192.

[5] Cf. Berg-Svensson, 1934, p. 36.

we meet with it again in the south-east of *Holland*, where, in parts of Gelderland and Utrecht, in Noord-Brabant and Limburg, it serves as the common wheeled-vehicle (Oudemans, 1926, p. 56; it is also known to have been in use in the Frisian Islands, Leuss, 1903, p. 204). The cart occurs in *Belgium* (Enquêtes 1, 1924, pp. 51—52; Heckscher, 1925, p. 282) and in the provinces of the *German* Rhine (Mitzka, 1934, p. 16; Wrede, 1922, p. 44, Fig. 15; see Hoffman, 1932, p. 221 for Rhine-Hessen and Pfalz). In great parts of *France* the cart is the normal vehicle. Here it is to be found in the west and central districts, but the waggon replaces it in the north and east (Brunhes, 1926, pp. 207—212; Flagge, 1935, pp. 160—163). From what is known, the cart was everywhere used in the *British Isles* in olden times and, as we have seen, the one-horse cart reached the north-west of *Spain* from France (Thede, 1933, p. 264). In the Alpine districts, the cart was the sole wheeled vehicle in use (Savoy, see Goldstern, 1922, 1, p. 8; for *Switzerland*, Rütimeyer, 1924, p. 297; Stebler, 1903, pp. 304—306, 382).[1]

The one-horse cart's greatest area of expansion, however, is in Asia. Here it may be said to be the normal wheeled-vehicle in all the central parts of the Continent. We find it in *Turkestan* (Schwarz, 1900, pp. 331—336), and it is used by the *Kirghiz* (Sommier, 1885, p. 585) and *Kalmuck* (Pallas, 1776, 1, p. XII, Pl. 1). It has also gained ground amongst the Turkish people in South Russia, and especially amongst the *Tartars* in *Crimea* (Ermans Archiv XVII, 1858, pp. 91—93; Matériaux pour l'ethnographie de la Russie 3, 1926—27, pp. 105, 107; cf. Georgi, 1776—80, p. 85), as well as in *Astrachan* (photog. in Hungarian National Museum, Budapest). Berthold Laufer has drawn attention to the fact that Hippocrates states that the cart was used by the nomadic Scythians, and Chinese annals also mention that Turkish tribes in Asia used the cart (Laufer, 1920, p. 193). According to Rockhill, the one-horse cart occurs in *Mongolia* (1894, pp. 17, 24, 32 etc.; cf. Consten, 1919, 1, Pl. 49 etc.; a Buryat cart of the same kind, Findeisen, 1934, p. 219), and it is the common vehicle throughout the whole of the North of *China*, where there seems to be entire absence of the pair-draught cart (for Chinese cart geography see Laufer, 1910, pp. 198—202; Wagner, 1926, pp. 158—163). Its extension into *Manchuria* is obviously and principally due to the influence of Chinese culture (James, 1888, pp. 217, 312), and the same may be said regarding its spread into the Amur country, where it is used by various tribes (v. Schrenck, 1891, p. 378; Stötzner, 1930). Though only as an exception, it has been used in *Corea* (Schmeltz, 1891, p. 62; James, 1888, p. 353; cf. Pogio, 1895, p. 229), and in conclusion, it is to be met with on *Formosa* (Fischer, 1900, p. 47), on the *Philippines* (Karutz, 1898, p. 337) and on the *Marianne Islands* (Costenoble, 1905, pp. 77, 79). Its occurrence on these places is undoubtedly thanks to Chinese influence.

We have now been able to prove the existence of a vast and somewhat coherent area where the one-horse cart has been the normal means of transport.[2] This area is quite distinct from that which shews the expansion of the pair-draught cart. It is interesting to note that when, as an exception, a *singly*-drawn cart appears within the latter area, it by no means refers to a two-shafted cart.[3] Undeniably remarkable is the fact, that North China (wheeled-vehicles, it

---

[1] The one-horse cart as a conveyance occurs in Roumania (Kanitz, 1875—79, 3, p. 256/257). Moszynski, 1929, p. 637 mentions the appearance of the two-wheeled cart also in Poland, but in all probability it is not an original national element.

[2] That the one-horse cart, and carts in general, may have spread relatively late within the great areas, is natural. W. Koppers is of the opinion that the Turks were not familiar with its use from the beginning (Schmidt-Koppers, 1924, p. 534).

[3] See, for example, reproduction of a sculpture with picture of cart and horse, by des Noëttes — Indian work from 15th century (1931, Fig. 106). Here only one shaft is used, and this is placed at one side, to enable the horse to be right in front of the cart. A similar example is seen on a Roman sarcophagus relief — des Noëttes, 1931, Fig. 73. Cf. other carts from Bulgaria (Kanitz, 1875—79, 1, p. 196/197), from the Kirghiz (Byhan, 1923, p. 236) and from the Marianne Islands (Zeissler, 1922, p. 124). Available reproductions of antique carts are sometimes less reliable and it may be assumed that this method was preferable.

is well-known, have never been in use in South China) has a clearly defined position in the world of the one-horse cart which, in some measure testifies to the inner Asiatic origin of Chinese culture.

In Sweden, and Europe generally, the single-draught cart is almost exclusively drawn by the horse, but there are exceptions where the ox is found taking the place of the former. The ox is then saddled to the cart with a single yoke, quite different from the pair-yoke used in South Sweden. Sometimes a wooden kind of shoulder-saddle, which resembles the horse-saddle is used. Here are quoted some words of Anders Tidström from Skedevi in Dalarna, 1754. He says "they have the custom of driving with oxen singly, and use saddles for the ox as well as the horse. Last winter, a farmer started off on the long journey to Gävle and back, and profited thereby, in that the ox consumed less than half of the forage, and he returned with his ox."[1] We have an excellent reproduction of a one-draught cart drawn by an ox, yoked with the kind of wooden shoulder-saddle mentioned above. It dates from the beginning of the 19th century, and is from Tröndelagen, in Norway.[2] It should be noted that the ox as a beast of burden belongs otherwise to the southeast of this country.[3] As far as is known, the ox, as a rule, has not been used singly, to any extent, in Europe. But, there are occasions on which the horse has other substitutes than the ox. It may suffice, perhaps, to call to mind the Dutch cart, drawn by dogs and even sheep,[4] and of carts in France, Italy and Spain which are drawn by mules. On the other hand, the ox, yak and buffalo are more usual for single-draught carts throughout East Asia, including China, Mongolia etc. In many parts of Central Asia they also occur, alternatively, with the horse. Here, oxen driven tandem are not rarely to be seen, that is to say they are yoked one before the other, instead of abreast.

The tandem driven horse is quite usual in many places in Europe. In the Northern Countries it can by no means be regarded as a popular custom,

---

[1] Notes on travels, now in Uppsala University Library. — As early as the 18th century, propaganda was made for a more extensive use of oxen for draught purposes (an order, dating from 1762, published by Modée, Publique förordningar, 7, p. 5329). During the latter half of the 16th century, oxen were rare in the north of Sweden. The few which existed were undoubtedly to be found on estates and vicarages. The boundary seems to be approximately, between the upper and lower mining districts of Dalarna. Some of the accounts given for various districts are sporadic. See Forssell, 1872—83, p. 35 and the tables. At the end of the 18th century, oxen for draught purposes were usual in Jämtland, see Burman, 1930, p. 54; 1571 offers no available account of the use of oxen. The province belonged at that time to Norway. It is remarkable, however, that from the neighbouring province of Härjedalen there are two single yokes for the ox, dating as far back as 1642 and 1669. These are now in the Nordiska Museet. For the use of oxen in later times in Västerbotten and Norrbotten, see Erixon, 1933, p. 195, note.

[2] Dreier-Lexow, 1913, p. 34.   [3] Erixon, 1933, p. 195.   [4] Oudemans, 1926, Fig. 16.

PLATE XIX

1. Hay-cart. Hudene, Västergötland. Photog. G. Ewald.

2. Cart, as seen on an engraving from Gothenburg, by Elias Martin 1787 (?).

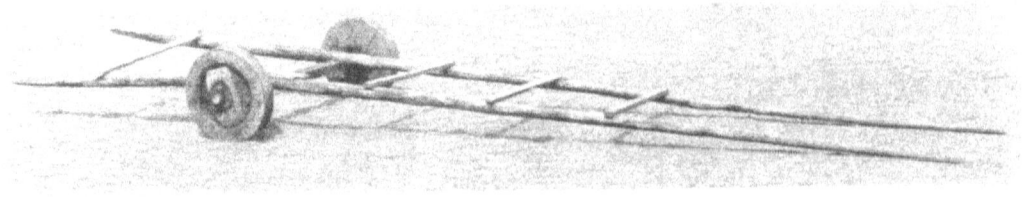

3. Hay-cart. Vilhelmina, Lappland. Nordiska Mus. 183,471.

PLATE XXII

1. Sledge with attached slide-car. Svinhult, Östergötland. Photog. A. C. Hultgren.
2. Sledge with attached slide-car. Borgsjö, Medelpad. Photog. Louise Hagberg.

3. Sledge with attached slide-car for wood-transport. Säter, Dalarna. Photog. G. Berg.

but in England it exists as a tradition from olden times[1], whilst its occurrence in France is not unknown.[2] Strange to say, in North Russia, the sledge has similarly been driven tandem.[3] In Western Europe the driver generally rides the foremost horse which is almost necessary, in order to be able to steer the vehicle. It has occurred, however, irrespective of tandem. One learns from reproductions that it must have been the usual manner of driving in days gone by, but it has been out of date in Europe, in more modern times.

A single instance is known in Sweden from Askim, in Västergötland, where statement is made by A. G. Barchæus, 1773, as follows: "when the horse has the cart behind him, empty or full, the rider, whether man or woman, always holds the halter; reins are unknown to them" (Barchæus, 1773, p. 8). From the same time, Abraham Hülphers tells that peasants in Nyland in Finland, "rode with stirrups and without reins, when driving their carts" (Hülphers, 1760, p. 30). The custom lived on to a later date in West Carelia (Grotenfelt, 1915, 21). Adam Olearius from Narva in Estonia reproduces a cart whose driver rides the horse (Olearius, 1656, p. 115). On European pictures of carts from the 15th and 16th centuries, this method of driving seems to the general rule.[4] The fact that reins were not at this time commonly used with the one-horse cart, though already usual in Mediterranean culture, and used generally, both for pair-draught carts as well as waggons, as early medieval manuscripts shew, should throw light on the early history of the cart. For this reason I shall return to the subject in the next Chapter. Meanwhile, it should be noted here that, in Central Asia, drivers riding the horse are very usual in connection with single-horse carts (for Turkestan, see, for example, Schwartz, 1900, p. 333; Kirghiz, Sommier, 1885, p. 585; Buryats, Findeisen, 1934, p. 219).

As to whether in Asia the ox superseded the horse as regards the single-draught cart, is a question which needs investigation on very broad lines, and this would be out of place here (cf. p. 143). That such, however, wa sthe case in the North, is pretty certain and obvious, as may be seen from the later character of the harness itself. Judging from the above, one feels obliged in my opinion, to keep the two types of vehicle (the single and the pair-draught cart) distinct and, at that, regardless of animal. Both ox and horse could easily be used with either vehicle. During the Middle Ages, horses in pairs were harnessed to the cart by means of the pole, as may be seen from manuscripts dating from that time.[5] We have a reproduction illustrating this in Sweden. It is on the "Broddetorp frontal" which originates from a church in Västergötland, and is considered to be Swedish work from the latter part of the 12th century. The representation shews the figure of a cart, in a medallion, drawn by two horses (in another medallion a similar vehicle is drawn by a pair of oxen). The altar-frontal was executed under Danish influence (Jutland),

---

[1] Fine illustration in Luttrell Psalter, p. 76. From 17th century, Hartley-Elliot, 1928, Fig. 40 a; from 18th century, Hartley-Elliot, 1931, Fig. 19 b.

[2] See for ex. Haberlandt, 1912, p. 8.

[3] Schrenk, 1848—54, I, pp. 11—14; Zelenin, 1927, p. 131; cf. from Åbo, Goeteeris, 1615—16, p. 227.

[4] Irish examples from 18th and 19th centuries, Haddon 1908, pp. 177, 201.

[5] See, for example, des Noëttes, 1931.

and according to Poul Nörlund, reverts to ornament in ivory, on English reliefs.[1]

In the Historiska Museet, Lund, Fig. 39, there is the earliest evidence in our country of a single-draught cart with horse. It is an engraving on a copper cross. In those days, as far as can be gathered from pictures, vehicles of that kind were in common use in Western Europe. Of course it cannot be denied that later tides of culture may have had some influence on the introduction of the one-horse cart into the North. A more detailed analysis of some of the cart's constructive elements tends to shew that its expansion must have occurred on a wide basis, and consequently must be assigned to an early epoch. The fortuitous nature of pictures available from the early Middle Ages must not be allowed here, or elsewhere, to pronounce without further notice a terminus post quem, in cases, where national civilization affords the possibility of a more plausible point of view.

To begin with, it is remarkable that we have not a few examples in Sweden of carts with solid, instead of spoke-wheels, that is to say, wheels, disc-shaped instead of being comprised of rim, spokes and hub. In the following account I have excepted the solid wheels of wheelbarrows and other primitive vehicles, as well as the fore-wheels of the so-called "trein-waggons" (cf. Chap. VIII).

In *Bohuslän*, carts with solid wheels occurred as late as about 1870 (Västerlanda, E. u. 4330). I personally know them from Eda, in *Värmland* (two solid wheels in Arvika Museum), S. Finnskoga (a solid wheel, in Nordiska Museet, 183,925) and from N. Ny (two wheels, Nordiska Museet, 174,544, personal notes and photographs). The wheel from S. Finnskoga is in one single piece, cut from the trunk of a sturdy pine; the wheels from Eda and N. Ny are turned. All are equipped with axle-box and rim of iron. In *Dalarna*, especially in the western and northern parts of the district, carts with solid wheels were rather common. I personally know of roughly hewn, thick wheels — not turned, from Järna (according to Ola Bannbers) and Leksand (personal notes), but these have also occurred elsewhere. Turned wheels were known in Lima (Nordiska Mus. 98,735) and Malung (Gahn-Adelswärd, 1765, p. 25, E. u. 5168) Svärdsjö (pers. notes), Våmhus (personal notes), Mora (Linné, 1734, p. 268; Gahn-Adelswärd, 1765, p. 25; S. Liljeblads Memor. Diarium 1797, MSS in UUB; Forsslund 1921, p. 14; personal notes; Nordiska Mus. 69,255 and 71,515), Sollerö (E. u., photog. Lärka; Forsslund, 1921, p. 120), Rättvik (Tidström's travels, 1754, MSS in UUB; Gahn-Adelswärd, 1765, p. 25: "some in Rättvik" also), Orsa (Hülphers, 1757, p. 131; Gahn-Adelswärd, 1765, p. 25, E. u. 3906; Nordiska Mus. 179,942, example in Gammelgården) and Älvdalen (Gahn-Adelsvärd, 1765, p. 25; Levander, 1914, p. 50; Bälter, 1922, p. 39; Nordiska Museet 71,630, Pl. XVI: 1). Carts with solid wheels occurred in *Härjedalen* (Älvros, Pl. XVI: 3, these were not turned; another specimen may be seen in the Jämtland Museum, Östersund; Sveg, Nordiska Museet, 127,016, with nicely hewn thin wheels), and *Jämtland* (Offerdal, design by N. M. Mandelgren in the Nordiska Museet; Ström, E. u. photograph; both having wheels not turned; Marieby, E. u. 5422). They are known from *Ångermanland* (Ramsele, E. u. 5541; Graninge, E. u. 4167), *Västerbotten* (Burträsk, Nordiska Museet, 177,030, two wheels made of two discs of wood nailed together), and *Norrbotten*, (Nederkalix, Hülphers, 1789, p. 197). Amongst the new settlements in the Lapp

---

[1] Thordeman, 1927; Nörlund, 1926, pp. 53, 205.

Fig. 39. One-horse cart. Engraving on a copper cross from 12th century. Historiska Museet, Lund. After C. G. Weibull.

Territory, Tärna and Vilhelmina, for instance, may be mentioned (Nordiska Mus. 183,468, 183,471, Pl. XIX: 3; E. u. 645).

One sees from the above that the disc-wheel had a distinct, westerly expansion, cf. map, Fig. 40. It is not at all likely however, that it was always limited to these parts. An odd disc-wheel found here and there in other parts of Sweden confirms this assumption. Such an example was found in a swampy meadow in Söderbykarl in Uppland, 1932, which is obviously of ancient date (the wheel is now in Söderbykarl Museum). The disc-wheel undoubtedly shared the fate of so many other culture elements, by being displaced at a comparatively late date by innovations from the South. In this case it was the spoke-wheel.

As a matter of fact the above exclusively concerns the roughly constructed wheel of one or more planks nailed together, and not the turned or nicely hewn, disc-shaped wheel from the north of Värmland, Dalarna and Härjedalen. Judging from its distribution, the latter kind constitutes a later specializing within the group, though according to Linné and Hülphers, they appeared in the middle of the 18th century.[1] It would not be out of place to compare these wheels with turned or hewn piles for store-houses from about the same district. Sigurd Erixon has proved that these piles spread from the west of Jämtland down to the north of Bohuslän. He surmises that the expansion took place in the 18th century and that it originated in Norway, where they date back to the 17th century.[2] Turned disc-wheels have been used in

---

[1] Linné, 1734, p. 268; Hülphers, 1757, p. 131.
[2] Erixon, 1933, pp. 268—271, (with map). It should be mentioned in this connection that in 1571, a turner was amongst the inhabitants of Mora (Forssell, 1872—83, p. 75).

Norway also, as the preserved pair from Telemark and Sogn (Gransherad in Telemark, Nordiska Museet 60,322; Årdal in Sogn, example in the Heiberg Collection, Ambla). It is interesting to note that these two solitary specimens, the only Norwegian examples I know of for the moment, originate from south-west Norway. Erixon has pointed out the west-European connection of the round store-house piles and in so doing particularly referred to England. Solid wheels of finely hewn or turned forms are also known from Ireland.[1] A connection here is not unlikely, and we get still another proof in support of Erixon's hypothesis that the culture-invasion to Sweden over the Norwegian boundary sometimes indicates west-European influence.

If we should now look more systematically into the expansion of the solid wheel outside our own country, we come across it in several places in *Norway*. During the investigation mentioned in the preface, I obtained information as to its existence in olden times in most of the districts from Vestagder in the south to Finnmark in the north, and in some places, it is employed even today. Of course this expansion is both irregular and scattered. In the south-east it would seem to have entirely disappeared in later years (Östfold, Vestfold) and I am unable to make any statement as to Hedmark. But it has been quite common in Sörtröndelag (a cart with such wheels is reproduced by Dreier-Lexow, 1913, p. 34) and Nordland; also in Vestlandet, especially in Möre, Hordaland and Rogaland (a similar cart is reproduced from Möre, see Norges jubileumsutstilling, 1914, p. 19; from Rogaland a similar one, Hasund, 1932, p. 102 and Anda, 1881, pp. 41—42). The solid wheel seems to have been used to a similar extent in Telemark. Examples with which we are familiar are big and rough, in some cases consisting of two rounded planks, fastened together like the one from Västerbotten recently quoted (information from Skjåk, Opland). Wheels made of single pieces of wood or of planks about a quarter of an ell thick and belonging to the 18th century are known from Setesdal in Austagder (Giellebøl, 1780, p. 70). Information concerning the turned wheels from Telemark and Sogn is to be found above. It is to be regretted that I have so little to state as regards *Finland* in this connection. Carts with solid wheels have been employed, however, in North Österbotten (Paulaharju, 1922, p. 19) and in sundry places in east Carelia (Grotenfelt, 1915, pp. 21—25; Sirelius, 1919—21, 1, p. 399; Itkonen, 1932, p. 407). At an earlier date, with the exception of Russian Carelia (see Carelia under literature for Finland), they seem to have occurred in north-east *Russia* (Moszynski, 1929, p. 635). It should be remembered that we know the north-European solid-wheel carts principally from *Scotland* and *Ireland*, not omitting *Wales*, where, in the two former, they were quite commonly in use (Haddon, 1908, pp. 173—178, 196, 200; Fox, 1931, p. 190). The cart with solid wheels which Leopold Rütimeyer met with, in the valley of Chamonix, in the south of *Switzerland* is worthy of note (Rütimeyer, 1924, p. 297). It may probably have some connection with the appearance of the solid wheel in *Italy*, but I am not aware of any example of more modern date from the northern parts of the country. On the other hand, it is usual both in the south of Italy and Sardinia (Wagner, 1921, pp. 66—72). One finds it on the *Pyrenean Peninsula* in many places, but it is commonly employed in Portugal and the northern and north-eastern mountain regions, as well as in the provinces of the Basques (Krüger, 1925, p. 195, 1927, p. 74). From here it may be traced to the Azores (Haddon, 1908, pp. 181, 183) and to the Canary Isles. *Greece* and *Bulgaria* are not unacquainted with it (Vahl-Hatt, 1922—27, 4, p. 143; Moszynski, 1929, p. 635). The types vary exceedingly, but the wheel with the two semi-circular perforations round the nave, as seen on the ancient Danish find, most frequently occurs. Quite similar is the case in countries exterior to Europe where the disc-wheel has been in use. In *Caucasus*, for example, (see Buschan, amongst others, 1926, Fig. 416), in *Asia Minor* (for Armenia, Rohrbach, 1919, p. 38; Endres, 1916, p. 41), in *Further India* (Rütimeyer, 1924, p. 300) and in *China* (see, for example, Wagner, 1926, Figs. 21 and 24; from *Mongolia* there is an example in the Pitt Rivers Collection, Oxford; cf. Vahl-

---

[1] See, for example, Haddon, 1908, Pl. IV.

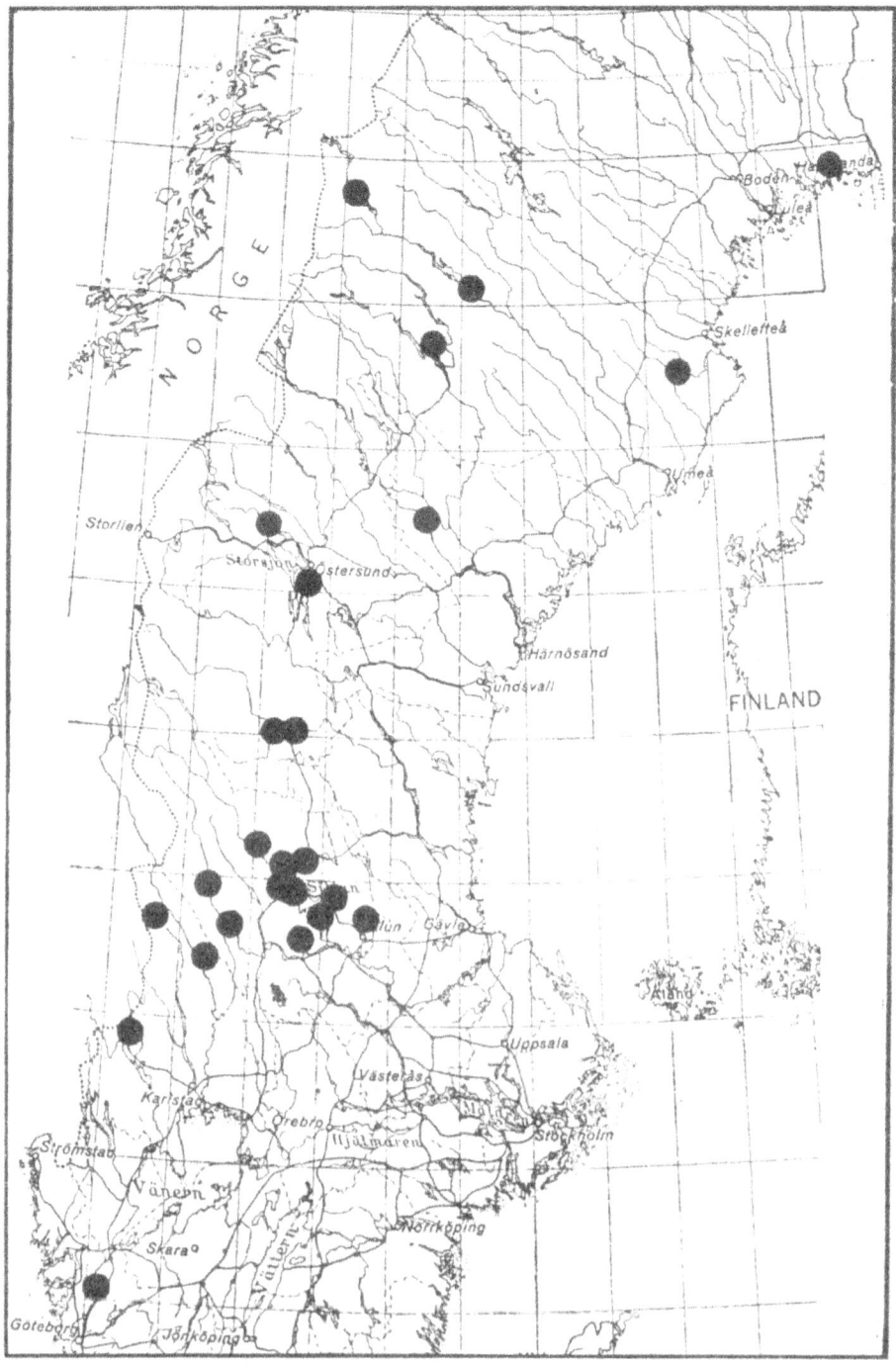

Fig. 40. The distribution of disc-wheels on carts in Sweden.

Hatt, 1922—27, 3, p. 162; for *Formosa*, Fischer, 1900, p. 302). The closely related details must obviously be regarded as culture coincidences and they should be looked upon as relics of a more uniform expansion.

In one such relationship only is the occurrence of the solid-wheel cart in Sweden fully intelligible. This does not refer to any temporary improvisation, even though the type often appears in places where wheeled-vehicles came into use at a comparatively late date. It should coincide instead, with the oft experienced advantage of this type of cart to that having spoke-wheels. It answered excellently when driven on soft, loose ground into which the wheels could easily sink. It was used in Dalarna at a later date mainly to cart manure, for expeditions to the mountain dairy farms etc. In more modern times, however, accounts shew that it was put to a much more all-round purpose, including that of a conveyance.[1]

There is yet another observation which tends to confirm a suspicion that there existed a relationship between the disc-wheel in the north and south cart provinces. From Salmis, in the east of Carelia, states Gösta Grotenfelt concerning the wheels of manure-carts which he has photographed, that they "are solidly fastened to the axle-tree which revolves with the wheel when the cart is in motion."[2] The axle is quadrangular in shape, and the wheels are wedged into place on the outer side. I know of no Swedish analogy but it is interesting to note, that a similar manure-cart has been employed in Setesdalen in Norway. In 1780 a topographical author writes that "its peculiarity is that the axle is not fixed, but lies loose and goes round with the wheels."[3] That this is no contingency is quite obvious from accounts from Nordland, bearing a later date. From Ofoten, my informant relates, that on carts of this kind "the axle revolves in a circular groove made in the shafts of the cart; the axle is square, and is fastened on the outer side of the wheels, with wedges." The carts of Beiarn were very similar, but the wheels of these had each its separate axle, fixed side by side, underneath the cart.[4] This was considered to give the wheel more freedom of movement, so that the one could move when the other stood still, yes, indeed, even go forward whilst the other went

---

[1] The inference of Fahrholz that the spoke-wheel cart in Ariège, in the Pyrenees, should be the precursor and the prototype of the disc-wheel cart, would seem unlikely (Fahrholz, 1931, p. 147). Mahr who appears to have adopted the idea that the disc-wheel had an independent origin in various places, was labouring under a misapprehension, and was led astray by Haberlandt's faulty statement, 1926, p. 396, that the wheel of the Basques should have been a tree-trunk with a transverse incision (Mahr 1934, p. 53). Such wheels are unknown from Europe and have never occurred there (Krüger, 1927, p. 74, note 4; they are supposed to be known, however, from Chile).

[2] Grotenfelt, 1915, p. 21; Sirelius, 1919—21, 1, p. 363, makes similar mention.

[3] Gielleböl, 1780, p. 70.   [4] According to my inquiries.

backward. It will be recognized that the foregoing account alludes to the famous "groaning cart" of Mediterranean coastal districts, so called because of the creaking noise it made. Frequent descriptions have been given by classical writers. As far as the question of expansion goes the type is closely connected with the disc-wheel, but this relationship is not without exceptions as there are many examples with fixed axles. We have already seen that whilst resembling the Mediterranean type both the ancient wheels from Dystrup and Tindbæk have had naves for stationary axles. Groaning carts have left traces behind them elsewhere than in the North. The British Isles principally should be mentioned in this connection. In the Pitt Rivers Collection at Oxford there are models of two similar carts from Yarmouth, in Norfolk, and there is evidence of their appearance in Yorkshire.[1] Those from Scotland and Ireland are especially well-known.[2] Another interesting model of a cart from the south of Russia is in the Oxford Museum. Here, "the wheels revolve both with and on the axle, which is loosely kept in place with wooden staples". From the Zyryan there is noted a cart with revolving axle in connection with disc-wheels.[3] For the appearance of "groaning carts" on the Pyreneean and Apenninean Peninsulas, I beg to refer Readers to Fritz Krüger, for illustrations and literature references.[4] Exterior to Europe, carts of a similar kind may be found, for example, in Turkey, on the Philippines, in Formosa and in China.[5]

That the revolving axle had a wider and less scattered expansion in earlier days, within which region present occurrences should be regarded as survivals, obviously goes without saying. The cart with the block or disc-wheel, and revolving axle, won its distribution as the older type, but was displaced and modified later on, by newer ideas.

The revolving axle with its solid-wheels has played a great rôle in discussions concerning the origin and early history both of the wheeled-vehicle, and wheels. It undoubtedly came to the North fully developed, but at the present moment I have no reason to take up the various theories for closer investigation. A characteristic common to them all, may be said to be their speculative and far from practical nature. It is to be regretted that the problem of the wheel's origin has been treated in such a general manner and, without, as a rule, any very real substantiation of facts, such as we know them from ancient finds and

---

[1] A wheel belonging to such is to be found in Science Museum, London; Walker, 1814, Plate.
[2] Haddon, 1908, pp. 173—178.   [3] Manninen, 1934, p. 233.
[4] Krüger, 1925, p. 195 and 1927, p. 75. Owing to similarities between the north-west Iberian cart and the Roman plaustrum, Krüger is inclined to regard them as a Roman culture-element (1927, p. 75). He, himself, however, indicates its occurrence exterior to the Roman culture-zone, which renders such a theory less likely.
[5] Cf. literature quoted earlier in the chapter; from Amur, Ermans Archiv, 18, 1858, p. 31.

picture-subject.[1] For the sake of discussion and in connection with foregoing statements I refer Readers to an excellent survey by Hugo Mötefindt.[2] The idea that the wheel originated in the log or roller, which was placed under a platform or sledge, seems to hold pretty good, but it has not yet been explained — and this is the main point — as to how its antecedent was fastened to the framework of the cart.[3] Eduard Hahn and G. Forestier differ in points of view. They maintain that the wheel appeared on the scene in connection with quite another object than the vehicle.[4] There should be no reason for attributing any actual value to these views. The latter is by far too theoretical and, as is not unknown, the former adheres to a batch of teaching which in the later years of ethnological investigation has become an exploded idea.

One point may be conceded with certainty, however, and this, from a purely culture-geographical view, that the disc-wheel is the older form which lies behind the evolution. In all probability the wheel had its origin in interior Asia, and from thence spread to the various parts of Asia and Europe.

Similarly unravelled is the question as to how the successor of the disc-wheel, that is to say, the wheel with spokes and rim came into existence. Mötefindt points out that the "breaking through" of the solid wheel, purely "typologically" should have led to a spoke-wheel, but this idea, which is founded mainly on picture-subject from the classical antiques, is little convincing.[5] Is it not far more reasonable to share the opinion of A. C. Haddon, that long after the solid-wheel had been in use, it "was discovered that it was not necessary to make the wheel solid, and various expedients . . . were devised to lighten the wheel and yet retain its strength"? — Haddon also gives a brief insight into his line of thought regarding the evolution, and avers that the four-spoked wheel known from the antiques, and from pictures on rock-carvings, is the parent of the original spoke-wheel.[6] Other methods of holding the wheel together with a rim have been in use from olden times, and might be considered as mere transitional forms in the stages of evolution towards the spoke-wheel, but as far as we know, there is no example from the North.[7] The spoke-wheel

---

[1] Mötefindt's essay, 1918, constitutes an exception, but through limiting himself for example, to European subject-matter, he has not been able to arrive at any definitive solution (cf. Horwitz' critique, 1933, p. 736).

[2] Mötefindt, 1918, pp. 31—35.   [3] Cf. Horwitz, 1933, p. 728—730.   [4] Cf. Forrer, 1932.

[5] Mötefindt, 1918, p. 44. Cf. also Haddon's disinclination towards this idea, 1908, p. 188.

[6] Haddon, 1908, pp. 178—191. Two notes from Hareid and Vartdal in Möre in Norway where the cart is included amongst the later culture-elements, enlightens one that about 1870 the "cross"-wheel — instead of the disc-wheel — with a wooden cross which formed four spokes, was in use (revolving axle?). Cf. from Rogaland, Anda, 1881, pp. 41—42.

[7] The wheel constructed of four pieces of wood surrounding the nave is known, for example, from Dalmatia (Moszynski, 1929, p. 637; M. indicates its employment as a plough-wheel in other places as well), Bosnia (Hoernes, 1882, p. 89) and Switzerland (Rütimeyer, 1924, p. 298; Forrer, 1933; cf. Haberlandt, 1926, p. 396). Closely akin is Mötefindt's so called ancient Italian wheel, a type familiar from one of the wheels

varies little in our country, on the whole, and the differences which occur are non-essential.[1]

The idea for fitting the spokes into the rim may probably have been taken from the sledge. There is undeniably a certain correspondence between the simple runner-sledge and the solid-wheel on the one hand, and the built-up sledge and the spoke-wheel on the other. As to whether there is any value in this analogy and if so, to what extent, is impossible for me to judge with the material-subject I have at hand. It should not be out of place to add a few words here about the rim of the spoke-wheel. As a general rule, and almost always in Sweden, it is formed of a number of felloes joined together with tree-nails, one for every two spokes. In other parts of Europe, and in Asia, the rim consists of a long piece of wood bent artificially. We might be justified in spending more time on this type as such wheels are known in Denmark from olden times. I refer to the famous Dejbjerg waggons from the early Iron Age (cf. p. 154). The wheels of this precious relic are shod with iron and a piece of metal is fastened over the joints of the rim. Later on, the curved rim had a distinct easterly expansion.

It is found to have spread to the eastern parts of *Finland* (Manninen, 1934, p. 235). *Esthonia* (Manninen, 1934, p. 235; Leinbock, 1932, p. 35), *Latvia* (Bielenstein, 1907—18, 2, p. 543; Hupel, 1774—82, 2, Pl. V), *Poland* (Pitkiewiez, 1928, Fig. 129, 150) and *Russia* (Zelenin, 1927, p. 137, Vjatka district and Kiew district; Ukraine, Moszynski, 1929, Figs. 519 and 520, 2), and far into Siberia, not only in the Russian culture district (Yenisei district, Makarenko, 1913, Fig. 23) but also in *Turkestan* (v. Schwarz, 1900, p. 331, with good description of process of making; Olufsen, 1911, p. 352). v. Schwarz reminds that Strabo, quoting Eratosthenes, mentions the supple branches of trees from which the wheel was made in India (v. Schwarz, 1900, p. 357). And lastly it was used by the various tribes of the *Amur* district, where it consisted of three pieces (Stötzner, 1930; the Indian cart-wheel may have been similarly constructed). The method of rendering wood supple for the making of wheel-rims, by means of a steaming or boiling process was known to the ancient Greeks and Romans (Blümner, 1875—87, 2, p. 326). Petersen mentions a similar wheel found at la Tène (Petersen, 1888, p. 37).[2]

---

in the Mercurago find. Its construction may have evolved from the type we learnt to know through the prehistoric wheels from Dystrup and Tindbæk. It is well-known from antique reproductions and until lately it occurred amongst the Spanish Basques (de Aranzadi, 1897), and in England (wheel of a turf-cart from Yorkshire, in Science Museum, London). That its expansion is not limited to Europe is evidenced by its appearance in Manchuria (Munsterhjelm, 1922, p. 25; James, 1888, pp. 217, 312) and in Exterior Mongolia (Consten, 1919—20, 1, Pl. 49, 2, Pl. 61). The Indian wheel is of quite another type. Each new pair of spokes is fixed into the nave whilst the old spokes are allowed to remain, thus causing variance in thickness (an excellent description, Grierson, 1885, p. 28—29; similar kind of wheel in Afghanistan, Markowski, 1932, p. 111). At present there is not sufficient subject-matter concerning all these wheels to render it possible with safety to place them in the history of culture.

[1] The method of inserting the spokes in a zigzag fashion to strengthen the wheel is without doubt a comparatively new feature. Personally I know it from various Swedish districts: from Östergötland (Hägerstad, E. u. 1451), Dalarna (Rättvik, example in Matsgården, Östbjörka; Säter, Nordiska mus. 32,271), Medelpad (Indal, Burman's diary, 1799, MSS in the Archives, Östersund) and Västerbotten (Degerfors, personal notes).

[2] In modern wheel-wright technics the lithe rim occurs alternatively everywhere (oldest evidence from Switzerland, 1810, Feldhaus, 1914, col. 531). In Sweden, so-called swamp-carts have this kind of rim, and

From this expansion, it is evident that it is necessary to regard the occurrence of the supple wheel-rim as an important factor in the disquisition of the origin of the spoke-wheel. Kazimierz Moszynski asserts that wheels of this kind are of a later date than those with felloes.[1] This is very unlikely however. On the contrary, one would wish to regard the wheel with its rim of felloes as a younger substitute, brought about, for instance, by an increased skill in craftsmanship. Besides, the spoke-wheel should undoubtedly be recognized as being of interior-Asiatic origin, and in consideration, one could scarcely expect to see this from the present expansion of the type in Europe. It seems as if its kinship with the sledge with artificially curved runners, will prove to be of special interest in this connection (cf. with these sledge-runners, p. 59).

In conclusion, some interest should be devoted to the frame-work of the cart. In our country as elsewhere it is rich in variety, and we are able to boast of some excellent illustrations of types. The simple platform was, as a matter of fact, comparatively little employed, owing partly to wheel difficulties experienced under loading, and to difficulties in connection with the loading accommodation itself. In order to avoid these inconveniences various modifications have been resorted to. In certain parts of N. Sweden a guard of thin wood was adapted to the wheel and this widened the floor considerably, Pl. XVII: 2. This type of cart was mostly used for harvesting purposes, and with its newer contrivance spilling was diminished.

Carts with wooden guards were employed in *Ångermanland* (Bjurholm, E. u. 4374; Gideå, according to Dr. L. Björkquist, Härnösand; Graninge, E. u. 4167); Ramsele, E. u. 5541; Multrå, Nordlander, 1933, see "Ask"; cf. Arenander, 1906, p. 12), *Hälsingland* (Järvsö, Schissler, 1753, p. 76, Hellström, 1917, p. 314, E. u. photog.; Ljusdal, E. u. 541; Ovanåker, Nordiska Museet 110,644; cf. Broman, 1911 ff., 3, p. 42), *Härjedalen* (Älvros, Nordiska Museet 126,788) and *Dalarna* (Orsa, Torsång and Hedemora, pers. notes).[2] I know of a similar cart from Svärdsjö in *Dalarna* having the same guard, but this is comprised of arched juniper laths (E. u. photog., Pl. XVII: 1). Dr. J. Granlund has met with such a cart also in Dorotea, *Västerbotten* (photograph E. u.). In *Småland* carts of the latter type are very usual. The rails are of juniper or hazel, Fig. 41. I have met with this kind of framework in central and north-east parts of the district (Åsheda, Lannér, 1765, p. 19; Lenhovda, according to Herr Hjalmar Gustafsson, Dädesjö; S. Solberga, E. u. 3602; Uppvidinge district, according to Herr J. A. Göth, Klavreström; Tolg, Alsheda, Vetlanda and Korsberga, according to Dr. J. Svennung, Uppsala; Gladhammar and Gemserum, Barchæus, travel notes, 1775, MSS

in this case it consists of chips of wood, but this must be a later specializing. Such occur in Småland and in Västergötland, particularly for hay-harvesting in meadow-land. The wheels hinder the carts from sinking into the moss. They are always drawn by hand (Kalm, 1747—51, 1, p. 20; Nordiska Museet 160,962) Man-haulage, even without rims of chips is above all a speciality for Småland and Östergötland, but otherwise it occurs elsewhere in south Sweden. It is known from the end of the 18th century (Vetlanda, Småland, Hilfeling's diary during a journey to Gothland 1799, MSS in the Royal Library).

[1] Moszynski, 1929, p. 635.
[2] Smaller wheel-guards are also to be found elsewhere, but these appear to be of later origin (this refers to Norway also). They appear also on quite modern trunk waggons. The guard is simply a development of the very simple wheel-guards consisting of a board of some kind and seen on carts with rails.

THE CART

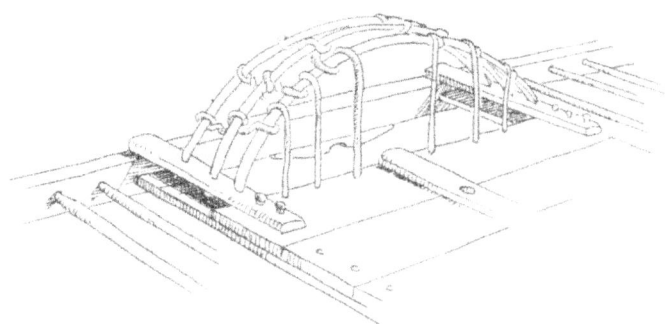

Fig. 41. Wheel-guard of hazel-wood from a hay-cart. Central Småland.
After a sketch by Gunnar Ell.

in UUB; cf. Gadd, 1871, p. 52 and Elgh, 1749, p. 35, concerning "Kryp," as this vehicle is generally called).[1]

A. G. Barchæus mentions wheel-guards of wood from Gemserum in Småland as follows, ". . . either with a small wooden guard for each wheel or with arched laths." One must assume as highly probable that some connection existed between the Norrland and Småland occurrences of wheel-guards on carts. It is worthy of note that the type occurred before 1750 in Hälsingland (the same year marks the decease of Olof Broman who mentions it in his Glysisvallur) and not long afterwards in central Småland (Lannér). One would rather be inclined to think that it was invented in Norrland and spread to Småland verbally. I have, however, not been able to discover anything in the way of document or print by means of which it could have otherwise been brought about.[2] There does not seem to have been any real discussion in "economic" literature as to the improvement of the cart, on any greater scale, before the latter half of the 18th century.[3]

Another method for preventing the wheels to collide was to make the platform of the cart concave, and this, in addition, afforded better accommodation for the load. Fig. 42 gives some idea of such a floor, nailed to the inner sides of curved branches in their natural state, which could be tilted backwards over the upturned ends of the shafts. In the carting of manure a loose end is used with an inserted plug, which leans inwards and when loaded upon is kept in place.

The cart with the concave platform belongs to *Värmland* (N. Ny, personal notes; E. u. photograph), *Dalarna* (Malung, Gahn-Adelswärd, 1765, p. 25; Lima, Gahn-Adelswärd, 1765, p. 25, personal notes, E. u. photog.; Floda, Cederblom, 1923, Pl. 46; Äppelbo, Linné, 1734, p. 342; Rättvik,

---

[1] Guards of a similar kind have occurred on wheels in Västergötland (an example in Skara Museum; Lyrestad, E. u. 4203).

[2] Concerning activities for the scientific stocking of farm implements, and its special connection with Ångermanland, see Berg, 1931 and 1932 (b).

[3] See, for example, Faggot-Chydenius, 1764; Hushållnings Journal, Oct. 1783, p. 79; Forsseman, 1789.

Fig. 42. Cart with disc-wheel and semi-cylindrical body. Älvros, Härjedalen. Nordiska Mus. 127,016.

Tidström's notes on his travels, 1754, MSS in UUB, Gahn-Adelswärd, 1765, p. 25; Våmhus, personal notes; Mora, Linné, 1734, p. 268, Gahn-Adelswärd, 1765, p. 25, Liljeblad's Mem. Diarium, 1797, MSS in UUB; Forsslund, 1921, p. 14; E. u. photog.; Nordiska Museet 69,255 and 71,515; Sollerö, Forsslund, 1921, p. 120; E. u. photog.; Orsa, Hülphers, 1757, p. 131, Gahn-Adelswärd, 1765, p. 25, Nordiska Mus. 179,942, personal notes; E. u. 3906; Älvdalen, Levander, 1916, p. 70; Nordiska Museet 71,630, cf. Grieg, 1928, Fig. 13) and *Härjedalen* (Sveg, Nordiska Museet 127,016).

The concave platform thus shews an expansion similar to that of the turned or hewn disc-wheel. It is worthy of remark that the movable floor, as illustrated by Linné was already being employed in upper Dalarna about 1730. At a much later date as will be seen, this practical contrivance was not in use in places already enjoying a more modern culture, and not even was it employed for carting manure. From this, one is disposed to believe that the semi-circular platform experienced its Swedish expansion relatively late. In Norway one hears occasionally of a cart with concave floor (for instance from Möre in Vestlandet[1]), but it does not seem to have been usual, and one cannot at present suppose the type being of Norwegian origin. It is more reasonable to suppose this platform's predecessor to have been the concave sledge-floor in use, both in Sweden and Norway, and especially in upper Dalarna, not forgetting its earlier and wider expansion in our land (cf. p. 66). The platform of the cart does not exactly resemble the floor of the sledge, in that the latter is wider at the back than the fore, but to this, one need not attach too great importance. Abraham Hülphers called attention to the resemblance between the floor of the cart and sledge and states that in Orsa "carts with concave floors were seen, which were driven on runners, in winter."[2]

A cart with a kind of a square box-like frame was a normal type both in our country and elsewhere, and its uses were many and various. It was employed in the transport of all kinds of goods. The peasants used it on journeys

---

[1] From answers received to my enquiries.
[2] Hülphers, 1757, p. 131.

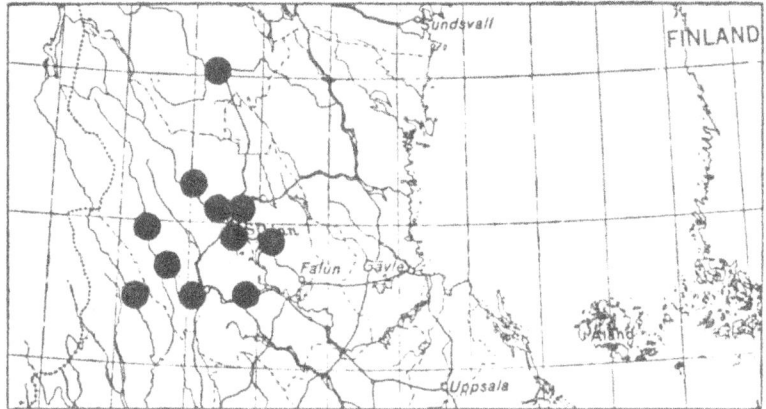

Fig. 43. The distribution of the semi-cylindrical body on carts in Sweden.

to the mills and towns. The back could be removed at will to facilitate the loading. In the north of Sweden, for example, in Dalarna, Gästrikland and Norrbotten, the cart went by the graphic name of "box-cart" (kistkärra).[1] Sometimes too it was called the "sack-cart" (säckkärra)[2] and in the western part of Västmanland it was known as the "mountain-cart" (bergskärra).[3] Special arrangements were made for different occasions, for instance, when iron-bars were transported, the bars were stuck through holes made at the back and the front of the cart.[4]

It stands to reason that this "box-cart" is the forerunner of the conveyance. Not so very long ago it was quite common in many parts of Sweden that no other vehicle than the ordinary cart for porterage existed. Although in the middle of the 17th century certain kinds of carts were to be found amongst the higher classes, it was more than a century before they were in common use with the peasants in the more advanced Swedish country-sides. To deal with the various spring-constructions, adapted sometimes under the seat, sometimes under the body itself, but copied as a rule from the four-wheeled waggons which determined the evolution would, I find, be out of place here. Suffice it to note that as already said the conveyance was also in use in many districts, where the four-wheeled waggon was the normal vehicle.

---

[1] Hülphers mentions a cart-"box" (kista) (1789, p. 125). "Box"-carts are found in inventories from the end of the 18th century, from Gästrikland (for example, Hille, 1772, Nordiska Museet, Archives).

[2] Liljebjörn, 1865, p. 40 (Värmland); personal notes from the south of Dalsland.

[3] Sigurd Erixon states that the term "mountain"-cart (bergskärra) occurs in the inventories of peasants, as early as the 17th century (Skultuna bruks historia, 2, MSS).

[4] Photograph of a painting of the great market-place, Västerås, the middle of the 19th century. Otherwise the bars of iron could be placed, at a pinch, on the top of the "box"-cart (Linné, 1746, p. 230; cf. Sahlin, 1931, p. 105 and Gothenburg's Museum Year Book, 1933, p. 106). Holes in the "box"-cart were also used for the carting of planks, in Mo, Dalsland (E. u. 492).

On the other hand, something must be said about the "box-cart" which in very great parts of our country and even external to the real cart provinces, was used for carting manure. It is a cart made to turn out its load and is equipped therefore with the contrivance recently explained, with the exception that the body of this cart is square. Above the axle-tree an extra bar is fixed which revolves, and by means of which the cart may be tilted backwards in order to unload. The tilting was managed by binding the box to one of the shafts with withy-cords or an iron hasp. Such manure-carts were mentioned about the middle of the 18th century in the various parts of Sweden by "economic" authors.[1] It is highly probable that the old "wippekärra," named in the inventory after the decease of Professor O. Verelius in Uppsala, 1682, was of this kind.[2]

The somewhat irregular expansion of this vehicle for the carting of manure, in the various parts of the country, absolutely indicates that it came into use at a relatively late date.[3] We have evidence that direct propaganda was made on its account.[4] In this connection there are analogies from other quarters. H. C. P. Kiesewetter tells how such a cart at the beginning of the 19th century was brought to Flotbeck, the Holstein estate, from Scotland.[5] Such carts were common in England and it is not unlikely that English influence of the 18th century's agricultural methods may have considerably furthered its expansion.[6]

More ancient than the manure-cart which could be tilted, it would seem, was the cart with the stationary body. The horse was unharnessed for unloading, in order to push the shafts up in the air. According to evidences from Dalarna, Hälsingland and Ångermanland[7] such manure-carts have been in use till later times. They have been found in Finland[8] and in Esthonian Ingria too.[9] The stationary body is generally longer than the one which can be tilted.[10]

The normal vehicle used for bringing in the harvest of corn and hay in Central Sweden is a cart with a rectangular body, erected with the help of paral-

---

[1] Kalm, 1747—51, 1, p. 281 ("in many places in Sweden"); Broman, 1911 ff., 3, p. 42 (Hälsingland, first half of 18th century) and Crælius, 1774, p. 365 (north-east of Småland; the cart appears to have been without a back end).

[2] Linköping's Diocesan Library, Cod. B. 130. Fru E. Svärdström drew my attention to this instance.

[3] Manure-carts of this kind have also been used in Scania (Rönneberga, Wigström, 1891, p. 18; Munka-Ljungby, E. u. 236; Dagstorp, E. u. 193).

[4] Osbeck, 1796, p. 26.   [5] Kiesewetter, 1807, p. 50.

[6] The "tilt" cart was commonly used in Finland also (Grotenfelt, 1915, pp. 21—25; Manninen, 1932, p. 35).

[7] Ljusdal, Hälsingland, E. u. photog.; Angermanland, Rieck-Müller-Högberg, 1920, 2, p. 222. It is certainly the same type Kalm investigated near Enköping in Uppland (1746, p. 4).

[8] For example, Grotenfelt, 1915, Fig. 26—27. (Carelia); Hermans, 1918, p. 91, (Österbotten).

[9] Manninen, 1928 (a), p. 54.

[10] With the method itself for unloading, cf. from middle of 16th century, Agricola, 1556, p. 348.

lel wooden staves on, and between the shafts, which form the framework of the base, Pl. XVIII. Sometimes a square framework was formed of open-work rails and sometimes, as the illustration shows, the staves were interlaced with slender cross-bars; in the latter case the wedge-like pegs were omitted at the back of the cart. Loose back and front ends are very common in the west of Sweden, Pl. XVIII: 1. The type is usual with slight variations in Småland and throughout the greater parts of the cart's distribution zone. The simple wheel-guard was rarely missing, especially in the west of Sweden. Of later years in many instances, movable rail-sides, inserted into the base, have taken the place of the wicker-body, and in the course of its evolution, these side-rails were gradually exchanged for horizontal bars (for example, in Bohuslän and Dalsland). From the writings of Abraham Hülphers we learn of carts with such loose lattice-doors from Ångermanland, which were removed for unloading, and the fodder was pitched into the barn with a kind of fork.[1] Suchlike practical considerations have influenced the structure of the hay and corn cart in many ways.

It would not seem incredible that the cart with rails and the cart which could be tilted, each in its own peculiar way, won ground at the expense of the waggon. Reinhold Broocman, in his "Hushåldsbok" of the year 1736, recommends the cart for hay and corn harvesting, in preference to the waggon, though he considers that much grain is spilt by the shaking of the former.[2] From 18th century accounts of the employment of the concave platform, and especially as regards Dalarna, one can conclude that the cart with rails is of comparatively later date in some parts of Sweden. On the whole, however, earlier Swedish evidence of the latter is rather unusual, probably, and perhaps mostly, because it was so very familiar to travelling and topographical authors, that its occurrence was not deemed worthy of special note.

In the west of Sweden, besides the cart with rails, there is another type varying in appearance, Pl. XIX: 1. Carl von Linné describes it as follows, from the surroundings of Alingsås: "The carts, in this place, consisted of a ladder laid across an axle with a pair of wheels of the usual kind; the rails were formed of staves which were bent under the rungs of the ladder crosswise, whilst the upper ends bent outwards to a suitable width, thus rendering other rails unnecessary."[3]

---

[1] Hülphers, 1780, p. 364.

[2] Broocman, 1736, 2, p. 78. The remedy recommended by Broocman, of placing a sheet and quilt in the cart has been carried out in many places both within and without Sweden, Grau, 1748, pp. 28, 30; Lannér, 1765, p. 19; Hersoug, 1932, p. 47, Hedmark, Norway; Wagner, 1921, p. 71, Sardinia etc.
Kiesewetter, 1807, p. 50, recommends the cart generally, even for carting hay and grain.

[3] Linné, 1746, p. 145.

I recognize this type from *Bohuslän* (Norum, Valla and Solberga, E. u. photog.; Västerlanda, E. u. 4330), *Västergötland* (Hudene, E. u. photog.; Nårunga, according to Dr. E. Klein, Nordiska Museet 174,501; Mjöbäck, E. u. 5259); Horla, E. u. photog.; Bollebygd, example in Borås Museum; cf. from Edsveden, Kullander, 1896, p. 32; cf. picture from Gothenburg 1787(?), Kjellberg-Clemensson, 1933, p. 118) and from the most southern part of *Dalsland* (Frändefors, personal notes). The carts from Nårunga and Horla are constructed with staves instead of laths but they still preserve their semi-circular form.

The origin of this type of body, together with the semi-circular platform, should be sought for amongst sledges. Sledge-bodies of corresponding type are also known from Västergötland. Fritz von Dardel's aquarelle of a wolf-hunt dated 1849, Pl. XI: 1, provides an excellent illustration.

The body made of rails, in its various forms, and acting as upper framework of the cart, is known from many parts of the European cart zone and is to be met with on earlier reproductions.[1] The greatness of the consistancy throughout the whole of the vast area is remarkable. This forceful evidence impels one to conclude that the upper framework spread to some extent from a coherent base. This does not exclude, of course, the undoubted probability of oft recurring influence both from the sledge-body and even the waggon's upper-framework. An influence such as this amongst other things, seems to have swayed in our land, rendering a closer investigation of the railed-body from a Swedish standpoint of little value.

---

[1] See, for example, Luttrell Psalter, Pl. 77, 99. The Mayster of the Game (about 1412), reproduced by for example, Zeissler, 1922, Fig. 182, and a 15th century wall-hanging, reproduced by Piton, p. 106. Excellent accounts of railed carts are given by Encyclopédie ou Dictionnaire raisonné, under Charron.

PLATE XXIII

 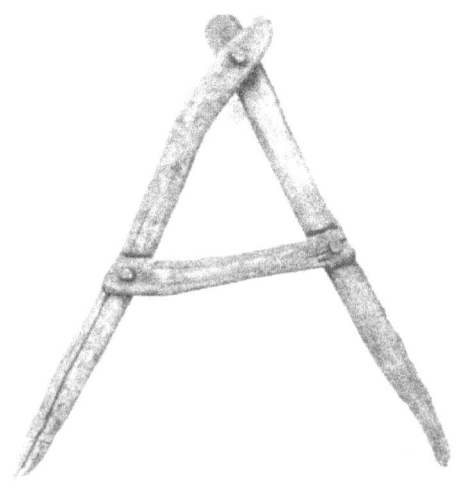

1. Trailing a plough. Hällstad, Västergötland. Photog. G. Källman.
2. Plough slide-car from Fageltofta, Scania. Nordiska Mus. 95.200.

3. Slide-car for turf-transport. Antrim, Ireland. After Cyril Fox.

PLATE XXIV

1. Wheel-sledge for hay-transport. Ed, Dalsland. Dalslands Museum, Ödeborg.

2. Wheel-sledge with a single runner at the fore. Ström, Jämtland. Nordiska Mus. 187,866.

PLATE XXV

1. Wheel-sledge for corn-transport. Nysätra, Västerbotten. Nordiska Mus. 177,028.

2. Wheelbarrow used for hay-transport in the swamps. Fagerhult, Scania. Nordiska Mus. 173,277.

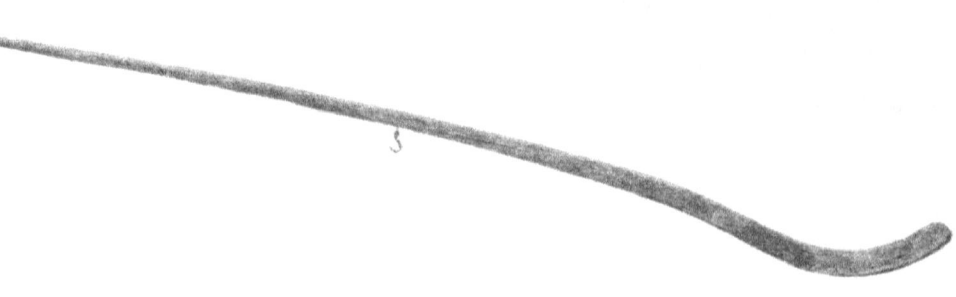

3. Draught-pole. Tystberga, Södermanland. Nordiska Mus. 183,939.

PLATE XXVI

1. Draught-pole. Mangslög, Värmland. Photog. Nils Keyland.

2. Wheeled-pole. Burs, Gotland. After a drawing by P. A. Säve.

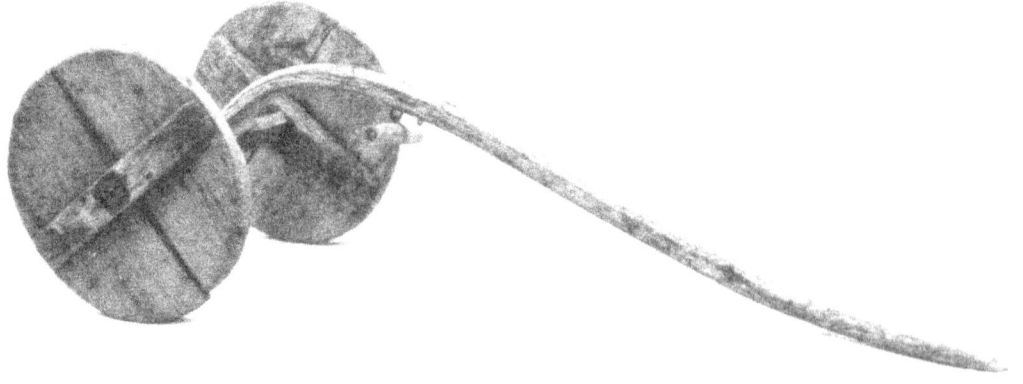

3. Wheeled-pole. Leksand, Dalarna. Nordiska Mus. 187,732.

CHAPTER VI

THE SLIDE-CAR AND THE ORIGIN OF THE CART

In what might be termed a pioneer publication, A. C. Haddon evolved the close relationship which of necessity exists between the one-horse cart and the implement known here as the slide-car. Haddon's basis was the subject-matter with which he was familiar from the British Isles, where the slide-car and the cart have existed and served side by side with each other. He describes a number of primitive carts from Scotland and Ireland and regards them as "simple modifications of the slide-car which ... was in contemporary use with them, with the addition of wheels." One type of cart was "nothing more than a wheeled slide-car, if the term be allowed, in which a round wicker-basket is jammed between the shafts just behind the pony."[1] The resemblance between these implements had not escaped the notice of earlier observers, amongst whom, the alert Finnish priest, F. P. von Knorring, in 1833 alluded to the cart in Savolax and Carelia as a probable "improvement or correction" of the slide-car.[2]

Neither Haddon nor von Knorring were acquainted, however, with the vast expansion of the slide-car, and their expositions were of a far too local nature. With a greater subject-matter the relationship between the cart and slide-car calls for a further investigation, and an immediate statement of facts referring to the occurrence of the latter, within, and exterior to Sweden would seem appropriate here.

The slide-car consists of two poles or shafts joined by cross-bars, and a small platform. The horse or other beast of burden is harnessed between the shafts whilst the back part rests on, or is drawn along the ground. The draught-animal is generally the horse, and sometimes man-haulage is employed. There are also combinations between other vehicles and the slide-car. As far as Sweden is concerned I propose to deal with these three groups, each separately.

---

[1] Haddon, 1908, p. 173.
[2] von Knorring, 1883, 1, p. 86.

The most southerly instance of a horse-drawn slide-car is in *Småland*. The reference is dated 1775 and is from Algutsboda: the slide-car is employed instead of the cart. The upper ends of the shafts were fastened to the horse, whilst the narrow ends trailed along the ground. "This is the poor man's conveyance in Småland. Such trailers were used mostly on stony ground and for the carting of rye from the forest clearings" (Barchæus, notes on travels, MSS, in UUB; cf. Hyltén-Cavallius, 1864—68, 2, p. 67). It is in *Dalsland* that we next meet with the car, and here it is used to carry the dead, a custom which has been very common in many of the roadless country-sides in the northern parts of our land (Edsleskog, E. u., according to N. I. Svensson). In *Värmland* it served as in the foregoing (Östmark, Keyland, 1923, p. 105; S. Finnskoga, Axelsson, 1852, p. 85; example in Nordiska Mus.; Hammarstedt, 1912; Nyskoga, MSS of N. Keyland in the Nordiska Mus.; Brunskog, E. u. 1436), and for the transport of herring, salt etc., to and from the mills, from the nearest road (Nyskoga, MSS of N. Keyland, Nordiska Museet; Gräsmark, E. u. 4632; Köla, for bringing home the rye, E. u., copy from a document, in Västsvenska folkminnesarkivet). We find it employed in *Västmanland* (Skultuna, according to Prof. Sigurd Erixon; Säby, according to Dr. S. T. Kjellberg, Lund; Ramnäs, example in Västerås Museum, for carting hay in the forest; Hällefors, for transporting the dead, picture in Finnbefolkningen i mellersta Sverige och sydöstra Norge, MSS of A. Segerstedt in Historiska Museet, Stockholm, reproduced in Suomen suku 1, p. 312 and Syrjänen, 1931, p. 297; Ramsberg, for transporting the dead, MSS of R. Blumenberg, in the Örebro Museum; in Ramsberg, there is a charcoal-works which got the name of "Bårhävarsbotten," because the slide-car was exchanged for the cart, according to Fröken Maja Forsslund, Kopparberg; Ljusnarsberg, according to Fröken Forsslund). In the mining district which goes down to *Nerike*, the slide-car has been used for transporting the dead to Church (Kvistbro, Hofberg, 1878, p. 37). Its uses were more varied in *Dalarna* (Grangärde, for carrying the dead, Hülphers, 1757, p. 522, for the dead and for the transportation of elk, pers. notes; Äppelbo, to and from the dairy-farms, according to Herr Ola Bannbers; Lima, E. u. 4142; Malung, for the dead, according to Herr Bannbers,[1] and Herr Erik Helmers, Gothenburg; Hedemora, for transport of hay according to Dr. K. A. Gustawsson; Svärdsjö, Gottlund, 1817, pp. 65, 118, E. u. 3890; St. Tuna, to the dairy-farms, pers. notes, E. u. 4137; Vämhus, for transporting the sick from the forest, E. u. 945; Mora, for the dead, Forsslund, 1921, p. 144; Ore, to the dairy-farms, E. u. photog. Pl. XX: 1; Orsa, E. u. 3906; Älvdalen, E. u. 4307). In *Hälsingland* (in Bjuråker, for the dead and other transportations, Wengelin, 1893, p. 176; Delsbo, for the dead, Lenæus, 1764, p. 122; Ljusdal, E. u. 860), *Härjedalen* (Lillherrdal, according to Herr O. Gunnarson, Stockholm) and *Jämtland* (Klövsjö, for the dead, Pl. XXI: 1, and to the dairy-farms, also drawn by oxen, E. u. 4115; Laxsjö, for the dead, for carting goods, and for the huntsman's bag, etc., E. u. 865; Mörsil, E. u. 5520, picture in Jämten 1931, p. 12; Oviken, picture in Jämten 1932, p. 72). In the more northern provinces it is to be met with almost everywhere, for example, in *Medelpad* (Stöde, Nordenström, 1769, p. 32), *Ångermanland* (Bjurholm, E. u. 3307; Ramsele, E.u. 5541; Tasjö, Modin, 1916, p. 98) and *Norrbotten* (Nederluleå, Nordström, 1925, p. 189, according to Dr. E. Brännström, Uppsala).

To the foregoing, which is to be found on map, Fig. 44, may be added two instances of the slide-car's occurrence at the close of the 17th century in Stockholm and its immediate neighbourhood. On W. Swiddes' famous engraving of Stockholm's Stortorg, in Erik Dahlberg's Suecia Antiqua et hodierna, one sees a slide-car employed for the transport of a barrel.[2] Swidde was a very accurate draughts-man, and studied the figures in the landscape on special request. We have preserved Dahlberg's own drawing of Tyresö Church in Sörmland and on this we are met with the same car loaded with

---

[1] After the funeral, the shafts, bearing the initials of the deceased are left by the wayside, propped upright against a certain tree. Cf. similar marking of shafts, in Värmland's Finn-district, Prinzinger, 1914, p. 170.

[2] Dahlberg, 1716, Pl. 54 (signed 1699). — About Swidde's studies of details, see Vennberg, 1925, p. 133.

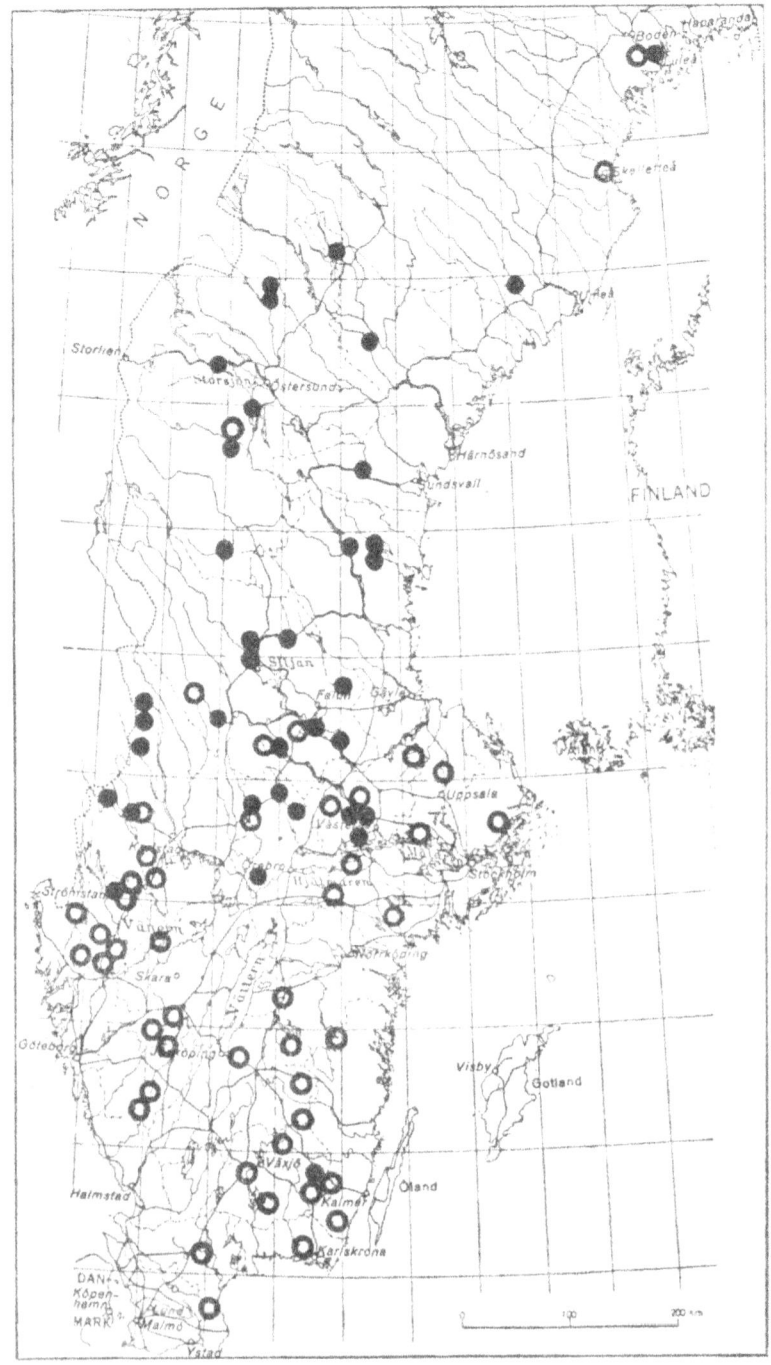

Fig. 44. The distribution of slide-cars in Sweden. Filled circles = horse-drawn. Open circles = man-hauled.

barrels, as on the engraving.[1] The former is of a more specific form and has upright staves at the back to prevent the load from gliding off. The driver is seated on the barrel. There are two similar slide-cars on an engraving 1676 of the massacre at Stockholm 1520; the picture is said to revert to a lost woodcut from 1524. The cars are loaded with upright barrels filled with corpses.[2]

The slide-car drawn by the horse has a fairly uniform expansion over the northern parts of our country. The scanty evidence from the districts furthest north fail to give a correct idea of the real occurrence of the vehicle. The vast northern territory with its sparsely populated country-sides is incapable of rendering reliable subject-material for a cartographical account, which would do justice to the quantitative occurrence of a culture-element. Evidences from the Småland of 1775, and the not less important Sörmland Suecia engravings go to prove that the slide-car was more common in olden times, further down in the south of the country. Additional support in my opinion, is the expansion of the man-hauled slide-car.

The hand-drawn slide-car is used almost exclusively on low-lying plains for carting the hay to drying-places, Pl. XX: 2. Often, as illustrated, a semi-circular body of bent wood is erected to prevent the hay from gliding off. Marsh-hay has played an important rôle in the economy far into later times, even in the south of the country.

The slide-car appears in *Scania* (Gumlösa, Linné, 1749, p. 273; Brösarp, according to Dr. G. Gustafsson), *Blekinge* (Almundsryd, Håkansson, 1932, p. 13; Listerby, according to Dr. M. Hofrén, Kalmar) and on *Gottland* (picture in the Nordiska Museet, Archives; Gustavson, 1931, pp. 69—70). Further on in *Småland* (from Algutsboda, Barchæus, notes on travels, 1775, MSS in UUB; Torsås, E. u. 223; Madesjö, drawing "about 1800" in Nordiska Museet, Archives; Sjösås, E. u. 240; Väckelsång, E. u. 4557; Öja, E. u. 4301; Kråkshult, E.u. 5573; Näshult, E. u. 7172; Forserum, E.u. 4265),[3] *Östergötland* (Sund, E. u. 6005; Hycklinge, E. u. Sigurd Erixon; Ekeby, E. u. 3621, *Västergötland* (from Jäla, E. u. 438, Mjöbäck, E. u. 5259; Otterstad, E. u. 3889; Örsås, ex. in Fristad Museum; Brunn, drawing in E. u.; Torsö, Nordiska Mus. 184,812; Sjuhärad district, E. u. 436; N. Säm, E. u. 4066). In *Dalsland* the slide-car is very familiar (Frändefors, pers. notes; Ödeborg, pers. notes; Dalskog, E. u. 492; Bolstad, Edsleskog, Mo and Töftedal, notes from N. I. Svensson) as it also is in the south of *Värmland* (Bro, E. u. 429; Borgvik, E. u. 892; Brunskog, E. u. 1436). Amongst the districts higher up in the country, may be mentioned *Södermanland* (V. Vingåker, Pl. XX: 2, Hülpher's notes on travels, 1759, MSS in UUB; Husby, E. u. 5343; cf. with Rekarne, Ericsson, 1883, p. 46), *Uppland* (Lillkyrka, E. u. 4066; Riala, E. u. 4298; Tensta, E. u. 5402; Östervåla, Eriksson, 1925, p. 104), *Västmanland* (Fläckebo and Gunnilbo, according to Dr. S. T. Kjellberg, Lund; Grythytte, pers. notes), *Dalarna* (Grangärde and St. Tuna, pers. notes; Malung, according to Herr O. Bannbers; cf. Västerdalarna, Dalarnas Hembygdsförbunds tidskrift 1926, p 41), *Jämtland* (Klövsjö, E. u. 4115), *Västerbotten* (Skellefteå, Jirlow, 1928, p. 207), *Norrbotten* (Nederluleå, Nordström, 1925, p. 189) and far north into the Norrbotten Lapp-country (photog. Borg-Mesch in Nordiska Museet, Archives).

---

[1] Dahlberg, 1716, Pl. 182. The drawing reproduced by Karling, 1933, p. 75.
[2] Stockholmsbilder från fem århundraden, 1923, Pl. 1.
[3] Cf. Hyltén-Cavallius, 1864—68, 2, p. 67.

Evidence of the hand-drawn slide-car covers its Swedish expansion area fairly well, as we see. Comparison should be made with the map. One might be led to suppose that the type recently considered once belonged to the horse-driven category, and was developed for a specific purpose. It is possible that we shall be obliged to count with both types side by side, and evidence is forthcoming, as we shall see, that the hand-drawn car is possibly the older. Strange is the fact that its occurrence northwards seems to be more sporadic.

Under any circumstance, it is not possible to assume the hand-drawn slide-car as an expansion from the north. In order to acquire some enlightenment as to the part played by the slide-car in Swedish culture, it is necessary to consider those vehicles, of which the slide-car appears to be a part. This should be contemplated from the view of the slide-car's once vaster and more frequent occurrence throughout the land.

Most common is the coupling together of a sledge and a slide-car, Pl. XXII: 3. Such an arrangement has been used for comparatively many purposes, and is known both from Central and Upper Sweden. A cross-piece of wood was fastened to the front of the slide-car and this was attached to the sledge. Sometimes a similar piece of wood was attached at the back also.

In Sjuhärad district in *Västergötland* such a vehicle was employed, equipped both with its back wooden attachment and basket, for the transport of potatoes, manure etc. (E. u. 436). They are said to have been used mostly in Mark (information from Mjöbäck, where they also occur, E. u. 5259; Kinnarumma, Västgötaordboken's Collection in Landsmålsarchives, Uppsala). They also occur in central *Småland* (Sjösås, E. u. 240; Torsås, E. u. 223; N. Hestra, E. u. 3891) and in *Östergötland* (Vårdsberg, E. u. 3917). In *Värmland* we find them transporting twigs and branches and wood for making charcoal (Glava, Bergström-Wesslén, 1922, Fig. 29; Blomskog, according to Herr P. H. Nilsson, Stockholm), *Västmanland* (for wood, V. Våla and Nora, pers. notes; Karbenning, E. u. 4865; Norberg, E. u. 4097), *Dalarna* (Säter, Pl. XXII: 3; Svärdsjö, E. u. 3890; in Idre it is said to have been used for transport of the dead, according to Herr O. Gunnarsson, Stockholm). Such "trail-porterage" is known from *Härjedalen* (Jämten 1927, p. 60), *Jämtland* (Föllinge, Frödin, 1927, p. 121; cf. Jämten, 1925, p. 176 and 1931, p. 27), *Ångermanland* (Graninge, E. u. 4167) and *Medelpad* (Borgsjö, with a kind of platform for the carting of wood, E. u. photog. Pl. XXII: 2). In the most northerly districts, in the Lapp country of Västerbotten for instance, it appears to be quite common. I know of evidence from Åsele (according to Dr. R. Jirlow, Nordiska Mus. 183,428 and Vilhelmina (E. u. 1284, 645, for wood, fodder and stone transport).

In many instances the principle of this vehicle approaches that method of transport treated in the foregoing, Chapter IV. Connection with the slide-car seems beyond doubt. In the south of Sweden, or rather, in parts of Småland and in the south of Östergötland the vehicle corresponds in some respects to the implement illustrated by Pl. XXII: 1. It will be noticed that a simple sled is attached to the runners of a short sledge of the usual type, by means of treenails.

I know this form from the following provinces: *Småland:* Sjösås (according to Herr J. A. Göth, Klaverström), Urshult (E. u. 5623), Väckelsång (E. u. 4557), Linneryd (E. u. 5588), Kråkshult

(E. u. 5573), Torsås (E. u. 223) and S. Vi (according to Herr Hj. Johansson, Västervik, E. u. 5623). Compare with an annotation by M. Cræ̈lius from the north-western district (Cræ̈lius, 1774, p. 370). From the very south of *Östergötland*, Svinhult (E. u. photog.) and Sund (E. u. photog. 1930).

This type of trailer, which sometimes resembles a real sledge was excellently suitable for carting big loads, thanks to the long runners which enabled certain ease of movement. Its limited expansion is of exceedingly great interest. It is highly probable that we have here to deal with a local development of a comparatively late date, in the form of a trailer of the above description, which has been evolving for some time.

After this investigation of what is known of the slide-car in Sweden, we will proceed with its occurrence exterior to the country. In *Norway* it prevails over the greater part of the land. It seems that its appearance is considerably less in the Lapp districts and south-westerly areas. Excepting the north (Nordland and Troms), we meet with both horse-transport and man-haulage. In connection with the former, it appears, as in Sweden, to be employed principally for carting goods to the dairy-farms and for transporting the dead. On the whole, and especially in Östlandet it is of the same type as our own (cf. from Höland in the province of Akershus, Gielleböl, 1771, p. 312; from Nes in the same province, Beretning om Akershus landbrukshöiskole, 1933, p. 24; from Lier in Buskerud, Essendrop, 1761, Pl. p. 202/203). Further north (evidence from Sogn and Fjordane, S. Tröndelag, Nordland and Troms[1]) a specific form is to be met with. The terminals curve upwards and the platform for the load is between these and the shafts. This type also occurs in Finland and is known from the most northern parts of Sweden.[2] A type with a short fore-sled forthcoming in various country-sides should not be omitted (Östfold, for wood; Hedmark; Opland; Rogaland, Anda, 1881, pp. 38—39; Hordaland where one notes very developed forms of the same type[3]; Sogn and Fjordane; Möre). There are instances which show that the slide-car has undergone a similar development as in Carelia (cf. below), in other words, traces have been inserted into the rear as in the case of the ordinary sledge (example from Sogn in Heiberg's collection, Amla).

As regards *Finland*, the slide-car seems to have been used to excellent purpose, as in Sweden and Norway, for the carting of hay by man-craft and for the transporting by horse, of every conceivable thing. In the former recurs the semi-circular body of curved willow-osiers in Österbotten (Hermans, 1918, p. 77; without the semi-circular body from Satakunda, Helminen, 1931, p. 201). A still more primitive man-hauled slide-car, consisting of two birch-trunks held together by crossbars, was used in Savolaks (Grotenfelt, 1899, pp. 186, 257, 259; the same type was sometimes drawn by the horse). From Österbotten and Tavastland, horse-draught slide-cars are known from the middle of the 18th century (Rudenschöld, 1738—41, pp. 23, 174; cf. En tur genom Österbotten, 1883, p. 84). Further north there occurs as previously mentioned a more evolved form with up-turned ends (Sirelius, 1912—21, 1, p. 384; Paulaharju, 1922, p. 19; v. Knorring, 1833, 1, p. 86). In the western parts of Finland the slide-car evinces a strong tendency towards a more sledge-like vehicle. One striking feature in this connection is the built-up body on the ends of the shafts trailing along the ground. This addition tends to steady the vehicle (Grotenfelt, 1915, p. 7; Sirelius 1913 (a), p. 1; Finland, 1923, p. 165; the normal form occurs also, see Itkonen, 1932, p. 407). Probably this development was influenced by the sledge, and constructional details would seem to assert that this is so.

Amongst the East-Baltic countries I am acquainted with the slide-car from *Esthonia* and *Latvia*. From the former, Manninen, 1934, pp. 229—230, Rahvateadoslikud Küsimuskavad, 1931, p. 11;

---

[1] Employed for the transport of wood, in winter, in places too steep for the sledge.
[2] Hellström, 1917, p. 195; from Nederluleå according to Dr. E. Brännström, Uppsala.
[3] Olsen, 1914—24, pp. 119—122, gives a good illustration and description of such a type from this place. He is acquainted with it from Sunnhordland and Hardanger in Hordaland, and from Ryfylke in Rogaland. It is not only used for carting stones, but even for transporting wood (answer to enquiry).

Hupel, 1777, 2, Pl. IV, for hay-harvesting; Wormsö, hay-harvesting, according to a student from the same place, 1926, and from the latter, photog. Gunnar Ullenius, 1930 (hay-harvesting and hand-drawn).

The occurrence of the slide-car in *Russian*-Carelia constitutes an immediate extension from its Finnish expansion zone. Even here it has gone so far with its built-up body in development towards the sledge, that nothing is left in common, save that the shafts are formed in one with the runners (Grotenfelt, 1915, p. 7.) But the normal slide-car occurs, and is drawn by the horse (Weule, 1912, p. 102). The vehicle is in use in other parts of Russia, especially in Great and White Russia, as well as in the north-eastern districts (Moszynski, 1929, p. 629; cf., from the vicinity of Leningrad, and of Moskow, Gaimard, 1838—40, 2, Pl. (254), (260). It is of special interest that the same kind of slide-car with upturned terminals, as seen in the northern parts of Finland, in Sweden and in Norway, is employed in White Russia (Moszynski, 1929, p. 629). It occurs also amongst the Bashkir (Rudenko, 1925, p. 239). In Ukrainia, further south, I met with a picture of the slide-car. It is to be seen in the Hungarian National Museum, Budapest, Pl. XXI: 2. The *Zyryan* use the car to bring home the hay. Branches and leaves are allowed to remain and often two vertical branches are stuck in at the back (Manninen, 1932, p. 279; 1934, pp. 229—231; Sirelius, 1908, illustration, p. 36, type with up-turned terminals). On the other hand, there is unmistakable evidence of its occurrence in Central Europe. From what Professor Arthur Haberlandt has informed me, it is known on the mountain regions of *Silesia*. During military service in Bressanone, in the north of the *Tyrol*, has Professor Haberlandt also come across them (cf. Haberlandt, 1926, p. 395). Hints as to a more extensive use of the present slide-car come from sundry places in the Alps, where one meets with the "combination" vehicle, the little sledge and the trailer. We find it in Engadin, Tessin and other districts in the south of *Switzerland* (Huber, 1919, cf. 33—35; cf. a toy-sledge in Landesmuseum für sächsische Volkskunde, Dresden). Sometimes, as is seen in Switzerland and the Tyrol, one of its component parts is a pair of wheels. (Photog. from Merano published in Svenska Dagbladet 6.IV. 1930.) Vehicles consisting of a little sledge and a trailer are found in the Carinthian Alps in *Austria* (Zeissler, 1922, p. 25) in the Alps in *Hungary* (winter vehicles, Anzeiger d. Ethnog. Abteil. des Ungarischen Nationalmuseums 8, 1916, p. 135), and in the *Roumanian* Siebenburgen (Teutsch-Fuchs, 1905, p. 161). In *Montenegro* the slide-car is used together with a fork-shaped trailer, pair-drawn (cf. p. 141; Haberlandt 1917, Pl. 4, 12); the same is to be met with in the Tatra mountains in the Polish Carpathians (Moszynski, 1929, p. 629) and amongst the Tatars in Russia (Pallas, 1793—94, 2, Pl. 3 A). In all these places it is employed for transporting wood, over very rough and rugged ground.

Still stronger evidence as to the slide-car's antiquity and expansion over the greater parts of Europe, comes from the British Isles. A. C. Haddon has given an account of its appearance and purpose in *Scotland* and *Ireland* and in addition has given information concerning its older forms. It is drawn by the horse and in appearance, coincides on the whole with the type used in Sweden, though the trailer seems much shorter as a rule. A basket is mounted for the transporting of such things as peat and fodder, and it is put to all-round uses (Haddon, 1908, pp. 164—166; cf. Mitchell, 1880, pp. 96—98). It occurs in Wales also (Peate, 1929, p. 68; Fox, 1931, p. 190).

The slide-car has spread considerably amongst the Russian settlements in Siberia. It is used for transporting straw, hay, sacks of corn etc. One finds the north-Russian, north-Finnish and north-Scandinavian types with upturned ends, and sometimes the basket-work body is there between its two shafts (Zelenin, 1927, p. 134). von Schrenk says about the Russian sledge drawn by oxen in the Amur districts that, "the thick runners are combined with the shafts and this renders them clumsy and unpractical" (v. Schrenk, 1891, p. 498). That our form is customary also, may be derived from a photograph of a funeral procession, published by Fritjof Nansen (Nansen, 1914, Pl. 344, 345). We are able to gather to what extent the slide-car was esteemed as a means of conveyance amongst the Siberians, when we read Wilhelm Radloff's account of how, when exploring amongst the Kalmucks in the Altai districts, he had such an equipage made for his wife. His words would seem to imply that the vehicle was unfamiliar to the Kalmucks (Radloff, 1860, p. 574).

But this cannot be said of all the Siberian peoples. The *Ostyak Samoyed*, *Kamassintzy*, and *Kirghiz*, each and all employ the slide-car. In some instances it may with certainty be due to Russian influence. The Ostyak-Samoyed transported elk in the summer-time from the forests

(Donner, 1915, p. 93). The Kamassintzy used the slide-car with its branches and leaves, and drawn by the horse, for bringing in the hay. Kai Donner points out that twenty or thirty years ago, the Kamassintzy were hunters and game-keepers (reindeer) and that, at that time, they had no need of this contrivance. He also finds that the neighbouring Russians and Tatars are unacquainted with the slide-car and consequently surmises that the Kamassintzy themselves invented it. But obviously this is a mistake (Donner, 1915, pp. 91—93). The Kirghiz use the slide-car as a conveyance, sometimes drawn by the horse and sometimes by the camel "for the transport of heavy loads." The car was often equipped with rails at the back to prevent the load from gliding off (Prinz, 1913, pp. 168, 172—174; Byhan, 1923, Fig. 240).[1]

To Captain Sigurd Sternwall, Stockholm, I am indebted for an account of the existence and the employment of the slide-car in *China*. This is of immense interest. Captain Sternwall tells that in the rugged mountain country-sides of the provinces Hupeh and Szechuen, it is drawn by the horse or donkey. It is used in the late-autumn for the bringing down of fuel and has for this purpose a basket made of leather or plaited osiers. The basket is supported behind by two wooden pegs. The harness includes a pack-saddle. In the Yangtze delta a similar slide-car is used without basket or body. It is drawn by the buffalo for carting home reeds, which are used as fuel. The buffalo is not harnessed with a pack-saddle, but wears only a very primitive belly-band to which the shafts are fastened.

A more thorough and systematic study of ethnographical literature as regards China would doubtless bring to light much more than is known in this connection. An interesting combination of two vehicles is met with in the *Phillipines*. It resembles, one might say, two slide-cars coupled together, and is drawn by the buffalo (Zeissler, 1922, p. 32; illustration, unsatisfactory). The sledge from *Siam*, after Paul Leser, which is used to transport agricultural implements, and for harvesting, with its runners and shafts, should be regarded as a slide-car, though as in the Amur district and Carelia it is otherwise constructed as a sledge (Leser, 1927, p. 43; another example is preserved in the Science Museum, London, Catalogue of the collections, 1926, p. 12). It seems highly probable that Chinese influence is to be counted with here, but absence of subject-evidence renders it precarious to judge.

The only explanation of the slide-car's vast and widely-spread expansion is undoubtedly its High Antiquity. Its irregular character should be viewed as being due to its existence, in many instances, as a survival, which has been preserved, owing to quite specific circumstances. Amongst the latter might be accounted, the advantages such a contrivance offers on occasions of transport over rugged ground, an employment for which wheels are scarcely adapted. Less practical would the simple runner-sledge be, as in summer-time, it must of necessity be used only for shorter transportations. Arthur Mitchell clearly defines the advantages of the slide-car in preference to the wheeled-vehicle when he writes: "We too often fail to see, in what we call rude implements, that suitability for their purpose, in the circumstances of their actual use, ... When I saw what these carts were employed in doing, namely, transporting peat, ferns and hay from high grounds down very steep hills entirely without roads, I saw that the contrivance was admirably adapted for its purpose and that wheeled-carts would have been useless for that work ... It is not always an evidence of capacity or skill, to use elaborate or fine machinery. A rough, rude tool may for certain purposes be the most efficient, and may shew wisdom

---

[1] The slide-car from Turfan in east Turkestan is mentioned by v. Le Coq, 1911, p. 90.

both in its contriver and employer."[1] Mitchell's hypothesis that the evolution was from cart to slide-car falls through because of faulty assumptions).

With a sturdy conservatism the slide-car has held its ground in the mountain districts of the various parts of Europe, whilst the more open country-sides have been earlier reached by newer culture influences existing within the area of the vehicle.[2] And this preservation is due to the suitability of the car on difficult ground. Much earlier however, its expansion was not limited in this manner, and today, as we have seen from many examples from Sweden, it is used to advantage on regulated roads. During the Great War it was employed as an ambulance on the Balkan front.[3]

Not rarely is it seen that implements of another character, more or less incidental, have been transported over rough country in a manner which closely coincides with the slide-car and, which, upon a certainty, implies a knowledge of the latter. In Romfartuna in Västmanland when the harrow was transported to the field, as a rule, two poles were inserted within its frame and the machine was trailed along the ground by a horse or an ox.[4] In Finland the harrow is transported upside-down, with its poles, as a slide-car.[5] The same is done in Olonetz in Russian Carelia.[6] In Finland the "forked"-plough, upside-down, is transported to and from the field in the same manner, and according to Sirelius the same method is used by the Zyryan people.[7]

An important criterion touching on the age of the slide-car is to be derived from its expansion amongst the Prairie Indians of North America. A. C. Haddon has already referred to these Indian "trailer" types, consisting, as a rule of two tent-poles harnessed to the backs of pack-horses. On this vehicle might be placed lighter loads, and even children, aged persons and the sick were transported in this manner, during the continuous removals incurred on hunting expeditions.[8] A similar trailer is known from the earliest exploring days through Coronado de Castañedas in his Relacion de la jornada de Cibola 1540.[9] Later on, according to Clark Wissler, the slide-car (travois) was com-

---

[1] Mitchell, 1880, pp. 96—98.
[2] The slide-car is included in military equipment and is used by the artillery of the Swedish army, Nordisk familjebok, see Släpa. Eric von Otter, an officer in the Swedish army had a slide-car made in Turkana in East Africa, for the transport of a safe. von Otter, 1930, p. 326.
[3] Horniman Museum, 1925, p. 19.   [4] E. u. 3275.
[5] Sirelius, 1919—21, 1, Fig. 194.   [6] Schrader, 1917—29, 2, Pl. 22.
[7] For ex. Gottlund, 1817, p. 65; Sirelius, 1919—21, 1, Fig. 204, p. 270.   [8] Haddon, 1908, p. 164.
[9] This shews how unreasonable is J. Loewenthal's assumption that the Indians got their knowledge of the slide-car from the Swedes. He writes, "if we suppose that the Dakota prairie-tribes got the slide-car from the Cree tribes of the plains, and call to mind that the Finns (from whom Loewenthal knows the vehicle), take in most of their culture-forms from the Germanic people (Swedes), so may we here assume a Scandinavian influence (Swedish) as far as the Algonkian(!)," Loewenthal, 1920—21, p. 214.

monly used "in the Missouri-Saskatchewan area."[1] But the draught-animal was not always a horse however, sometimes it might be a dog even.[2] As the horse is post-Columbian in America, one has presumed the dog as being of earlier date. The investigator who most emphatically endorses this theory, is Clark Wissler and he has frequently returned to the problem.[3] As he seems unacquainted with the occurrence of the slide-car in the Old World, he considers connection with Asiatic culture extremely unlikely. From my point of view, however, such a connection may very well have existed. It should be of interest, if the hand-drawn slide-car were found in use in northern Asia to-day (concerning Sweden, see p. 132). But another possibility would seem to present itself if the dog-drawn slide-car, once in general use throughout Asia, due to the common employment of the horse, became later on, entirely extinct. Parallels of the dog as draught-animal for the sledge, in North Asia, would not of itself render such a supposition unlikely. However, Kaj Birket-Smith has drawn attention to the insignificant rôle played on the whole by the dog, as draught-animal amongst the Indians, and stated that it would scarcely seem as if the "dog traction among the Indians is at all a pre-Columbian element."[4]

Clark Wissler has endeavoured to explain the slide-car's autochthonal origin amongst the Indians, by drawing attention to the manner in which several of the tribes saddle their tent-poles to the sides of the draught-animal. But this method may be regarded as more incidental. In these cases burdens were also packed on the tent-poles. Improvised "trailers" of a similar kind are known from elsewhere. The Swedish migrant Lapps sometimes fastened their tent-poles to the last of the rein-deer on the march.[5] In other places, building materials are transported in this manner. Once the harnessing technique is mastered, the rest is quite easy.[6]

It is scarcely probable however, that a slide-car could have originated from these methods, and still less likely would it seem, within a culture-district, where the pack-saddle seems not to have been more generally employed in

---

[1] Wissler, 1910, p. 91, gives excellent accounts of its occurrence amongst the various tribes.
[2] Wilson, 1924, pp. 216—221, 275—288, gives a detailed illustration of the slide-car for dog and horse, amongst the Hidatsa Indians.
[3] Wissler, 1910, p. 91, 1912, p. 32, 1914, p. 12, 1922, p. 32.
[4] Birket-Smith, 1929, 2, p. 169. Religious reasons may have played a part here. Cf. Koppers, 1930, p. 369.
[5] von Düben, 1873, p. 113; Petterson, 1888, p. 30; Wiklund, 1899, p. 32; Demant-Hatt, 1913, p. 185.
[6] Similar pack-saddle arrangements, for poles, boards etc., I know from Norway, Hordaland, answer to my enquiries; Iceland, Bruun, 1928, p. 323; Turkestan, v. Schwartz, 1900, p. 338; Atlas Mountains, Schröter, 1925, p. 783; several places in the north of Africa, British East Africa, Lindblom, 1931, p. 75, and South America, Zeissler, 1922, p. 12.

pre-Columbian times. In addition, and according to Birket-Smith, it appears that the conical tent with poles, is a late type in America, "and the question is, is the Travois not earlier then than this"?[1] It must not be overlooked, that the Indian slide-car, with its poles meeting at the fore, in a V shape, does not quite coincide with the Eurasian, but this can be a natural adjustment suited to dog-draught, which had its survival in the slide-car.

The probabilities being in the majority seems to me an argument in favour of an existing connection from very ancient times, between the slide-car's expansion area in the Old and New World.[2] Could it be proved that also in Asia the horse-drawn slide-car had behind it, in the history of culture, a predecessor drawn by the dog, would much which seems so vague, appear quite natural. As matters now stand, the contrivance is closely allied to the horse, and to some great extent, it spread, undoubtedly, in connection with the expansion of this domestic animal. At least, such is the case in Europe, and should the horse be accounted to have served as model for other draught-animals, the same might be said of Asia. That the slide-car belongs to an earlier stage in the evolution than the cart, is evident, but the circumstances are very complicated, and differ exceedingly in the various culture-areas.

Fritz Flor, who counts with a time-honoured "pre-Indo-Germanic" horse culture has ascribed the slide car to a proto-Samoyedic culture which he has personally investigated.[3] He bases his assumption a good deal, as far as the Northern Countries are concerned, on the find of a "net stick" or chisel made from the bone of a horse, from the Ancylus period, in Kolsan, Nordtröndelag, Norway. Flor accordingly regards the find as evidence of the occurrence of the tame horse already at this early age.[4] But as similar bones were found in a shell heap in 1920, near Uddevalla, in Bohuslän, such a view is considered groundless.[5] Scientific research seems to agree that the wild horse once inhabited Scandinavia though it may have been extinct at a comparatively early age.[6] There is no forthcoming reliable evidence of the tame horse in the Northern Countries before the end of megalithic time. On the other hand Otto Rydbeck indicates probabilities that the tame horse appeared in connection with the

---

[1] Birket-Smith, 1929, 2, p. 168.
[2] Fritz Flor considers this connection fully substantiated as fact. Flor, 1933, p. 56. — Flor's reference to Nansen's picture of a burial with slide-cars, as evidence of the occurrence of the vehicle amongst the Tunghuz is a mistake. — For the whole problem concerning the connection between North America and North Eurasia cf. v. Richthofen, 1932 (a).
[3] Flor, 1930 (b), p. 83.
[4] Flor, 1930 (b), pp. 201—204.
[5] Ringström, 1928, p. 13.
[6] Cf. Nordgaard, 1932, p. 34; Isberg, 1930, p. 398.

one man's grave or the battle-axe culture.¹ Rydbeck is of opinion that, in Sweden, during the Later Stone Age, an agricultural people penetrated the area already inhabited by indigenous dwellers (megalithic culture, which according to Rydbeck came from England) and afterwards, during the passage-grave period, the more nomadic pastoral-race came from the south bringing the domestic horse with them. During the period of the grave-cist the two peoples joined forces. One of the most valuable supports of the theory which indicates connection between the tame horse and the battle-axe culture is the speed and force with which the former spread throughout the North of Europe, an expansion which calls to mind the spread of the horse amongst the North American Indians in post-Columbian times. Archeologically it is not yet clear, where in Europe the domestic horse originally belonged, but when J. E. Forssander suggests the Steppes of S. Russia where it is known from the early dyne-dwellings, one is inclined to believe he is right.²

The vast expansion of the slide-car and its High Antiquity renders A. C. Haddon's inference that the single-horse cart, as known in the British Islands, autochthonally should have evolved there, an utter impossibility. Such a theory ignores too entirely the cart's similarly wide-spread and ancient expansion. On the other hand, the leading idea in Haddon's theory should be considered as fully correct and indisputable. The single-horse cart has evolved from the slide-car, but this occurred in very ancient times and probably in connection with the earliest employment of the tame horse by the Altaic peoples.

One of the evidences of existing kinship between the single-horse cart and the slide-car is that the cart, from the very beginning was driven from horseback. This way of driving the cart is quite unknown within the culture province of the pair-cart, and may be an indication of the single-horse cart's seniority. Riding the horse has the advantage of dispensing with the bit.

The custom of riding the draught-horse of the slide-car is common both in the north of Asia and in the east of Europe. We find it, for example, amongst the Kirghiz, Kamassintzy and Bashkir, in Ukrainia, Russian Carelia and Savolaks in Finland.³ I know of it in Sweden and Norway as little as from the

---

[1] Rydbeck, 1930 and 1934; Forssander, 1933, pp. 210—213. The well-known Ullstorp cranium from Scania belongs to the Grave-Cist Period or Early Bronze Age. Flor states that the horse was killed with a knife-thrust in the forehead, similarly as was the reindeer amongst the Siberian peoples. Flor, 1930, pp. 113, 153.

[2] Forssander, 1933, p. 213. For actual research as to whether the Indo-Europeans learnt the tame horse culture directly from the Altai or through the Uralians or Ugrians, are N. European conditions, as Koppers also points out, of relatively less importance (Koppers, 1934, p. 186).

[3] See earlier account of the slide-car's occurrence at these places. The same custom is found in the Phillipines, Zeissler, 1922, p. 33, and amongst the North American Indians, Descamps, 1930, Fig. 10.

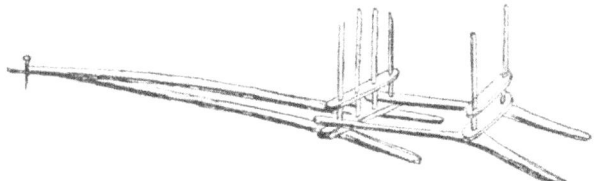

Fig. 45. Comprised Tatarian slide-car for transport of wood. After P. S. Pallas.

British Isles, but this may be due to a later development, connected with the appearance of the present-day horse-saddle.

The very harnessing of the slide-car and the single-horse cart with the "pack-saddle" idea suggests similarities.[1] It might seem appropriate in this connection to infer the pack-saddle as the possible antecedent of the Northern saddle-pommel. We are now touching on an area, however, which has not yet been satisfactorily investigated and to draw further positive inference from the various harnessing arrangements scarcely seems possible.

That the single-horse cart had its origin in the slide-car I find to be an unconditioned fact, as absolute as the certainty of the close relationship existing between these vehicles and the horse. There is, however, a parallel contrivance to the slide-car which is used for pair-draught, and which I will refer to here as the "forked" slide-car, Fig. 45. This type seems to be of great import in the development of the vehicle, an import which, one may say, has been sadly neglected. Though it is not possible to carry on any lengthy investigation here, a few indications are undoubtedly in place, especially as the type has occurred in Sweden.

The forked slide-car seems more particularly at the moment to have a South-European expansion but has, earlier, of a certainty, been quite common also in South Asia. Evidence of its occurrence, at my disposition is scanty, and this scarcity may perhaps be due to the dominant position attained by the pair-cart. L. F. Cammiade has published a slide-car of this kind from the Godavari district in *India*, mounted with a basket-work body, and drawn by a pair of yoked oxen "at the apex of the runners." "The advantage of the vehicle is that it can be used over rough, stony ground that would smash the wheels of an ordinary country cart, and it can slide down and up muddy watercourses and gullies where an ordinary cart would stick" (Cammiade, 1925). The fore-part of the vehicle reproduced by P. S. Pallas, from the *Crimea*, which is used for transporting wood from steep mountains consists of such a forked trailer (Pallas, 1803, p. 136, Pl. 3 A). In *Montenegro* and *Servia* in the Balkan Peninsula there are simple and combined vehicles of the slide-car construction (Haberlandt, 1917, p. 122, Pl. IV, 11 and 12. Examples may be seen in the Ethnographical Museum, Belgrade, concerning which I have been informed by Dr. E. Klein). According to K. Moszynski, the forked slide-car is used elsewhere in the east of Europe. It is of a similar formation to that used for transporting the plough which will shortly be mentioned and is used for the transport of stone and agricultural implements (Moszynski, 1929, p. 630). In *Roumania* it is used in combination with a wheel-axle, according to Mr. R. K. Trichkov, Vratza. Extraordinarily enough the vehicle has also been employed in Africa (Betchuana in the Transvaal, Anučin, 1899, p. 144), and undoubtedly must it be a question of European influence.

[1] See the instructive illustration of a cart, harnessed in this manner, by Linné, 1747, p. 230.

To these quite too few instances of the forked slide-car as an all-round vehicle may be added, however, its employment as transporter of the plough, which occurs over the greater parts of Europe. Paul Leser has specially investigated the various methods of getting the plough to and from the field.[1] He states that in some places the farmer carries the plough on his shoulders and sometimes it is put on the yoke of the oxen.[2] The ordinary custom in Europe was to convey the plough by means of a "trailer", which consists of two slenderish poles coupled together at the ends and held in place with a cross-bar. The ploughshare was laid in the triangle to the fore, and the free ends trailed on the ground, Pl. XXIII: 1.

The triangular plough slide-car has been common in our country, on agricultural plains, even though, with time, it has been exchanged for other types, especially in connection with the iron-plough. It was used in *Scania* (Fågeltofta, Nordiska Museet 95,200; Lyngby, E. u. 233; Väsby, notes and picture from 1830 in the Mandelgren Collections; Lund, Linné, 1749, Pl. 3: two ploughs with trailers; cf. Scanian law, Chap. 69, "àrderdrög" (the plough trailer) and Rietz, 1867, under Ärja with information from various Scanian places), *Halland* (Frillesås and Värö, Rietz, 1867, under "Plogsläpa" and "Ärja"), *Småland* (Sjösås, E. u. 240, Väckelsång, E. u. 4557; Kråksmåla, E. u. 6559), *Västergötland* (Solberga, Sundén, 1903, p. 6; Hällstad E. u. 2885; Kölingared, E. u. photog.; cf. Rietz, 1867, under Släpa, and Säve, 1869, p. 170), *Gotland* (Follingbo and Hejdeby, E. u. 577; Burs, E. u. 585), *Östergötland* (information from most of the districts, in E. u.),[3] *Västmanland* (Skultuna, E. u. 2441; there does not seem to have been a cross-bar, the contrivance could be folded) and *Uppland* (Söderbykarl, E. u. 3415; Våla and Tierp, according to Dr. M. Eriksson, Uppsala; there is only one pole here, the other was supplemented by the steering pole). This type of slide-car is known to me from *Finland* (Vilkuna, 1933, p. 10). It has been very common in various parts of *Germany*. Leser has brought forward instances from Pfalz, Hunsrück, Eifel, Westerwald, Bergisches Land, Rheintal, Hannover, Mecklenburg and Böhmen (Leser, 1927, p. 38); example from Hannover in Bomann Museum, Celle). It also occurs in *Switzerland* (Schweizerisches Idiotikon, under Schlitten, col. 777). According to Kasimierz Moszynski it is used in slightly varying forms in *Czecho-Slovakia, Poland*, White and Little *Russia*, in the south of Great Russia and in the west of *Bulgaria* (Moszynski, 1929, p. 630; cf. Leser, 1927, p. 38; according to the late Professor Boris Sokolow, Moscow).

It seems indisputable that this kind of "plough" slide-car spread in connection with the plough at a very ancient date.[4] Its vast expansion in conformity to type is impossible to explain otherwise. Under such circumstances this must be understood to be a specializing of a more generally used vehicle and, by so doing, the assumption, that in the south-east of Europe there existed

---

[1] Leser, 1927.

[2] To Leser's example from Sardinia may be added examples from Switzerland, Atlantis, 1931, p. 349, the Pyrenees, Fahrholz, 1931, p. 74, and Persia, v. Gennep, 1913, p. 75. The method has occurred alternatively here in Sweden according to accounts from several places in Östergötland, for example, Heda (E. u. 4261).

[3] In some parts of the district, from the slide-car has developed a "plough-cart", which is, in reality, the slide-car equipped with a pair of wheels. W. Howitt describes a similar arrangement from the middle of the 19th century, in the surroundings of Heidelberg as follows: some of the peasants "instead of this forked bough (the triangular plough slide-car) have a little frame with a pair of wheels to put behind. A sort of carriage is thus formed, and the peasant lays his harrow on the top and drives to the field" (Howitt, 1842, p. 26). Cf. from Belgium Loewenthal, 1918, p. 204.

[4] This undoubtedly calls to mind Lesers "Pflüge mit Krümmel," cf. p. 106.

a widely expanded forked slide-car as universal vehicle before the pair-cart, is considerably substantiated.[1]

The "plough" slide-car and the "forked" slide-car are closely associated with the ox as draught-animal, and this brings us face to face with a distinct contrast between the North-European horse-complex and the Mediterranean ox-complex. Asia affords a similar contrast, but I am unable to develop this opinion further. This contrast is especially evident in the south-east of Europe where the culture-districts meet. In Ukraine, we have seen how the slide-car is used for the horse, and the pair-cart for the ox, whilst amongst the Crimean Tatars and in Montenegro the vehicle consists of a forked slide-car coupled together with a simple slide-car etc.

On the other hand, the contrast between the single and pair-draught vehicle must not be taken to indicate their independent origin. Without doubt there exists a connection between them. Berthold Laufer emphatically states that the cart must be ascribed to the mutual culture-elements of China and Western Asia "which go back to a remote prehistoric age." According to Laufer, to these belong "the mode of agriculture, the cultivation of wheat and barley, tilling of the field by means of the plough drawn by an ox, methods of artificial irrigation, cattle-breeding, employment of cattle as draught-animals, the composite bow, the cart based on the principle of the wheel and the potter's wheel."[2]

The question is, has the single horse-cart got its wheels from the already completed pair-cart or is the contrary possible? The solution of the problem is dependent on what research will have to tell about interior and historical connections in Asia of the culture of the horse and other beasts of burden. Ethnology seems to have good grounds for counting with the North-Asiatic pastoral cultures as an inspiring element in the rise of cattle-rearing. "It is possible," says Wilhelm Schmidt, "that we have to thank the peoples of the north-easterly districts, that is to say the real cattle-breeders, for the invention of the wheel, and in consequence, of the waggon also."[3]

Under all circumstances it is quite obvious that the wheel itself could not have been brought about through a combination of sledge and cylinder, but that it must have originated in connection with the development of the slide-car, or forked slide-car.

---

[1] It is not improbable that the simple runner-sledge of the forked type, as it occurs in Spain, in Sweden and elsewhere, in some cases reverts to real forked slide-cars. In Urshult, Småland, there are said to have been such forked slide-cars as a variation of the ordinary forked runner-sledge (E. u. 5623).

[2] Laufer, 1914, p. 185. Cf. Laufer, 1931, pp. 538—539.

[3] Schmidt-Koppers, 1924, p. 101. Cf. Flor, 1930 (b), p. 15: "Ethnological facts make it quite plain nowadays, that oxen were only employed in South Asia, in religious rites, and that their taming was due in the first place, to influence from Siberian pastoral tribes."

CHAPTER VII

THE WHEELED-SLEDGE AND WHEEL-BARROW

In sundry parts of the west of Sweden there is a sledge equipped with a pair of wheels, which serves as a summer vehicle. The contrivance varies in form. Sometimes it has the appearance of a rather ordinary sledge fitted with axle and wheels, or it consists of a small sledge and a pair of wheels which together support the platform. The vehicle is almost exclusively used at harvest times to bring in the hay and corn.

It is used in *Bohuslän* ("more generally in the mountain districts," Holmberg, 1842—45, 2, p. 78, 1848—49, p. 62). *Dalsland* (Holmberg, 1848—49, p. 62; Ed, example in Dalslands fornsal, Ödeborg, Pl. XXIV: 1), *Västmanland* (Gunnilbo, according to Herr A. Nygren, Västerås), *Dalarna* (Ål, E. u. 4158; Malung, Mandelgren, 1889, p. 129, for transport of boards), *Härjedalen* (Storsjö, Mandelgren, 1889, p. 129), *Jämtland* (Berg, according to Dr. R. Jirlow; Ström, Hellström, 1917, p. 336, Nordiska Museet 187,866, with a roughly made runner at the fore, instead of a small sledge, Pl. XXIV: 2; Borgvattnet, example in Jämtlands Museum, Östersund, similar to the Ström example; from the southern part of the province, according to Professor S. Erixon), *Ångermanland* (Graninge, E. u. 4167 for carting boards) and *Västerbotten* (Nysätra, Nordiska Museet 117,028, Pl. XXIV: 1; Vilhelmina, E. u. 1285, 1293; according to Herr H. Palmgren, Umeå, it is common in many parts of the province).

Of these all too few examples, the Västmanland may be due to a contingency. The others, as we see, group themselves towards the districts bordering on the Norwegian frontier in the same manner as did the solid-wheel cart.[1] One might otherwise infer the wheeled-sledge in Sweden to be an internal development of the summer-sledge as it appears at harvest times throughout the central and southern parts of our country. Such an association would thus not seem unnatural. In Norway, however, the wheeled-sledge is quite common, but it is unknown in Finland, for instance. It is not possible to dismiss the idea of a connection between its occurrence in the two Scandinavian countries.

---

[1] The experiments of the 18th century were obviously of quite another character as they aimed at a combination of the qualities of the sledge and waggon. Such attempts are to be found written in Vetenskapsakademiens handlingar, 1744 (pp. 211—215) and in "Bondestolpe," the curious publication of J. P. von Wulfschmidt, the first edition of which came out in 1771. Sledges of this construction were intended to facilitate movement on bad roads.

PLATE XXVII

1. Waggon from a rock-sculpture at Risbed, Askum, Bohuslän. After G. A. Gustafson.

2. Waggon from a rock-sculpture at Langön, Tossene, Bohuslän. After G. A. Gustafson.

3. The Dejbjerg waggon. About 100 B.C. National Museum, Copenhagen.

PLATE XXVIII

1. Waggon with »nailed» beam-construction. Burseryd, Småland. Nordiska Mus. 83,952.

2. Waggon with »cylinder» beam-construction. Svinhult, Östergötland. Photog. A. C. Hultgren.

3. Waggon with supports from the back wheels and with two poles and shafts. Västerstad, Scania.

PLATE XXIX

1. »Trein-waggon» for hay-transport, with solid front-wheels. Nössemark, Dalsland. Photog. G. Berg.

2. »Trein-waggon», probably from the north of Scania. The open-air Museum at Lyngby, Copenhagen.

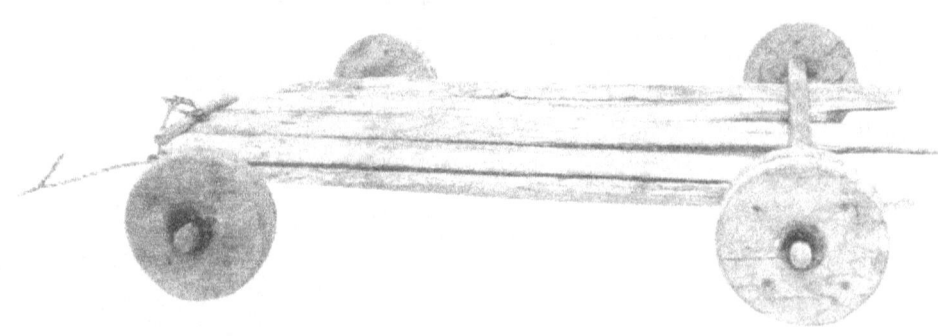

3. Hay-waggon from Hede, Härjedalen. Nordiska Mus. 173,410.

PLATE XXX

1. Waggon from Rackeby, Västergötland. Nordiska Mus. 115,352.

2. Waggon from Landa, Halland. Varberg Museum.

The wheeled-sledge appears in Norway in slightly different forms throughout the greater part of the country. I know them, employed on the whole as in Sweden, from every province excepting Finnmark, Troms and Hedmark. As regards Hedmark, this can of course be due to fortuitous circumstances, but it is of interest to note that the vehicle is not so well known from the neighbouring provinces of Dalarna and Värmland. Older evidence is from Nord-Tröndelag.[1] Strange to relate the cart is called "hjulsläde," wheeled-sled, in many places, even in districts where both a two-wheeled vehicle and a real wheeled-sledge are in use.[2] As a rule this would imply that the cart appeared in these parts as a younger culture-element, and supplanted the sledge.

In many places, both in Sweden and Norway, the wheeled-sledge is said to have made its first appearance in more modern times. Its employment has been restricted to rural districts with rough and rugged ground. Intimation of its inclusion amongst agricultural implements is not either lacking. J. N. Wilse, in 1779, writes from Östfold that he should deserve a reward who could construct a kind of hay-sledge or waggon, suitable for the district. One has tried with small front wheels on a sledge, he says.[3] And from Flatdal in Telemark, 1786, H. J. Wille writes that one has *begun* there to use the sledge with *wheels at the fore*.[4]

One might count with an internal development from summer-sledge to wheel-sledge in Norway too. But strange to say the latter occurs in various parts of Europe, and in such a manner as to render possible a west-European influence similar to that assumed in Chapter V on the part of the turned disc-wheel. The vehicle thus recurs in England and in the Alpine districts of Central Europe.

The wheeled sledge is known from Lancashire in *England* (Brown, 1758, 2, p. 45), Montgomeryshire (Sayce, 1933, p. 121), Radnorshire (Hennel 1934, p. 37) and Wales (Peate, 1929, p. 68; Fox, 1931, pp. 185—187). For *Switzerland*, see for ex. Huber, 1919, Figs. 18, 26, 28—30, 32 and 34; Stebler, 1903, pp. 303, 306—308; Freuler, 1906, p. 7, Figs. 14, 18—20; Brockman-Jerosch, 1929—31, 1, Figs. 60, 2, Figs. 82 and 139; Friedli, 1905—28, 1, p. 340, 3, p. 554. From the Alpine districts of *France* are occurrences of the wheel-sledge mentioned by Brunhes, 1926, p. 206, by Flagge, 1935, pp. 156—160, and from Styria by Meringer, 1907, p. 279.

---

[1] Schöning, 1773—75, 2, p. 153 (Overhalla); Nilsson, 1816, p. 149; drawing by N. M. Mandelgren in the Nordiska Museet (Stiklestad); drawing by F. von Dardel, 1857, photog. in the Nordiska Museet, Archives (Levanger). Illustrations of other wheeled-sledges from other parts of Norway, see, for ex. Anda, 1881, p. 41 (Rogaland); Östlid, 1929, 1, p. 441 (Östfold).

[2] Especially in Nordland. But the cart is called "hjulslede," wheeled-sledge, also in Sogn and Fjordane and as far south as Vest-Agder (answer to enquiries). Cf. "Hjulsläde" in modern Icelandic means wheelbarrow (Blöndal, 1920—24).

[3] Wilse, 1779, p. 230. Wilse has personally experimented with wheeled-sledges for winter use (p. 285). Cf. Gielleböl, 1771, p. 94.

[4] Wille, 1786, p. 189.

Ludwig Flagge states in his last publication, that the wheeled-sledge from Provence evolved internally from the summer-sledge with influence from the cart.[1] Cyril Fox has endeavoured to construct a similar internal development of the Welsh wheeled-sledge.[2] It might be considered within bounds, however, to presume possible a mutual expansion basis. Often the main features coincide within the various expansion areas. It is quite obvious that its distribution is not of any great age. The whole question requires a closer investigation which points to the agricultural-economic literature of the 18th century.

As far as Sweden is concerned it remains to add that the wheeled-sledge with absolute certainty obtained its expansion through Norwegian influence. This was facilitated, however, by the earlier common use of the summer-sledge at hay-making time and the harvest. Wherever the wheeled-sledge made its first appearance it was naturally an evolution of the summer-sledge.

Similar influence of the wheeled-vehicle is in evidence elsewhere. Many wheelbarrow-like contrivances may be mentioned in this connection. The wheel as a detached element borrowed from the cart, has been adapted to other implements.

The real wheelbarrow which may be described as a barrow with a wheel at the fore, and pushed backwards by means of shafts is of fairly young origin in Sweden. It is almost entirely missing from the oldest farm inventories, and it has never been in common use. In many of the country-sides, one meets with some notification or other that it was introduced during the latter half of the 19th century. Sometimes it only refers to newer forms of the implement. The construction of the railway has carried this culture-element along with it.[3] But long before indeed, the wheelbarrow put in its appearance in town and city culture as may be seen from illustrations, inventories etc. Its foreign origin reverts to the Middle Ages.[4] It is not unthinkable that renewed impulses as to the employment of this expeditious contrivance reached Europe in connection with south-Chinese influence which, during the 18th century made itself felt within its area.[5] It is interesting to note in this connection that, even

---

[1] Flagge, 1935, p. 158.

[2] Fox, 1931, pp. 186—188. The summer-sledge has been much used in England. See also, for example, Gomme, 1890, pp. 286—287, Hennel, 1934, p. 37.

[3] In Malung and Floda, in the province of Dalarna, according to Herr O. Bannbers; Ljusnarsberg in Västmanland, according to Fröken Maja Forsslund, Kopparberg and Frändefors in Dalsland according to pers. notes.

[4] For France, see Havard, under Brouette; Violette le Duc, 2, p. 41; van Marle, 1932, 2, p. 432; Lacroix-Serré, 1848—51, 3, Fol. XI/XII. Cf. from Lübeck, 1475, Mummenhoff, 1901, p. 11.

[5] Cf. with Leser, 1931, pp. 442—458; Berg, 1932 (a), 1932 (b), pp. 113—116.

in Europe it has occurred that two persons have engaged in managing the wheelbarrow, namely, one to haul and the other to push.[1] I personally know of the dog as draught-animal even in Holland and Westphalia, in Germany.[2] In the 18th century, in those countries of western Europe influenced by Holland, as well as in Holland itself, the wheelbarrow enjoyed a special popularity.

What is known as the Scanian swamp cart ("madakärra"), Pl. XXV: 2, is another development worthy of mention. It occurred mostly in the northern parts of the province but was also used in Fågeltofta in the South-east.[3] It was used for bringing in hay from swampy ground, which employment constitutes its relationship to the draught-carts treated in Chapter V, and to the man-hauled slide-cars of Chapter VI. Carl von Linné described and reproduced them in 1749 from Gumlösa as being used in variation with the slide-car.[4] Undoubtedly this is a localized evolution of the slide-car, due to the influence of other wheeled-vehicles.

The draught-pole with wheels is another contrivance presumably brought about in the same manner. In many parts of Sweden it occurs that water and milk are transported by hand-craft. The pail is hooked on to a long pole, one end rests upon the draught-man whilst the other trails along the ground. Personally, I know the implement from western Värmland, from Tystberga in Södermanland and from Nysätra in Västerbotten, in its primitive form. Pl. XXVI: 1, gives an illustration of a pole being trailed along the ground even in summer-time.[5] For summer-use the draught-pole is sometimes fitted with a wheel, otherwise a little runner is employed.

Evidences of the draught-pole with runner are from *Småland* (Hjorted, Hallingsberg and Locknevi, E. u. 1314; S. Vi, E. u. 5623; Hannäs, E. u. 4103), *Södermanland* (Tystberga, E. u. 735; Bälinge, Nordiska Museet 183,938; Gåsinge, E. u. 763), *Dalarna* (Rättvik according to Dr. R. Jirlow, Västerås) and *Västerbotten* (Nysätra, Nordiska Museet 177,033 and Jirlow, 1928, p. 208).

In many cases the contrivance is equipped with a runner which could be put on and taken off, but this is perhaps a more modern form, probably arising from the simultaneous use of the wheel which then took the place of the runner. The draught-pole with wheel, Pl. XXVI: 2, has a wider expansion however.

---

[1] Blok, 1897, 1, p. 94 (about 1663).
[2] Blok, 1897, 1, p. 16; Magasin, 1841, p. 136. For China, see for ex. Wagner, 1926, pp. 162—164.
[3] From Fågeltofta, according to Dr. G. Gustafsson. See for Scania, also Sjöbeck, 1927, p. 53.
[4] Linné, 1749, p. 273.
[5] Photog. from Mangskog by N. Keyland, in the Nordiska Museet, Archives; Nord. Mus. 183,939 (Tystberga), 177,033 (Nysätra).

I know of its occurrence from the following places. From *Småland* (see foregoing note from Hjorted and S. Vi; Kråksmåla, E. u. 6559; Linneryd, E. u. 5588), *Gotland* (chiefly Burs, Säves Gotländska samlingar, MSS in UUB, IV, p. 435. The implement is specially used here for the transport of tar), *Östergötland* (Tjärstad, photog. in E. u., Heda, E. u. 4622; Vårdsberg, E. u. 3917; Kärna, water was transported to the camp in this manner, see Barchæus, 1775, notes on travels, MSS in UUB; from the same place there is an illustration by P. A. Säve in connection with the Östgöta dictionary, MSS in UUB), *Södermanland* (see foregoing notes from Tystberga, Bälinge and Gåsinge, example in Nyköping Museum), *Uppland* (Tensta, E. u. 5402; Lillkyrka, E. u. 4066; Övergran, E. u. 3907; Söderbykarl, E. u. 3415; Sånga, Nordiska Museet, 185,475), *Västmanland* (in many places on the plains, pers. notes), *Dalarna* (Malung, according to Herr O. Bannbers; Ål, E. u. 4158; St. Tuna, E. u. 4137), *Västerbotten* (see Nysätra; Degerfors, Nordiska Museet 186,604 and Jirlow, 1928, p. 208; Burträsk, Jirlow, 1928, p. 208) and *Norrbotten* (Nederluleå, according to Dr. E. Brännström).

A variation with two wheels is also known to me from *Dalarna* (Leksand, Nordiska Museet, 189,732, Pl. XXVI: 3), *Ångermanland* (Bjurholm, E. u. 3307) and *Norrbotten* (Korpilombolo, photog. E. u.; cf. Hellström, 1917, p. 542).

The draught-pole with wheel could either be drawn or pushed. It undoubtedly has some connection with the tub-pole, a pole which, in many places in Sweden was used for transporting two-handled tubs. It dates here to the town-culture of the 15th century.[1] The draught-pole with two wheels and closely resembling the Dalarna, Ångermanland and Norrbotten type has been in use elsewhere in Europe. Reproductions were published for instance in Verantii Machinae novæ already at the close of the 16th century.[2] The form appears to be widely spread and occurs exterior to Europe.[3] It would not seem amiss to mention the little draught-pole here, which, for example, in North Germany is used to convey bread to the oven. It is also to be met with in Portugal.[4] Considering the vast expansion of the two-wheeled draught-pole, its Swedish occurrence may probably be due to foreign influence.

The facility with which the wheel is attached to a previously used instrument is worthy of note. On page 106, I pointed out a similar condition in connection with the plough. Amongst other phenomena of a like nature, it may suffice to draw attention to the wheel in a ropery which has been a very common implement amongst the Swedish peasants.[5] The net-maker's apparatus with its pair of small wheels is another example.[6]

---

[1] The tub-pole in use, may be seen in the draught-crafts' guild-statutes, Klemming, 1856, p. 184/185.
[2] Verantius, p. 18, Pl. 48.
[3] From Roumania, Teutsch-Fuchs, 1905, p. 150; cf. Findeisen, 1934, p. 232 (Transbaikal-Buryat).
[4] Messerschmidt, 1931, p. 121; cf. Bátky, 1906, p. 185 (Hungary).
[5] The Nordiska Museet has an example of this kind in preservation, from Tjärstad, Östergötland. Säve gives a description of one from Gotland (Gotländska samlingar, MSS in UUB III, p. 81). Cf. Klein, 1924, p. 309 (Runö in Esthonia) and Graves, 1921, p. 100 (Denmark).
[6] Cf. Manninen, 1931—32, 1, p. 222 (Esthonia) and with an example in the Hungarian National Museum, Budapest.

Berthold Laufer has shewn that the cart-wheel is of immense significance as an independent element. According to him the potter's wheel should be ascribed as a loan from the cart. It is only in this way that its coincidental expansion with the cart can be explained. It is certainly not due to any internal development in pottery technique.[1] Should Laufer's theory prove to be true, such objects of culture as the spinning-wheel and water-wheel were impossible of explanation otherwise than as being due to a prior knowledge of the cart-wheel. By entertaining such an assumption we gain still further proof of the cart as a fundamental factor within the South-Eurasian culture zone.

[1] Laufer, 1917 (b), pp. 152—160.

CHAPTER VIII

THE WAGGON

To the same extent that the two-wheeled cart is employed in agricultural pursuits in the north of Sweden, is the four-wheeled waggon, in this same function, restricted to the southern parts of our country. Similarly as the cart in specific and newer functions occurs within the waggon area, has the waggon, especially as a conveyance, achieved expansion of late years, here and there, within the province of the cart. But this cannot hide the fact that of old both vehicles have mutually experienced a distinctly restricted expansion in Sweden. I will therefore confine myself to bringing forward evidence of waggons which are known to me from the essential boundary zone, that is to say, from that same district for which in a previous Chapter I noted the occurrence of the cart, cf. map, Fig. 46.[1] A comparison with map, Fig. 38 should fully verify the above.

In *Bohuslän*, the waggon seems to be missing, at least in the greater part of the district; but, in 1653, in the neighbourhood of Gothenburg, one hundred waggons drawn by a single horse, or two oxen, or cows, were mustered on the occasion of the journey through Sweden of the English Ambassador, B. Whitelocke, Esq. (Whitelocke, 1653—54, p. 152). In the north of *Halland* the waggon is undoubtedly the most commonly used vehicle (the surroundings of Varberg, Barchæus, 1773, p. 77; Källsjö, Nordiska Museet, 90,204; Asige, Nordiska Museet, 105,485; Abild, Nordiska Museet, 86,257; Torup, Hofberg, 1880—81, p. 10; Esmered, Mandelgren 1889, p. 128). As regards *Västergötland* the circumstances are more complicated. Here, the waggon is especially centred, partly on the agricultural plains of Vänern in the north (Otterstad, E. u. 3889; Rackeby, Nordiska Museet 115,352; Tun, notes in E. u. by Dr. N. Keyland; Flakeberg, Nordiska Museet 124,168; Laske-Vedum, Ljunggren, 1913, p. 58) and partly on the Fal district in the east (the surroundings of Skövde, notes in E. u. by Dr. N. Keyland; Dala, Tham, 1796—97, p. 56 and Pl. V: 2; Åsle, Salander, 1811, p. 61; Jäla, E. u. 438; Göteve and Hagelberg, according to Dr. J. Götlind; Solberga, Sundén, 1903, p. 11). It occurs elsewhere too, for instance, in Mjöbäck (E. u. 5259), N. Säm (E. u. 4043), Ödenäs (according to Dr. N. I. Svensson, Vänersborg) and in Vadsbo district (Hova, photog. in the Agricultural Academy; E. u. notes by S. Svensson). In *Nerike*, the waggon practically dominates, if one excludes the mining district in the north-west. (Askersund, photog. E. u.; Kräklinge, Hedin, 1741, p. 19, and other places; St. Mellösa, personal notes; Glanshammar, E. u. 3654.[2] Its occurrence in Knista, etc., in the mining district, is seen from a communi-

---

[1] Only such examples are included, which, with certainty, indicate the use of the waggon as an agricultural implement and, as a rule, only in connection with hay-making and harvesting.

[2] That the waggon in St. Mellösa was used in olden times is gathered from mention of its occurrence in old country rectory inventories from 1591 (Löw 1922—24, 1, p. 53). This tempts one to believe that J. V. Wallander's above mentioned painting of the hay-cart, p. 108, was not taken from life.

cation in Nerikes-Tidningen (newspaper), 4. III 1929). I have already indicated that the waggon expanded as far north as Fellingsbro in *Västmanland* but it appears elsewhere on the plains of this district (according to Herr A. Nygren, Västerås). From olden times it has been very usual in the south of *Uppland*, especially this has been the case in the south-east parts of the district (Simtuna and Tortuna, according to Dr. N. E. Hammarstedt; Lillkyrka, E. u. 4066; Löt, Grau, 1748, p. 29; Kalmar, Grau, 1748, p. 27; Husby-Sjutolft, Grau, 1748, p. 22), otherwise it appears here and there (Alsike, according to Dr. R. Cederström; Alunda, according to Dr. S. Wallin; Morkarla and Söderfors, examples in Disagården, Gamla Upsala; cf. from Rasbo and Rasbokil, Floderus, Description of the parish of Rasbo and Kihl, about 1820, MSS in UUB: "for longer journeys the pair-waggon is used").

And finally, one should not omit a brief survey of the distribution of the waggon in *Småland*. It is not normal on the high-lands of the central parts of the district, but such is the case in the west (N. Hestra, E. u. 3891; Burseryd, Nordiska Museet 83,952; Villstad, Nordiska Museet 83,619; S. Unnaryd, E. u. 5623) and in the east (Väckelsång, E. u. 4557; Linneryd, E. u. 5588; Vaxtorp, E. u. 248; Torsås, E. u. 223; Ålem, notes in E. u. by Dr. N. Keyland; Mönsterås, Barchæus, notes on travels, 1775, MSS in UUB; Kråksmåla, E. u. 6559; N. Solberga, Nordiska Museet 85,229; the surroundings of Gränna according to Dr. E. Granlund, Stockholm; Tryserum, 18th century oil-painting at the estate of Fågelvik, photog. in the Nordiska Museet). That the hay-waggon is not quite excluded from Central Småland is seen from its appearance in, for example, Tolg and Härlöv (according to Dr. J. Svennung, Uppsala).

In the remaining provinces in the south of Sweden, in the south of Halland, Scania, Blekinge, on Öland and Gotland, in Östergötland and Södermanland the waggon may be considered predominant. It was not until a much later date that the waggon gained any ground in the north of the waggon's previously outlined northern boundary. The country estates may be regarded as the principal intermediary agents, but in the west of Värmland, in the 19th century,[1] the peasants were already beginning to employ it.

From the expansion of the waggon, one is able with absolute certainty to trace its close association with agriculture. In almost every district where, in olden times, agriculture occupied a prominent position, has this implement been almost of as great importance as the plough. The expansion of the waggon is not, however, to be solely accounted for as dependent on natural conditions, for example, as a vehicle for the plain, but not for the forest districts. This refers mostly to its employment as a conveyance.[2] But this was a secondary consideration, and as an agricultural implement, the waggon is closely connected with other culture-elements which display a similar expansion. It may suffice here to call attention to the employment of oxen, and the pole-plough also, and to a certain degree, to the more extensive spheres of mortised timber-construction,[3] the use of straw-thatching by means of sewing etc. That the, so to say, more negative culture boundaries which call attention to the absence of

---
[1] Personal notes; notes from E. u. by N. Keyland.
[2] Cf., for example, H. van Bretten's excellent description of his journey through Sweden, 1592. At the boundary between Scania and Småland they were obliged to ride horseback, but at Gränna, in the most northerly part of Småland they were able to get waggons again "as the ways were now tolerably passable."
[3] Erixon, 1931 (b), Pl. 1.

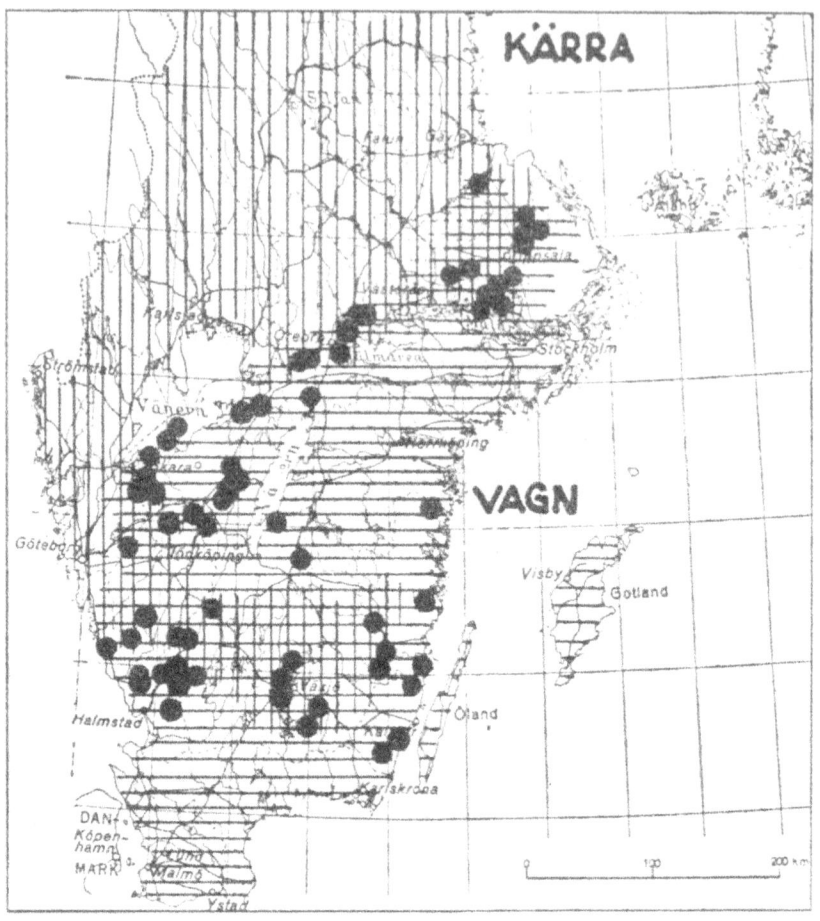

Fig. 46. The most northern distribution of the waggon in Sweden. 'Kärra' = cart. 'Vagn' = waggon.

various Old-World culture-elements, in the south of Sweden, just about coincides with the boundaries separating the cart and waggon zones, I have already touched upon (p. 108). Of special interest are the circumstances in Västergötland where, on the Kålland Peninsula, and especially in the Kålland district, the waggon has achieved predominance. In this connection attention should be given to the sturdy expansion of the use of inner buttresses — according to the "mesula"-construction in the science of building.[1] One must undoubtedly interpret these phenomena as ancient characteristics, of the kind, otherwise common to the district.[2] Inference was made when dealing with the two-wheeled vehicle, that the cart, especially as a conveyance,

[1] Erixon, 1931, p. 20, 1932, pp. 136—141.
[2] Lithberg, 1918, pp. 19, 26. — A waggon from Rackeby, as will be seen, is of a type unknown from Denmark. It is therefore improbable that the occurrence of the vehicle is dependent on south-west influence.

occurred side by side with the waggon, in sundry places within the expansion zone of the latter.[1]

It may appear strange that quite the oldest illustrations of waggons known from Scandinavia, namely, those on the rock-carvings of Bohuslän and the south-west of Norway occur within the later cart zone. Their home is, however, in districts having excellent connections and need not of necessity be considered to infer a wider-spread displacement of boundary between the various types of vehicle. One must also count with the fact that the one-horse cart, as already seen, is a newer culture-element whose expansion assisted in the confusion of the original connection.

Pictures of waggons are known from at least several of the rock-carvings in the west of Sweden, for example, at Rished, in Askum, Pl. XXVII: 1, Långön in Tossene, Pl. XXVII: 2, on a carving near Tossene Church,[2] on one north of Bottna Church at Nasseröd in Svenneby and at Hjälp-Edsten in Kville.[3] On the Rished carving the waggon occurs together with two pair-draught carts harnessed to horses. The waggons were drawn by oxen. The construction may quite clearly be seen, the wheels have four spokes and there is a beam with a forked-end which is fastened to the back axle-tree. On the Långö carving even, the pole is forked and attached to the fore axle-tree. Two lines mark the body of the waggon on the Rished carving. Gabriel Gustafsson calls attention to the small figures of human beings which surround the waggons and carts, probably drivers or task-masters. The pictures from Nasseröd and Hjälp-Edsten are without drivers and seem to be portrayed in front view. There are some waggons on Norwegian carvings very akin to those of Bohuslän. Mention should be made of two, the former, at Lilla Borge in Borge in Östfold,[4] the latter at Övre-Solberg, in Skjeberg, in the same district.[5] The waggon from Lilla Borge is drawn by a yoke of two oxen and the forked end of the pole is fastened to the front axle-tree.[6]

The attendant uncertainties which prevent the dating of rock-carvings are mentioned on p. 100. They must undeniably belong to distinctly varying ages.

---

[1] Cf. Gotland law refers to the waggon and cart alternatively, "waggon for oxen, or horse and cart" Chap. 26, MSS from the middle of the 14th century.

[2] See Gustafsson, 1886, pp. 491, 487, 486 (my more intimate knowledge of the carving near Tossene Church is from Gustafsson's reference "a four-wheeled waggon, in fragment").

[3] For the three last, see Ekhoff, 1879, pp. 159—161.

[4] Coll, 1902, p. 122; waggon reproduced also by Mötefindt, 1917, p. 220.

[5] My information concerning this carving comes from Dr. G. Gjessing, Oslo, through the kind mediation of Dr. S. E. Engelstad, Oslo. There are not less than four waggons.

[6] On a rock-carving in Angarn, Uppland there is a most simplified waggon, drawn by horse. Reproduced by Ekholm, 1921, pp. 96—97.

Especially is to be noticed, however, the appearance of the pair-cart and waggon on the same carving (Rished), from which it may be gathered that the vehicles were in use parallel with each other. Hugo Mötefindt has drawn our attention to analogous waggon-pictures on west-Prussian urns from the early Iron Age[1], and Wolfgang La Baume has devoted a great deal of time and attention to them. He is of the opinion that they originate, as a rule, from a period dating 800 B. C.—500 B. C. The waggons resemble those on the Bohuslän pictures, but always they appear to be harnessed to horses and not to oxen.[2]

The waggon pictures which appear on the sculptured stones of Gotland, from the year 1000, are of later date. The figures are in profile, thus of quite another type from those quite lately treated. In spite of the very primitive design executed in relief, one should dare to presume that the waggons are drawn by a pair of horses harnessed to a pole. On one of the stones from Levide, a man in the waggon is depicted as driving,[3] on the other from Alskog, two persons are seen in the waggon.[4] Pictures of waggons are also to be found on two weavings belonging to the Oseberg find, in Norway.[5] The latter may be goods-waggons, probably with block-wheels, and drawn by a pair of horses(?). The pictures can be dated to the early half of the 9th century. What remains of the Northern picture-subject of waggons[6] is of a considerably later date and therefore of less interest in this connection.[7]

There is included in this picture-subject, however, as is not unknown, two important finds of waggons from prehistoric times. One of these occurred about 1880, in Dejbjerg, in west Jutland. The find consisted of parts of at least two waggons and one of them has been reconstructed to a great extent, Pl. XXVII: 3. Owing to the rich decorations, it was found possible to date the waggons to about 100 B. C.[8] From the worn-out condition of the parts of the waggons, one might surmise that they had been long in use before they found shelter in the Dejbjerg bog.[9] Particularly interesting are the well preserved

---

[1] Mötefindt, 1917, pp. 221—226.
[2] La Baume, 1924, 1928, especially pp. 38—40.
[3] Reproduced by Enquist, 1930, Pl. 25: 2. — For dating and position in the history of culture, see Lindquist, 1933.
[4] Säve, 1852, the stone is in the Historical Museum, Stockholm. — There is also a newly-found unpublished similar stone from Ekeby from the same time.
[5] Reproduced by Dedekam, 1920, pp. 146, 148; Salvén, 1923, p. 3; Norsk Kultur, 1931, Pl. 4.
[6] A harvesting waggon, drawn by a pair of horses on a Churchpainting, from the 15th century, at Rinkaby, in Scania, should be mentioned. Reproduced by Bolin, 1933, p. 51.
[7] In Olaus Magnus, Charta Marina, and later, in the Historia de Gentibus Septentrionalibus, waggons drawn by reindeer are mentioned, but this seems very unlikely.
[8] Petersen, 1888.   [9] Petersen 1888, p. 33.

under-parts of the waggons with their forked-beams which, according to H. Petersen, were brought about by artificial means — "by heat."[1] The forked-pole provides us with a parallel to the waggon on the Långö carving in Bohuslän.

Petersen asserts that some of the earlier Danish bog-finds could be said to belong to waggons of the Dejbjerg type. Wheel parts have been found at Langaa, on Fyen, with artificially made rims of similar construction to the Dejbjerg.[2] There are analogies from the Rhine-Provinces, of which, the most important, is a waggon found in Ohnenheim, in Elsass, the year 1917.[3] This example originates from about the same time, and very much resembles the Dejbjerg waggon. According to Robert Forrer it shall have had some arrangement for fastening a canopy over the body of the cart.[4]

The well-known and richly carved waggon included in the Oseberg find, from the early half of the 9th century, is called to mind in conclusion. The construction of the under-part resembles those we met with in the other finds and pictures. The waggon was not equipped with a pole, but with an arrangement such as the sledges had, in the same find. This was the only deviation.[5] It can more nearly be described as two shafts, one for each draught-animal, and one feels compelled to assume that outer traces had been attached to the nave of the front wheels. Such traces have the waggons on the recently quoted textiles. It may be that the pair-cart was similarly harnessed. If so, we should immediately have an explanation of the extraordinary double (triple, but obviously through faulty carving) poles on one of the carts from Rished, Pl. XXVII: 1.[6] The Oseberg-waggon's concave platform is placed on curved tressles, and I know of no analogy to this. The body is clinker-built with a technique undoubtedly borrowed from boat-building.[7]

Sigurd Grieg views the Oseberg waggon as having served in the cults, and generally speaking, in like manner should the Dejbjerg waggon have been regarded.[8] H. Mötefindt opposes the idea, on the grounds that the characteristics of the latter are not in conformity with the cult waggon, and rightly

---

[1] Petersen 1888, p. 27.
[2] Petersen 1888, pp. 3, 29. Cf. p. 121.
[3] Concerning a find from Frenz in Düren, see Lehner, 1923.
[4] Forrer, 1923—24; a picture of the reconstructed waggon is also given in Eberts Reallexikon II, Pl. 181 b.
[5] See p. 65.
[6] Gustafsson, 1886, p. 492. Cf. p. 100.
[7] See Grieg, 1928, pp. 3—33. — Semi-cylindrical bodies though differently made are known from Carelia, Grotenfelt, 1915, p. 28, and Ukraina, Vahl-Hatt 1922—27, 4, p. 380. Finsch describes the body of a waggon as "the hollowed-out trunk of a poplar." Finsch, 1876, p. 312. The explanation under "Bultvagn" in Svenska Akademiens Ordbok, "manure waggon with semi-cylindrical upper-framework made from a hollowed-out tree-trunk," is unaccountable.
[8] Cf. Eitrem, 1923, concerning the Oseberg waggon.

asserts that quite too many vehicles, on the whole, are assigned to this category.[1] Our foremost interest, at this point, is to discover to what extent we have the right to make inferences from these magnificent specimens in connection with simpler waggons and their construction. In my opinion, from all points of view, it would be permissible. The excellent continuancy which prevails close up to our day, goes to prove this. Obvious is it, however, that the upper-part of the waggon was intended for some specific purpose, and thus far, it might have served the cults, but this should not be taken as primary.

In order to get some idea of the waggon's culture-historical position, one must make a survey of its expansion, exterior to Sweden. It has long been evident that the waggon, as we know it in our country, with front and back axle-trees connected together by a beam, shews limited expansion in Central Europe, and that it is practically unknown outside our part of the world. It has been said that a map indicating boundaries between the cart and waggon areas would be of immense importance to ethnological research.[2] Too little preparation work has unfortunately been done to allow of this, so I shall only be able to put forward a few points. Mention is only being made of such instances as refer to the farm-waggon, and where the occurrence does not depend on modern development.

In the northern parts of *Norway* there is no sign of the waggon at all, and even further southwards it is so young that tradition is fully aware of it.[3] On Åland, and in some of the south-west parts of *Finland* (Atlas of Finland, 1925, p. 140), as well as in the south-east of Finland, east of the Kymmene it is to be found, but it seems to have spread to the latter, through Russian influence, in comparatively newer times (Itkonen, 1932, p. 407). In *Denmark* the waggon is normal, and if certain of the Rhine Provinces (cf. p. 111) were excluded, one might say the same about *Germany*. In *Holland* also the waggon predominates (Oudemans, 1926, p. 56). *England* belongs to the cart's expansion area, and here the waggon gained its ground at a later date. It is due to Dutch influence. "The intrusion of the Dutch form 'waggon' (wain) into the English language during the sixteenth century suggests that the four-wheeled waggon was probably introduced from the Low Countries at this period, the new word being borrowed to differentiate it from the ruder two-wheeled wain hitherto employed." (Parker, 1925, p. 7.) From Holland also comes the Boer waggon in *South Africa* which, as is known, played an important rôle in olden times, and underwent a special development to some great extent (from comprehensive literature see Sparrman, 1783, pp. 60, 120, 127, 137; Schonken, 1910; Sayce, 1930). In *Belgium* and *France* the mutual connection between the cart and the waggon is more complicated, but it is obvious that the latter has a more north-east expansion (see, especially Brunhes, 1926, pp. 207—212). In *Spain* and *Italy*, waggons are generally only to be met with as processional vehicles (see, for ex. for Spain, Forrer, 1932, p. 91; for Italy, Peasant art in Italy, 1913, Figs. 376—378, Catalogo della mostra di Etnografia Italiana, 1911, p. 98).

Transferring our attention to the east of Europe we find the waggon predominant in all the *Baltic Countries*, and in the greater parts of *Russia* (for exceptions, see Chap. V). From Russia, it spread amongst the European peoples in Siberia and Turkestan. *Poland, Czechoslovakia, Austria, Hungary* and *Roumania* belong to the province of the waggon. In *Yugoslavia* and *Bulgaria* and

---

[1] Mötefindt, 1917. [2] Pessler, 1914, p. 162. [3] Cf. for another type p. 164.

in *the Balkan Peninsula* again we find it, but as Arthur Haberlandt states, it is certainly due to Donau influence (Haberlandt, 1917, p. 143). In other words, the waggon penetrated a zone where the pair-cart had long been at home.

Needless to say, there exists important picture-subject which lucidates the expansion of the waggon within the district of Roman provincial culture. There is no scientific survey at hand concerning this, so one must be satisfied with ascertaining that it neither opposes nor completes what we have hitherto gathered from ethnographical material. At the most, it proves that the boundary of waggon occurrences, at most points, was exceedingly conservative. It also evidences in its way, the High Antiquity of this expansion. On the whole, it may be said that the waggon created one of the acutest boundary lines between the Mediterranean and Continental-European culture.

Throughout the whole of its widely-stretched expansion area, from Holland in the west to the Urals in the east, from Bavaria and Bulgaria in the south, to the Swedish province of Västergötland and Åland in the north, the waggon is remarkably uniform as to its shape. Everywhere of old has the yoke of two oxen been normal, whilst the horse, in pairs, or singly, acted only as a substitute. Research has long been aware that this is to be understood as a manifestation of a culture which, in reality, belongs to North European area, but which does not directly permit of derivation from the "antique."[1] On the contrary, it is Roman provincial culture which took up this already extant culture-element.[2]

Should one desire a parallel to the waggon's expansion, and its position in the history of civilization, one cannot do better than turn to Paul Leser's so-called "four-sided plough." Certain important dissimilarities make their appearance, it is true. On the one hand, this type of plough is more widely spread in Europe and Asia than is the waggon, and on the other, it has a comprehensive expansion area also in the east and south-east of Asia.[3] Still more striking is the comparison, should we limit ourselves to the wheel-plough, that form of the four-sided-plough which has wheels to weight it down to the ground. If Trans-Caucasia, Armenia, and Persia are excluded, this form shews a similar expansion to that of the waggon.[4] In Chapter V, I have expressed my view that the European four-sided plough should be considered as a younger

---

[1] Refer to pp. 163—165 for two other four-wheeled types.

[2] See, for example, Mötefindt, 1917, p. 225. — The supposed origin of the waggon in Scandinavia is a mistake. — Cf. Leser's illuminating words: "Germanic agriculture originates, and especially as regards implements, absolutely independently of Rome. At the coming of Roman influence, the cultivation of the land stood as high as the Roman itself, and there are scarcely any enrichments in the way of implements". Leser, 1931, p. 567.

[3] Leser, 1931, p. 500.   [4] Leser, 1931, p. 515.

element than Leser's "Pflug mit Krümel" from the greater parts of Central Europe, which the former supplanted.

This is a very good analogy to the waggon's vigorous expansion within the pair-cart's old area. It is possible that the four-sided plough is an older culture-element than the waggon, the wheels taking the place of the "shoe" which was otherwise placed on the pole of the plough. A similar "shoe" occurs, according to Leser, both in great parts of Europe and in east Asia.[1] In like manner is the pair-cart concerned in the evolution of the waggon, as we shall see.

The distinguishing characteristic of the European waggon is the beam which connects the axle-trees of the front and back wheels. One meets with several different types however, some of them having decided geographical expansion. The simplest is the beam which goes right through the front axle and is fastened to the back axle, with or without a fork-like attachment. I know only a few waggons from a later date with such an unjointed beam, Pl. XXX: 1, namely from Rackeby, Västergötland and from St. Herrestad, Scania.[2] Otherwise this construction appears to belong to the east of Europe though here, as distinct from Västergötland, the beam seems to be fastened directly to the axle-tree. Such waggons occur in Latvia,[3] in south-west White-Russia, and in a great part of Little-Russia[4] as well as in Bulgaria.[5] In certain cases this can only refer to a more developed construction with a pivotted axle-pole above the front axle-tree.[6] The possibilities of turning a waggon with an unjointed beam are obviously very limited.

It is apparent that the ancient waggons from Dejbjerg and Oseberg are fundamentally of this type. We find here also that the forked-ends of the beam project from the back axle-tree thus rendering possible manual assistance in case of need. It is the same method which, at a much later date, was applied to a type of wicker-waggon in Sweden, used for hunting and travelling, and which was known as the "jutvagn." This was in reality only a construction with a revolving disc which recurs on German and south-Russian waggons.

---

[1] Leser, 1931, p. 501. The wheel-plough's direction of expansion in Europe was probably indicated by the appearance of the plough-wheel on page 120, the type with four diametrical spokes fitting into the nave. Exterior to the wheel's normal expansion area, for instance, Switzerland, Führer, Basel, 1931, p. 7, it occurs in Hanover, Leser, 1931, p. 68 and amongst the Kaschub, Moszynski, 1929, p. 637.

[2] E. u. 612.

[3] Hupel, 1774—82, 2, Pl. V.

[4] Moszynski, 1929, p. 639; Zelenin, 1927, p. 139; Matériaux pour l'ethnographie de la Russie 1, 1910, p. 54.

[5] According to Mr. R. K. Trichkow, Vratza.

[6] Pietkiewicz, 1928, Figs. 144, 145.

It brought about freedom of movement, but only to a certain degree, so that the waggon had to be repeatedly lifted at the back. On the rock-carvings from Rished, Långön and Lilla Borge may be seen the ends of the beam projecting distinctly backward, and evidencing in all probability, a similar state of affairs.

The construction most in use here in Sweden has a pivotted beam, a piece away from the front axle-tree. I do not know to what extent this form is in use outside our land, but it occurs in Esthonia and in parts of Germany and Holland.[1] Where the above mentioned "disc"-construction[2] or similar and more modern appliances occur, one has obviously no need of the pivotted beam. Here we meet with two distinctly specific developments; the Swedish waggons with the "disc"-construction is due to foreign influence.

In Sweden in more modern times it never occurred that the beam with the forked-attachment passed directly through the back axle, instead, the forked-attachment coming from the back axle, was hollowed to admit of the beam passing through, or it was nailed to the upper side of the beam. The former, I call the "cylinder" form, the latter the "nailed" form. In each case the waggon can be lengthened as occasion requires, by means of holes in the beam, Pl. XXVIII: 1—2.

I have met with the "cylinder" construction in the following places: *Scania* (Dagstorp, E. u. 193), *Småland* (Linneryd, E. u. 5588, Torsås, E. u. 223; Högsby, E. u. according to Herr M. Dyfverman; Solberga, Nordiska Museet 85,229), *Västergötland* (Flakeberg, Nordiska Museet 124,168; Otterstad, E. u. 3889; Göteve and Hagelberg, Collections for the Västergötland-dictionary, Dialect Archives, Uppsala; Rackeby, Nordiska Museet 115,352), *Gotland* (Burs and Sproge, E. u. 576), *Östergötland* (Hycklinge, E. u. after notes of S. Erixon; Svinhult, photog. in the Nordiska Museet; Ekeby, E. u. 3621; Ulrika and Tjärstad, E. u. after notes of N. I. Svensson), *Södermanland* (Julita, waggon dated 1744, in the collections at the estate), *Nerike* (St. Mellösa, according to Captain J. Nerén, Stockholm; Knista etc. in the mining district, E. u. 262; Hidinge, E. u. 769), *Västmanland* (the Koberg estate in the neighbourhood of Arboga, example in Västerås Museum), *Värmland* (S. Ny, E. u. 429, ox-waggons from estates) and *Uppland* (Lillkyrka, E. u. 4066; Söderbykarl, E. u. 3415).

The "nailed" construction occurs in *Scania* (Västerstad, E. u. photog.; Brandstad, E. u. 4041; Ravlunda, Nordiska Museet 118,167, 118,148), *Blekinge* (Kristianopel, E. u. photog.), *Halland* (Abild, Nordiska Museet, 86,257; Källsjö, Nordiska Museet 90,204; Asige, Nordiska Museet 105,485), *Gotland* (Fleringe, Nordiska Mus., 107,555; photog. in E. u.) and *Småland* (Burseryd, Nordiska Museet 83,952; Villstad, Nordiska Museet 83,619).

Mention should also be made of the occurrence of the later construction exterior to Sweden. We find it on *Åland* (Nordiska Museet 79,280, E. u. photog.; Grotenfelt, 1915, Fig. 34), in *Poland* (Moszynski, 1929, Fig. 518: 3) and in *Roumania* (Teutsch-Fuchs, 1905, pp. 149—150). Otherwise the other type is more usual, and is to be met with in *Denmark* (Själland, Olsen, 1914, p. 31; Ingvorsen, 1918, pp. 129—130), *Esthonia* (Manninen, 1925, p. 63; St. Rågö, E. u. photog.; Russwurm, 1855, Pl. XI), the *south of Russia* (model in Sammlung für deutsche Volkskunde, Berlin) and *Bulgaria* (Moszynski, 1929, Fig. 518: 4, Marinov, 1901, p. 123; according to Mr. R. K. Trichkov, Vratza).

---

[1] Manninen, 1925, p. 63; Oudemans, 1926, p. 55.
[2] Bomann, 1929, p. 126, gives an illustration of its shape.

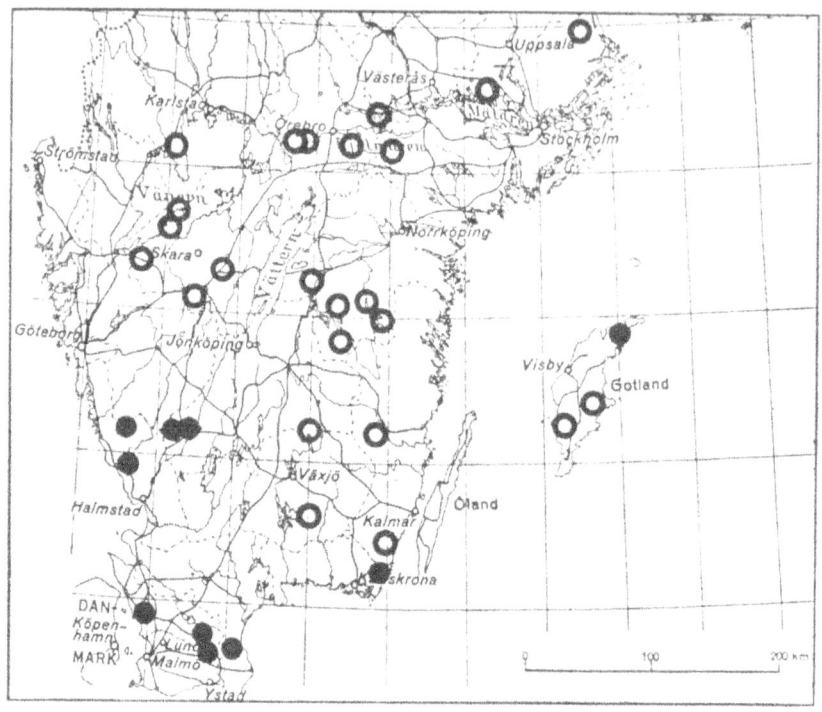

Fig. 47. The distribution of the "cylinder"-construction (open circles) and of the "nail"-construction (filled circles) in Sweden.

As may be gathered from the map, Fig. 47, the "cylinder" construction dominates in the northern and eastern districts of Sweden's waggon province. To this expansion may its appearance on Åland be included. On the other hand, all south Swedish districts together with Denmark and the east Baltic Provinces, have waggons of the other type. A more comprehensive study of its occurrence in Europe on the whole must, however, be made, before one can arrive at any definite conclusion as to the mutual relationship existing between the two types. Should one presume to judge according to the expansion in Sweden, the "cylinder" construction would seem to be the older which, in the rationalizing of the waggon had been supplanted by the former.

Th. Oudemans has clearly pointed out the existing relationship between the various kinds of beams as applied to front and back wheels of equal size. He writes, "in our day, we find waggons in sundry Dutch Provinces with small front wheels which were capable of rolling themselves right up to the beam, whilst, the older waggons had, without exception, large wheels which, when revolving, collided with the waggon bottom."[1] The same has been ex-

---
[1] Oudemans, 1926, p. 55.

PLATE XXXI

1. Waggon from Tving, Blekinge. Photog. S. Erixon.

2. Waggon with gate in the rails. Runö, Esthonia. Photog. G. Selling.

PLATE XXXII

1. Dung-waggon, Algutsrum, Öland. Photog. K.-A. Gustavsson.

2. Conveyance from Sällstorp, Halland. Gothenburg Museum.

perienced in Sweden, as well as in other parts of the waggon's expansion area.¹

No special freedom of movement, laterally, seems either apparent, in cases where the front wheels are lower than those at the back. Cf. Pl. XXX: 1. Later on, this problem was solved by a kind of erection on the front axle, as illustrated on Plate XXVIII: 3 from Västerstad, in Scania. Such a construction is not usual earlier, and should indicate an imported cultural innovation.² As regards conveyances, quite another method was adopted to avoid front-wheel discomforts. We generally find in the coaches and other kinds of waggons from the 18th century a beam with upward curving bows to leave place for the wheels.³

What remains to be said of the lesser wheels is, that, as wheels, they are undoubtedly of considerable age, though, as far as Sweden goes, they should in former times have been unexceptionally confined to the conveyance. The front and back wheels of the Oseberg waggon are equally high, and the same applies to the waggon on the Rinkaby-painting (p. 154), but the front wheels are lower than those at the back, on reproductions of waggons by Olaus Magnus, in Charta marina, 1538.⁴ We learn of the lesser front wheels from foreign reproductions also from engravings, in the 17th century.⁵ From this it may probably be rightly assumed that the solution which gave the waggon greater freedom of movement was discovered about this time. An 18th century debate seems to bring other reasons to light. When Erik Palmstedt drove along that rugged road between Västervik and Kalmar, in 1778, he wrote in his diary, that "the vehicles of the peasants are neatly made, with extraordinarily small front wheels, in comparison with those at the back, to cope with the hills".⁶ Carl Hårleman makes an opposing statement in his writings from Södermanland. He says "this seems to be as little credited by the people at large, as the idea that the larger front wheel gives the waggon easier movement than the lesser, an opinion which was shared by two peasant-coachmen only, during the whole of the drive" (from Stockholm).⁷

---

¹ For example in the east of Finland, see Grotenfelt, 1915, pp. 26. — *Esthonia*, instances given above; *Latvia*, Bielenstein, 1907—18, 2, Figs. 500, 505—508; cf. Fig. 495 and p. 541 concerning a type imported by Germany at a later date; *Poland*, Moszynski, 1929, Pl. XXIX: 2, Fig. 521; *White Russia*, Zelenin, 1927, Figs. 84, 85; *Ukraine*, Moszynski, 1929, Pl. XXVII: 2, and *Bulgaria*, Moszynski, 1929, Pl. XXVII, XXVIII: 1.

² Similar waggons, for example, on Åland, E. u. photog.; Grotenfelt, 1915, Fig. 34. Cf. Oudemans, 1926, passim.

³ See illustrations by Kreisel, 1927.

⁴ Brenner, 1886; it is of lesser importance, in this instance, if these waggons revert to Swedish or German prototypes.

⁵ Cf. Augostino Gallo 1569.   ⁶ Palmstedt, 1778—80, p. 11.   ⁷ Hårleman, 1749, p. 10.

11 — 35218.

It is very evident that the waggon with the type of beam recently considered could only have arisen through the coupling together of two pair-carts. The beam of the back cart would seem to have been inserted into the axle of the front cart, whilst that of the front cart, by means of a forked-attachment, was then made movable, in a verticle direction. This latter development of the pole has been sufficiently commented upon, and at this point it would be advisable to enter into the development, by means of which, the axle of the front cart was attached to the very harness itself. This coincidentally appeared when the horse superseded the ox, as draught-animal. There are, of course, places where the ox was succeeded by the horse quite naturally, and without any essential change in the harnessing arrangements. Carl von Linné gives a description bearing on this from Gotland, 1741. He writes, "the yoke was employed here when waggons were drawn by the horse. It consisted of a horizontal bar, to the middle of which was attached a ring, and through this, the beam was inserted. The bar hung in front of the horse, between the shoulders, and was held in place by means of two straps which lay across the withers of the animal."[1] Quite early, special arrangements began to make their appearance however, in connection with the employment of the horse. We have recently seen p. 155, that the Oseberg waggon has two beams and presumably is equipped with outer traces. The same arrangement occurs in later times, both in the North and in the East Baltic Countries, but the traces there are replaced by sticks inserted into the outer ends of the front axle. The Rackeby waggon is an excellent illustration of this method. From Västerstad, Hjärsås and Munka-Ljungby in Scania,[2] there is another fine example, and I personally know of instances from Öland,[3] Åland[4] and Latvia.[5] It is possible that we are face to face with an older method here, which was supplanted later, partly by harnessing with a "balance" tree and partly by the ordinary way of driving the horse singly before the waggon.

Robert Mielke avers that the use of the horse for draught purposes must, in some cases be of antiquity,[6] but in this respect it can scarcely be considered of the same age as cattle. On the contrary, the harnessed horse, between shafts,[7] so especially common in Europe, should obviously be regarded as a transmis-

---

[1] Linné, 1741, p. 174; Wallin, 1747—76, 2, p. 173, also mentions that horses were always used in pairs on Gotland.

[2] Pl. XXVIII: 3, E. u. 232 and 236.

[3] E. u. 1938 (N. Möckleby). — Cf. also from Lillkyrka, Uppland, E. u. 4066.

[4] Photog. in E. u. Here the beam is divided in the middle into two parts, and the same may be said of the waggons from Hjärsås in Scania and from Öland.

[5] Bielenstein, 1907—18, 2, pp. 549—551. [6] Mielke, 1917, p. 203.

[7] See Moszynski, 1926 and Zelenin, 1927, for illustrations. Cf. Bielenstein's map of the boundaries between the single and pair-drawn waggon in Latvia, Bielenstein, 1892, Pl. 6, p. 395.

sion between the pair-waggon and the single-horse cart. It can also be said that, in more modern times, it has not been so unusual in the west of Europe, in connection with tandem-driving.[1]

The theory that the waggon derives its origin from two carts is not new. J. G. Wilkinson put forward the proposition in his well-known work on Ancient Egyptian culture,[2] and other investigators, such as Hugo Mötefindt[3] and Th. C. Oudemans[4] are of the same opinion, but there are also those who maintain that the waggon is older than the cart.[5] In this case, the reference is to waggons which distinctly differ from the Central European type, in that the beam forms no part of their construction. The kind is not rarely to be seen on antique pictures, and has indeed been in use till more modern times. We meet with it, for instance, amongst the Italian pageant-waggons previously mentioned.[6] In these cases it is the superstructure which holds both the wheel-axles together. It probably resembles the well-known earthenware model of a Scythian waggon found in Kertsch.[7] The four-wheeled Indian waggon should undoubtedly belong to this group[8] and not unlikely also the Chinese four-wheeled waggon too.[9] We find ourselves thus confronted with another, and quite different development in the way of four-wheelconstruction. Should it be proved however, that this construction was normal in the south-east of Europe in olden times, it might with certainty be counted with, as predecessor of the Central European waggon, though the axles were connected in another manner.

In this connection attention should be drawn to the fact that such four-wheeled waggons without the beam have occurred in Europe also to some extent, though as a rule, for some more special purpose. Thus they are known from Sweden.

A low vehicle with roughly made wheels was employed to transport stone in widely separated parts of the country, in Småland, Dalsland, Nerike, Värmland and Västmanland.[10] A similar vehicle has been used for harvesting in

---

[1] See the Luttrell Psalter, 1932, p. 115.
[2] Wilkinson, 1837, 2, p. 120.　[3] Mötefindt, 1918, p. 37.
[4] Oudemans, 1926, p. 73. — Cf. van Erven Dorens, 1930, p. 223, who regards the theory solely in the light of a hypothesis.
[5] See Wahle, 1929, p. 233.　[6] See Waern, 1910, Pl. LXXII.
[7] Reproduced by Ebert, 1921, p. 96.
[8] The waggon-pictures on the urn from Ödenburg in Austria do not give a correct impression of the type, as a rectangular figure hides the under-carriage. The urn originates from the time of Hallstadt. See illustration, des Noëttes, 1931, Figs. 98—99.
[9] For the Chinese waggons, see Laufer, 1910, pp. 200—201.
[10] Cf. Björn Collinder's account from North Sweden, Olsen, 1914—24, p. 276.

Härjedalen, Pl. XIX: 3,[1] and in Norrbotten.[2] The type is not unknown in Norway, evidences have been met with in Vestagder.[3] Strangely enough a waggon, built on the same principles, but larger and much better made, is to be met with on the Orkney Islands.[4] A type normally low is known in England,[5] at Wormsö in Esthonia,[6] Hungary[7] and Servia.[8] With the subject-matter we have, it is impossible to judge to what extent there is any real connection, or whether it is an incidental evolution of the simple runner-sledge due to influence from wheeled-vehicles or, in other words, a development, similar to that of the wheeled-sledge dealt with in the last Chapter.

Waggons still in preservation, formed by the coupling together of two carts and which have not reached the final stage of completion, provide excellent illustrations of the waggon with a beam. Eduard Unger drew attention to a waggon of this construction on the Assurnassirpal obelisk, from c. 1200 B. C.;[9] and the singular example from Kashmir in Central Asia is worthy of notice.[10]

There is a waggon which serves to exemplify a similar coupling method, though it is actually a fully developed type.[11] It consists of a lower pair of wheels with shafts which form the fore part of the waggon, and a pair of wheels at the back, to the axle of which is fastened the platform. This latter rests on and is nailed to the front axle-tree. We call this type the "trein"-waggon, Pl. XIX: 1—2, and the districts in which it especially occurs in Sweden, are as follows:

In *Bohuslän* (Bullaren district, personal notes) and *Dalsland* (Frändefors, personal notes; Dalskog, E. u. 492; Ödsköld, E. u. 1427; Dalskog, Nordiska Museet 178,564; Nössemark, personal notes, Pl. XIX: 1; the two last have solid front-wheels). In *Värmland* (Köla, personal notes; Brunskog, E. u. 1436) where it spread as far as Malung in the west of *Dalarna* (according to Herr O. Bannbers). In *Västergötland* (Erixon, 1933, p. 253), *Småland* (specimen in Kulturhistoriska Museet, Lund, probably from here) and *Scania*, Pl. XIX: 2 (specimen in Open air Museum at Lyngby, Copenhagen; according to Herr K. Hansen and Dr. J. Olrik it probably came from Göinge district). In most of these districts the type appears only very sporadically and in Dalsland, for instance, where, at a later date, its appearance was comparatively common, tradition relates that it is rather young, sometimes dating only forty or fifty years. One can see how, in the capacity of mowing-machine and harvest-waggon, it is in the act of penetrating the area of the cart.

---

[1] Hede, Nordiska Museet 173,410.
[2] Arvidsjaur, according to Dr. E. Brännström, Uppsala.
[3] Laudal, answers to enquiries. — Probably it is a similar waggon to the one seen by Pehr Kalm, 1747 at Grimstad in Austagder. Kalm, 1747—51, 1, p. 73.
[4] Fox, 1931, p. 185.   [5] Jekyll, 1925, Fig. 162.
[6] A sketch owned by the Föreningen för Svensk Kulturhistoria.
[7] Ecsedi, 1928, pp. 16—19. The construction of these waggons coincide to the extent, that one axle is disconnected during the loading. Cf. Túri Mézáros, 1928, pp. 105—113.
[8] Glasnik o Bosni i Hercegovini, 1933, p. 130.
[9] See Ebert's Reallexikon, under Wagen, p. 242.
[10] Huntington, 1907, p. 20/21.
[11] The connecting together of waggons and carts to a "waggon-train" is on the other hand, of comparatively late date and will therefore be omitted here.

Sigurd Erixon has shewn how, in *Norway*, this waggon "finds its home in districts round the upper Oslofjord, and a bit of the way up in the Glåma valley." It appears to be spreading even here, and one finds it occurring also in Valdres (Erixon, 1933, p. 253). The opinion that we are dealing with a rather young phenomenon, probably gains support through its expansion exterior to Scandinavia. From *Holland* an account is given by Oudemans, 1926; it occurs there in the western parts of the province of Noord-Brabant (pp. 73—75).[1] To some extent, types akin, though not of a certainty related, are to be met with in *Carelia* (Grotenfelt, 1915, p. 28) and *Latvia* (Bielenstein, 1907—18, 2, p. 541, Fig. 495).

This cross between the cart and the waggon proves itself not necessarily to be of any great age, but viewed psychologically, it shews how a vehicle with larger body and greater accommodation was brought about.[2] In this connection it would not seem amiss to call to mind other combinations touched upon in Chapters IV and VII.

Proceeding to an investigation of the waggon's upper-framework we find that a normal type of body consists of two open framework sides with vertical rails.

This type may be adjudged old, though I have not been able to obtain evidence earlier than the 15th century.[3] It is quite common throughout the waggon's expansion zone, and with certainty it may be assumed to have spread simultaneously with the waggon on the whole. It is no doubt worth while to start with the Swedish subject-matter and investigate its origin and connection with the body of the cart, and the following will be found to give some account of special forms of framework which are to be met with in our country.[4]

In addition to the type of body recently described, there is one having supports which go down from the upper edge of the body to the axle-ends, Pl. XXX: 1. The supports may be found at both back and front wheels, but waggons with smaller front wheels have supports as a rule extending only from the back wheels. Franz Nopcsa first drew attention to the waggon with outer supports for the framework. We find it mentioned in his Work, Albania (1925), together with the first survey made of its expansion. He considers the type very probably

---

[1] Judging from photographs published in the weekly press, it should also occur in France.

[2] Indicated by Oudemans, 1926, p. 73. — Cf. the English "hermaphrodite"-waggons, Seebohm, 1927, p. 354, Hennel, 1934, pp. 31, 37.

[3] Painting in Rinkaby Church, Scania, reproduced, Bolin, 1933, p. 51; a picture in the Richental Chronicle for the Konstanz council, reproduced, for instance, Adametz, 1908, p. 9. According to Nopsca, 1927, p. 280, there is in Cordova, a relief with railed-sides which is considered Gothic. Railed framework is common in 16th century European picture-subject.

[4] The type with the body lying within two beams is entirely missing in Sweden, but in the east of Europe it occurs, for example, in Carelia, Grotenfelt, 1915, p. 28, Russia, see Moszynski, 1926, Fig. 519, amongst the Crimean Tatars, Ermans Archiv, XVII, 1858, pp. 91—93, and Cheremiss, Manninen, 1932, p. 222. This is the familiar Siberian Tarantas from the Yenisei district, about which Nansen, 1914, pp. 215—218 gives a good description.

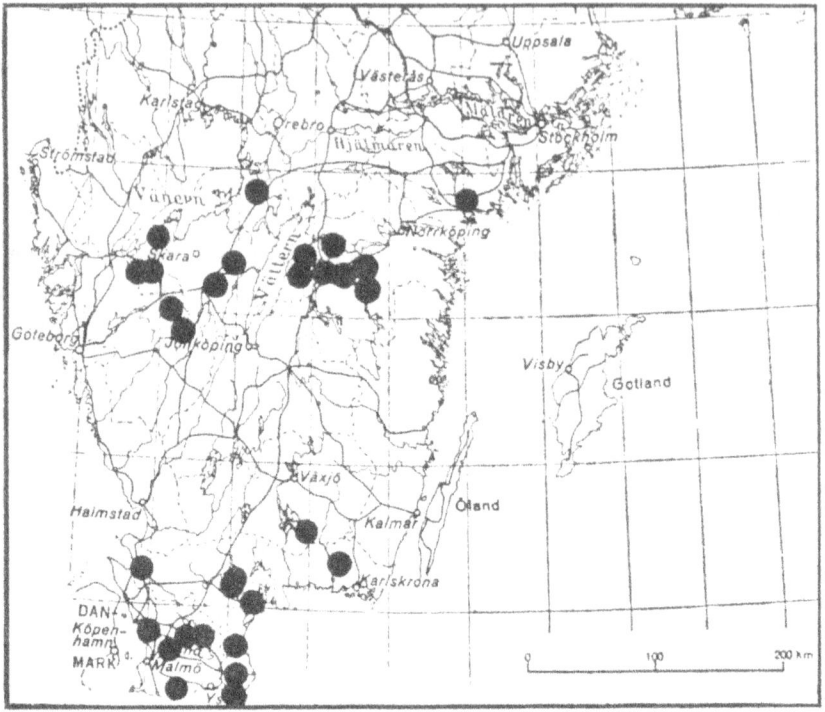

Fig. 48. The distribution of outer rail-supports on waggons in Sweden.

slavic.[1] Nopcsa also states in this Work that the "Slavic" waggon was employed in Russia, Bulgaria, Serbia, Croatia, Vienna, in the Northern Alps and westwards to the Rhine, whilst the type, without the outer supports, was spread in Bulgaria, Serbia, Bosnia, the Tyrol, Switzerland, Bavaria and Holland. In a supplement to his Work, Nopcsa puts it more exactly in the following words: the waggon with rails and supports "which found its way to Wurtemberg" is "an implement solely restricted to Poland and Ukrainia," whereas the waggon, minus such supports "whose north-west boundary was established in Holland, stretches from Petersburg to Moscow and from thence to Radomsko."[2] These statements of Nopcsa can in many instances be completed and rectified. Cf. map, Fig. 48.

In the first place the waggon with rails and supports was rather common in Sweden. It occurred in *Scania* (Vemmenhög district, Nordiska Museet 14,854; Löderup, see E. u. by Sigfrid Svensson; Ingelstad, Hörlén, 1914, p. 111; Ravlunda, Nordiska Museet 118,148 and 118,167; Västerstad, photog. in Nordiska Museet; Torna district, Forssell, 1827, Pl. 46; Löberöd, sketch from 1839 in an album, No. 1225, National Museum, Helsingfors; Harjager district, E. u. 623; Dagstorp, E. u. 193; Munka-Ljungby, E. u. 236; Knislinge, sketch by R. Mejborg, in the National Museum, Copenhagen; Hjärsås, E. u. 232; Kiaby, sketch by F. v. Dardel, 1833, photog. in Nordiska Museet, Archives; cf. sketch by G. W. Palm 1837, reproduced by Lindgren, 1933, p. 38, and in another 1834, reproduced in Ord och bild 1906, p. 250; in Scania, as a rule, supports extend only from the back

---

[1] Nopcsa, 1925, p. 139.   [2] Nopcsa, 1927, p. 280.

wheels), *Blekinge* (Tving, photog. E. u. Pl. XXXI: 1; usual in the province, E. u. 5588), *Småland* (according to Professor S. Erixon, who is acquainted with the type from the tradition in the northeast parts of the district; Tingsås, E. u. 5588), *Västergötland* (Rackeby, Nordiska Museet 115,352, Pl. XXX: 1; Dala, Tham, 1796—97, p. 56; Främmestad, photog. E. u., S. Erixon; Skölvene, S. Ving, Hagelberg and S. Kedum, according to Dr. J. Granlund; cf. from Edsveden, Kullander, 1896, p. 32[1]; a waggon of this kind is preserved, according to Dr. Å. Campbell, Uppsala, in Fristad's Museum; Dr. Sigfrid Svensson knows them from Horn), *Nerike* (according to Nerikes-Tidningen, March, 4, 1929) and *Östergötland* (Vårdnäs, example in Bjärka-Säby Museum; Skeda and Landeryd, according to E. u. by Maja Ericsson; Heda, E. u. 4622; Ekebyborna, according to mention in Dialect Archives, Uppsala, J. Götlind; traditional discoveries have been made in sundry places, according to Professor Sigurd Erixon, inclusive of Vadstena and Linköping surroundings). There are a few notices too, shewing occurrences of the type in earlier times, for example in *Södermanland*, (Svartsjö, drawing by Jean Eric Rehn, 1763, National Museum, reproduced by Kuylenstierna, 1923, p. 317; cf. Svärta, in later time, according to Dr. G. Jonsson), in *Stockholm* (engraving by W. Swidde, 1691, Suecia Antiqua et hodierna, Pl. 31) and *Uppland* (Löt, drawing by Grau, 1748, p. 29).

The expansion of the type coincides in Sweden, as we see, with the waggon's expansion on the whole. It is remarkable however, that I have not succeeded in coming across any evidence in Halland, and this draws attention to the fact that it appears to be absent from Denmark too. Throughout the country, it is noticeable that the type has long been on the decline, obviously dethroned by waggons of a more modern type. In this connection it might be mentioned that in a manuscript by I. Möllerheim dated to about 1720, on artillery technique, there is reproduced an armed-waggon with supports at both back and front wheels, which however, not unlikely, may imply foreign influence.[2]

In *Germany* the type is common over the greater part of the country. It occurs in Rügen (personal notes); in Hamburg (engraving, 1771 and lithography, reproduced by Hamburgs Vergangenheit u. Gegenwart, 1896—97, pp. 35,118; aquarelle, 1813, in Museum für Hamburgische Geschichte), in south-east parts of Hanover (pers. notes), Braunschweig (Andree, 1901, p. 242; pers. notes), Hunsrück (Daehne, 1930, p. 217), Rheinhessen (Hoffman, 1932, Fig. 46; according to Dr. G. Selling), Baden (Howitt, 1842, pp. 21—23), Schwaben (Gröber, 1925, Fig. 107; Walther, 1929, Pl. 13, 20), Bavaria (common everywhere, personal notes; cf. Mitzka, 1933, p. 46; Karlinger, 1925, Fig. 80; Volkskunst u. Volkskunde I, pp. 33, 111—113, II, p. 85; older evidence is numerous from the 17th and 18th centuries, see Hahm, 1928, Pl. 3, 1607, Karlinger, 1925, p. 177, 1648, Mummenhoff, 1901, p. 114, 1716, etc.), Saxe and south Brandenburg (pers. notes), also in Schleswig (models in the Landwirtschaftliches Museum, Berlin, and in the Museum für Volkskunde, Vienna; photog. in Volk und Rasse, 1930, p. 38; Zeissler, 1922, p. 129, 1728). In *Czecho-Slovakia* it seems to be common throughout the country (Schramek, 1908, p. 103; Blau, 1917—18, 1, p. 168; Hofman, 1928, p. 38; pers. notes), *Austria* (Heimatgaue, 1927, pp. 202—205; pers. notes from Upper and Lower Austria), *Hungary* (Magyar Nép Müvészete 1, 1924, p. 48; Anzeiger d. Ethnogr. Abteil. des Ungar. Nationalmus., 5, 1910, p. 6; A Magyar nemzeti múzeum 1909, p. 141, 1911, p. 36—53, pers. notes), *Yugoslavia* (in Slovenia, Croatia and the north-east parts of the country, Valvasor, 1689, 1, p. 105; photog. in the Nordiska Museet, Archives), *Bulgaria* (Vahl-Hatt, 1922—27, 4, p. 129; according to Mr. R. K. Trichkow, Vratza), *Roumania* (Papahagi, 1928—30, 1, pp. 58, 61, 2, p. 84; Oprescu, 1929,

---

[1] Kullander also mentions that the cart had similar outer supports, and this is verified by a photog. from Hudene, in the Nordiska Museet, Archives. It is probably due to influence from the waggon. Judging from a photog. reproduced by L'art populaire hongrois, 1928, p. 70, the same development occurred in Hungary.

[2] MSS in the Army Museum, Stockholm.

pp. 4, 6), *Russia* (Ukraina, model in Sammlung für Volkskunde, Berlin; Zelenin, 1927, p. 139; Moszynski, 1929, p. 643. — Crimea, Roskoschny, 1882—84, 1: 1, pp. 301, 329. White Russia, Zelenin, 1927, Fig. 85. — Dr. T. J. Arne has told me that owing to Russian influence, the type has spread to West Turkestan) and is to be found in *Poland*, (Schultz, 1918, Fig. 80: — "this kind of peasant waggon with small variations is spread throughout 'Congress' Poland"; Moszynski, 1929, p. 642; cf. Wiener Zeitschrift für Volkskunde 8, 1902, p. 217 (Huzuls) and Bolinder, 1928, pp. 240—257 (Bojks)) and *Lithuania* (photog. from various parts by S. Erixon and G. Ullenius, in E. u.; Vahl-Hatt, 1922—27, 4, p. 447).

From what has been said, it is seen that Nopcsa's latest publication is incorrect as far as the Polish expansion is concerned. The widely-spread expansion in Bavaria is remarkable also. In other words it is far more comprehensible than it appeared to be when attention was given to the vehicle. To characterize the type as "slavic" should be impossible, especially as regards its occurrence in Sweden.[1]

When Nopcsa indicated the waggon with outer supports as being probably slavic, he believed that the type, without the supports might be of greater age. Older picture-subject leaves us in uncertainty. The oldest evidence that I have found of such a waggon is a picture from 1512, of a car in the Emperor Maximilian's triumphal procession.[2] Engravings from Germany are known from the close of the same century.[3] Nothing, however, speaks against a much earlier general occurrence within its present area of expansion. The real object of the supports is not apparent regardless of the waggon's body construction. It seems to be associated with a looser and less well-built form. It would appear more reasonable to assume therefore, that this refers to an older type, which was superseded by improved and rationalized forms from the west of Europe. The European distribution of both types seems to endorse this presumption.[4]

So long as we are devoid of objects or picture-subject, it is impossible to date the appearance of the younger forms which may with certainty have occurred at a predecessive stage. It is worthy of note, that a type closely related to this construction is to be found amongst south-European processional cars, the upper framework of which is held in place by means of upright boards. Robert Forrer reproduces a similar Spanish waggon from the 16th or 17th

---

[1] Braungart's "Slavic yoke," by which term he indicated the type in Sweden, holds not good for the same reason. Braungart, 1914, pp. 188—274.

[2] Reproduced by Hirth, 1882, 1, p. 183.

[3] Liebe, 11, p. 90, 1573; Braun, 1575—81, 2, Pl. 45; Agostino Gallo, 1596, Plate.

[4] Cf. how Bruno Schier from quite another source asserts the existence of a Northern-East-germanic-Slavic-Alpine culture district, coinciding somewhat with the West-Germanic-German, 1932, pp. 11, 13. This appears to me as a stage only, in the evolution, behind which lies a comparatively uniform north-European culture, as distinct from that of the Mediterranean.

Fig. 49. Detail of a waggon with framework and projecting rails. Torsås, Småland. After a photograph by A. C. Hultgren.

century,[1] another example occurs on a relief in Chieri in Italy, dating from 1673[2] and several Italian waggons of the kind are still in preservation.[3]

As already mentioned, the waggon with open-work rails is the normal vehicle for carting purposes, here in Sweden. There are special types within the country, and in conclusion, I will mention a few of these which seem to be of general interest. It is noteworthy that two of these types seem very obviously to belong to the east of Sweden. To this category belong the Småland and Östgöta waggon-sides, Fig. 49. They are formed of horizontal bars with rails, few and far between, which project above the uppermost bar. They were used exclusively for the transport of wood, and were easily made.

Personally, I know the type from *Småland* (Sjösås, according to Herr J. A. Göth; Torsås, photog. E. u., according to Fröken Ingeborg Thorin, Åtvidaberg; Gullabo, according to Frk. Thorin; Vissefjärda, see E. u. by N. I. Svensson; Våxtorp, E. u. 248; Kråksmåla, E. u. 6559; Säby, see E. u. by N. I. Svensson) and *Östergötland* (Ljung, see E. u. by N. I. Svensson; Åtvidaberg district, according to Fröken Thorin). The type is of interest because of its resemblance to forms which occur elsewhere in Europe, for instance, may be mentioned, Bulgaria (Moszynski, 1929, p. 643). This manner, however, of increasing the carrying accommodation, in Sweden, may not improbably be of local development.

It should perhaps be mentioned here that the waggon-body especially in the west and south of Sweden — Halland, Scania and Blekinge — has frequently a construction resembling that of the cart from Västergötland (p. 127). The body of the waggon is almost concave, which is brought about by the laths or staves being interlaced in a curved fashion through the bottom, Pl.

---

[1] Forrer, 1932, p. 91.
[2] Touring Club Italiano, p. 84.
[3] Peasant art in Italy, 1913, p. 376; Catalogo della Mostra di Etnografia Italiana, 1911, p. 98.

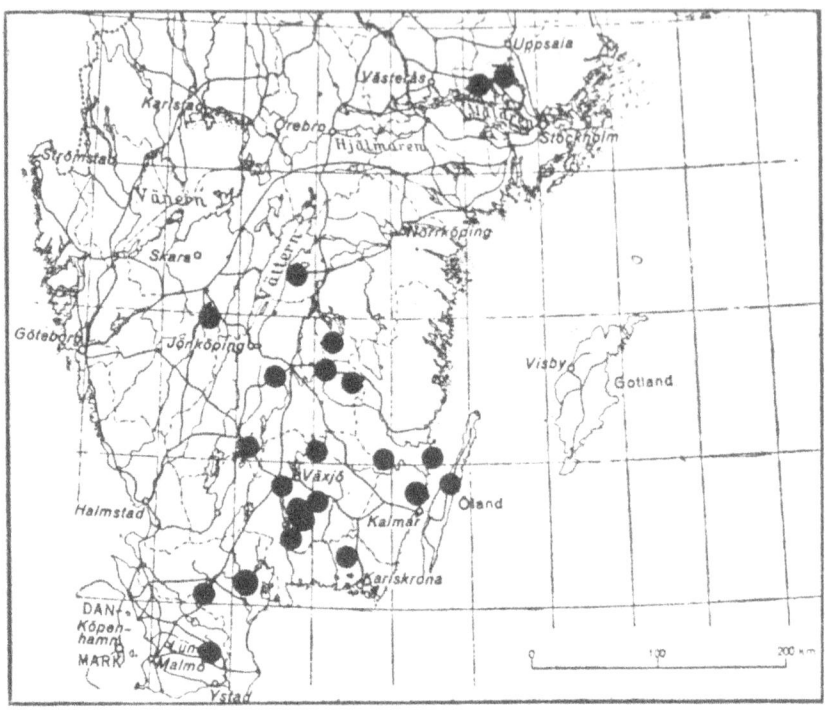

Fig. 50. The distribution of waggon framework with upward lengthened open-work sides in Sweden.

XXX: 2. Here we undoubtedly meet with influence from the cart and sledge platforms.

The waggon with the upward lengthened open-work sides, Pl. XXXI: 1, is, on the whole, mainly to be met with in the east of Sweden. A special erection is here attached to the rails, which considerably increased the accommodation for harvesting purposes, and this, on occasion, could be let down.

I know waggons with similar sides from *Scania* (Brandstad, E. u. 4041; Knisslinge, drawing by R. Mejborg in National Mus., Copenhagen; Brönnestad, Sjöbeck, 1927, p. 53), *Blekinge* (Tving, photog. E. u.; Almundsryd, Håkansson, 1932, p. 14), *Öland* (Köping, photog. E. u.; cf. Rhezelius, 1634, p. 20 and from Herr. O. Homman, information that the type is now general on the island), *Småland* (Sjösås, pers. notes; Jät, photog. E. u.; Hult, see E. u., by S. Erixon; Malmbäck, photog. E. u.; Ryssby, E. u. 6803; Öja, E. u. 4301; Mönsterås, Barchæus, notes on travels, 1775, MSS in UUB; Våxtorp, E. u. 248; Kråksmåla, E. u. 6559; Väckelsång, E. u. 4622; Linneryd, E. u. 5588; Kråkshult, E. u. 5573), *Östergötland* (common in the province, according to Prof. S. Erixon; cf. Erixon, 1932 (c), Fig. 3; Heda, E. u. 6005; Sund, E. u. 6005) and *Västergötland* (Solberga, Sundén, 1903, p. 11; probably only in the most south-easterly parts of the district). It occurs on *Åland* (E. u. photog. and notice by Herr O. Bannbers) and it is probably of the same type as that reproduced by Grau from Kalmar in Uppland, 1748 (Grau, 1748, p. 27; cf. for *Uppland* E. u. 4066, Lillkyrka, and E. u. 3907, Övergran, the occurrence here due to later influences). It is interesting to note that the type is known here in Sweden from the early half of the 17th century (Rhezelius). Foreign parallels apart from Åland — which follow Swedish tradition — are unknown to me.

Fig. 51 illustrates the Gotland bog bush-waggon. Here is seen an opening at the sides which are unusually high, and through this opening, the hay and corn is unloaded. As far as Sweden is concerned, this method is peculiar to Gotland. M. Crælius mentions rails of waggons from the middle of the 18th century, in Småland, which could be taken down to facilitate the unloading of hay. Crælius assumes some connection between these rails and the peasants out-houses, which latter, were simply low-built barns devoid of hay-lofts.[1] And the same undoubtedly applies to the large waggons of Gotland.

Exterior to Sweden I am able to indicate waggons with side-openings from Runö in *Esthonia* (Klein, 1924, pp. 293, 303), from *Latvia* (Bielenstein, 1907—18, 2, p. 552), *Czecho-Slovakia* (Hofman, 1932, pp. 33, 38, 75) and *Germany* (Gröber, 1928, p. 60, model of waggon from close of 18th century). This form appears to have experienced a certain expansion in Central Europe, and the East Baltic. Gotland especially was not insensible to impulses from these countries.

Of course the "box" shaped body occurs in our country in variation with the rail and post types, and was comprised of boards fastened together. It was specially used for the carting of manure, Pl. XXXII: 1. Pehr Osbeck has carefully described this vehicle from the south of Halland at the close of the 18th century. He expresses himself in terms of annoyance concerning the ineffectivity of the low side boards.[2] Similar kinds have been in use in Blekinge, on Öland, in Småland and Västergötland. Some specific evolution often took place. A. G. Barchaeus observed one instance in Mönsterås, 1775. The stakes which, on the waggon's right-hand side support the side boards, are forked at the top to hold both boards whilst unloading takes place.[3] I know the same type, in use today, from Algutsrum, Öland[4] and from Asige, Halland.[5]

Closely related to the body of the manure waggon is the "box"-shaped upper-part which, at a later date was used for various carting purposes in different parts of Sweden. It is from such types that most of our older conveyances originate. But the peasants in our country held fast, for a very long time, to the custom of using the ordinary harvest waggon as a conveyance for driving to town and Church etc. In the west of Sweden only, and in Halland, Pl. XXXII: 2, in particular, has the large conveyance resembling the low Saxe waggon become popular.[6] The "karm"-waggon spoken of in Gotland has doubtless belonged to this part also.[7]

---

[1] Crælius, 1774, pp. 366—367.
[2] Osbeck, 1786, p. 26.
[3] Barchæus' notes on travels, MSS in UUB.
[4] According to Dr. K. A. Gustafsson.
[5] Nordiska Mus. 105,485.
[6] Examples in the Gothenburg and Varberg Museums.
[7] Säve, Gotland collections, MSS in UUB, IV, pp. 130, 668 etc.; also notes from copies.

172 SLEDGES AND WHEELED VEHICLES

Fig. 51. Waggon with gate in the railed-side. Gotland. After a sketch by Gunnar Jonsson.

Conveyances as used amongst the higher classes, originate as is well-known, from the farm waggon. But one must not forget the tent-like upper-part which, of a certainty, has its origin in Central Asia.[1] To this "Kobelwagen," reverts in its turn also, the carriage with the hood.[2] The new element which especially evolves, is the introduction of springs. This development is still far from satisfactorily worked out. The oldest Swedish evidence of a spring-carriage known to me is from a vocabulary dated 1538, where "Pilentum" is translated as "suspended waggon."[3] It was not until the latter half of the same century that this type became more usual, and this was due to west European influence. Information is to be obtained both by way of documents and publications as to the expansion of these newer forms in our country, but I find it impossible to deal with the subject here.

---

[1] Cf. Laufer, 1910, p. 198, 1930, p. 14; Oelmann, 1927, p. 15.

[2] Concerning the earlier development of the conveyance, see Kreisel, 1927, pp. 13—31.

[3] Variarum rerum vocabula, p. 42: "sparwagn hengiande wagn." Cf. Strömbom, 1924, p. 278, import to Nya Lödöse (Gothenburg) of 6 "sporrevagnar." — Remarkable, but insufficiently noted is the fact that a spring-carriage is known from the 10th century amongst Slavic tribes in the south-east of Europe. The arab visitor Ibrâhîm ibn Ja'qûb, noted how their kings travelled in large, high waggons on four wheels with four posts from which, by means of chains, a body was suspended, in order to spare the traveller as much shaking as possible. Similar waggons were placed at the disposition of the sick and wounded, Jacob, 1927, p. 18.

LITERATURE

Aaltonen, E., 1931, Vanha Tammela. Porvoo.
Aario, L., 1933, Kuortaneelta löydetyn reen jalaksen ikä. In: Suomen Museo 40, pp. 15—17.
Adametz, L., 1908, Ueber das in der Ulrich von Richentalschen Chronik des Konstanzer Konzils befindliche Bildnis des Auerochsen. In: Zeitschrift für das landwirtschaftliche Versuchswesen in Oesterreich, pp. 3—21.
Agostino Gallo, 1569, Le Vinti giornate dell'agricoltura. Venice.
Agricola, M., 1556, De re metallica. Eng. translation by H. C. Hoover and L. H. Hoover. London. 1912.
Ailio, J., 1912, Zwei Tierskulpturen. In: Finska fornm.-föreningens tidskrift 26, pp. 257—282.
Ailio, J., 1917, Rev. Pälsi, 1916. In: Historiallinnen Aikakauskirja, pp. 37—39.
Ailio, J., 1922, Fragen der russischen Steinzeit. In: Finska fornm.-föreningens tidskrift 29, 1.
Aldén, G. A., 1927, Hemma och i Uppsala. Stockholm.
Almgren, O., 1912, Tanums härads fasta fornlämningar från bronsåldern. Hällristningar. In: Bidrag till kännedomen om Göteborgs o. Bohus l. fornminnen 8, pp. 473—575.
Almgren, O., 1932, Ture Lång i Skänninge, de tyska Rolandsstoderna och andra jättebilder. In: Arkeologiska studier tillägnade H. K. H. Kronprins Gustaf Adolf, pp. 176—194.
Almgren, O., 1934, Nordische Felszeichnungen als religiöse Urkunden. Frankfort on the Main.
A Magyar nemzeti múzeum. See: Értesítöje.
Anda, 1881, Aeldre redskapsformer. In: Tidskrift for Landmaend 8, pp. 33—45.
v. Amira, K., 1922, Die germanischen Todesstrafen. Munich.
Andree, R., 1901, Braunschweigische Volkskunde. Second ed. Brunswick.
Appelgren, Hj., 1882, Muinaisjäännöksiä ja Tarinoita Kemin Kihlakunnan itäisissä osissa. In: Finska fornminnesföreningens tidskrift 5, pp. 1—87.
Arning, E., 1887, Ethnographie von Hawaii. Report in Verhandl. der Berl. Anthrop. Gesellschaft, pp. 129—138.
Arning, E., 1931, Ethnographische Notizen aus Hawaii 1883—86. Hamburg.
Anučin, D., 1899, Sani, lad'ja i koni, kak prinadležnost' pochoronnago obrjada. In: Drevnosti. Trudy Mosk. Archeol. Obščestva 14, pp. 81—226.
Anzeiger d. Ethnogr. Abteil. d. Ung. Nat. mus. (Budapest).
de Aranzadi, T., 1897, Der ächzende Wagen und anderes aus Spanien. In: Archiv für Anthropologie 24, pp. 215—222.
Arbman, E., 1932, Några anteckningar från Borgsjö socken om jämtarnas färder genom Medelpad. In: Jämten, pp. 139—152.
Arenander, E. O., 1906, Kortfattad beskrifning af gamla ångermanländska ekonomibyggnader och jordbruksredskap. Uppsala.
Armbruster, L., 1926, Der Bienenstand als völkerkundliches Denkmal. Neumünster i. H.
Atlantis. Berlin-Leipzic.
Atlas of Finland, 1925. Helsingfors 1929.
Axelsson, M., 1852, Vandring i Wermlands Elfdal och finnskogar. Stockholm.

Balfour, H., 1898, Sledges with bone runners in modern use. In: Reliquary and illustrated Archaeologist. (London.)
Baltzer, L., 1881, Glyphes des Rochers. 1. Gothenburg.

Baltzer, L., 1891, Hällristningar från Bohuslän. Ny serie. Gothenburg.
Banner, J., 1912, Félhajo. In: Értesítöje 13, pp. 39—40.
Barchaeus, A. G., 1772, Berättelse angående landthushållningen. In: Västmanlands fornm.-fören:s årsskrift, 13, pp. 13—122.
Barchaeus, A. G., 1773, Underrättelser angående landthushållningen i Halland. Lund 1924.
Bátky, Zsigmond, 1906, Útmutató Néprajzi Múzeumok Szervezésére. Budapest.
Bellosics, B., 1913, Adatok a bácsbodrogmegyei sokáczok tárgyi néprajzához. In: Értesítöje 14, pp. 296—303.
Beretning om Akershus landbrukshöiskole, 1933, för år 1931—32. Oslo.
Berg, G., 1925 (a), Vägledning genom Skansens vagnhall. Stockholm.
Berg, G., 1925 (b), Lassånasläden. In: Från Nordiska museets samlingar, pp. 8—9.
Berg, G., 1928, Den svenska sädesharpan och den kinesiska. In: Nordiskt folkminne, pp. 19—24.
Berg, G., 1929, Kyrkåka och kappsläde. In: Svenska kulturbilder 1, pp. 51—64.
Berg, G., 1931, Den svenska tröskvagnen. In: Västerbotten, pp. 169—192.
Berg, G., 1932 (a), »Stundande skördar mödornas lön». In: Fataburen, pp. 101—116.
Berg, G., 1932 (b), Magnus Stridsberg och den svenska tröskvagnen än en gång. In: Västerbotten, pp. 109—111.
Berg, G., 1933 (a), Förhistoriska skidor. In: På skidor, pp. 142—169.
Berg, G., 1933 (b), Transportdon till lands. In: Nordisk kultur, 16, pp. 266—281.
Berg, G., 1934, Några nya myrfynd. In: Norrbotten, pp. 186—188.
Berg, G., 1935, Boskapsskötsel och fäbodliv. In: Vår hembygd, pp. 221—232.
Berg, G. and Svensson, S., 1934, Svensk bondekultur. Stockholm.
Bergfors, G. and Neander, A., 1928, Norrbotten. 1—2. Stockholm.
Bergmann, W., 1934, Studien zur volkstümlichen Kultur im Grenzgebiet von Hocharagón und Navarra. Hamburg.
Bergström, G., 1892—95, Arboga krönika. 1—2. Örebro.
Bergström, H. and Wesslén, G., 1922, Om träkolning. Third ed. Gothenburg.
Bielenstein, A., 1892, Die Grenzen des lettischen Volksstammes und der lettischen Sprache. St Petersburg.
Bielenstein, A., 1907—18, Die Holzbauten und Holzgeräthe der Letten. 1—2. St Petersburg.
Birket-Smith, K., 1927, Eskimoerne. Copenhagen.
Birket-Smith, K., 1929, The Caribou eskimos. 1—2. Copenhagen.
Birket-Smith, K., 1931, Rev. Wiener Beiträge zur Kulturgeschichte und Linguistik. 1. In: Anthropos, pp. 605—607.
Blau, J., 1917—18, Böhmerwälder Hausindustrie und Volkskunst. 1—2. Prague.
Blok, P. J., 1897, Amsterdam. 1. 's-Gravenhage.
Blümner, H., 1875—87. Technologie und Terminologie der Gewerbe und Künste bei Griechen und Römern 1—4. Leipzic.
Blöndal, S., 1920—24, Islandsk-dansk Ordbog. Reykjavik.
Boas, F., 1909, The Kwakiutl of the Vancouver Island. New York-Leiden.
v. Bode, W., 1930, Mein Leben. 1—2. Berlin.
Boding, J. D., 1747, Ångermanna Hushollning. Ed. Nätterlund. In: Norra Ångermanland. 1925.
Boerner, C. G., 1930, Handzeichnungen alter Meister des XV bis XVIII Jahrhunderts. Versteigerungskatalog 164. Leipzic.
Boerner, C. G., 1932, Kupferstiche alter Meister. Versteigerungskatalog 176. Leipzic.
Boëthius, G., 1922, Dalarnas samfärdsmedel. In: Dalarnas hembygdsförbunds tidskrift, pp. 100—128.
Boëthius, G., 1931, Hallar, tempel och stavkyrkor. 1. Stockholm.
Bogeng, G. A. E., 1926, Geschichte des Sports aller Völker und Zeiten. 1—2. Leipzic.
Bogoras, W., 1904—09, The Chukchee. New York-Leiden.
Bolin, S., 1933, Skånelands historia. 2. Lund.
Bolinder, G., 1928, Underliga folk i Europas mitt. Stockholm.
Bomann, W., 1929, Bäuerliches Hauswesen und Tagewerk im alten Niedersachsen. Second ed. Weimar.

Borchardt, L., 1907, Das Grabdenkmal des Königs Ne-user-rê. Leipzic.
Bore, E., 1891, Bärgsmanslif i början af 1800-talet. In: Svenska landsmål 5.
Borisov, A. A., 1906, U Samojedov.
Bottiglioni, G., 1914—15, Die Terminologie der Marmorindustrie in Carrara. In: Wörter und Sachen 6, pp. 89—115.
Bourlet, P. A., 1907, Les Thays. In: Anthropos 2, pp. 355—73, 613—32, 921—32.
Braun, G., 1575—81, Civitates orbis terrarum. 2—3. Cologne.
Braungart, R., 1914, Die Südgermanen. 1—2. Heidelberg.
Brenner, O., 1886, Die ächte Karte des Olaus Magnus vom Jahre 1539. Oslo.
v. Bretten, M. H., 1592, Aegyptiaca servitus. Heidelberg 1610.
Breuil, H., 1933—35, Les peintures rupestres schématiques de la péninsule ibérique. 1—4. Lagny.
Brockmann-Jerosch, H., 1929—31. Schweizer Volksleben. 1—2. Erlenberg-Zürich.
Broman, O., 1911—, Glysisvallur. Uppsala.
Broocman, R., 1736, En Fulständig Svensk Hus-Holds-Bok. 1. Norrköping.
Brown, R., 1758, The complete Farmer. 1—2.
Bull, J. B., 1916—19, Rendalen. 1—2. Oslo.
Brunhes, J., 1926, Géographie humaine de la France. 2. Paris. In: Hanotaux' Histoire de la nation Française.
Bruun, D., 1928, Fortidsminder og Nutidshjem paa Island. Second ed. Copenhagen.
Brännström, E., 1934, Med säljägare ute på Bottenhavet. In: Svenska kulturbilder, N. F., I, pp. 235—286.
Brüning, O., 1932, Der Flechtzaun im norddeutschen Küstengebiet. In: Niederdeutsche Zeitschrift für Volkskunde 10, pp. 89—105.
Bureus, J. T., 1886, Sumlen. In: Svenska landsmål, appendix 1.
Burkitt, M. C., 1929, Rock Carvings in the Italian Alps. In: Antiquity 3, pp. 155—164.
Burman, F., 1930, Anteckningar om Jämtland. Lund.
Byhan, A., 1923, Nord-, Mittel- und Westasien. In: Buschans illustrierte Völkerkunde 2.
Bälter, A., 1922, Myrslätter. In: Dalarnas hembygdsförbunds tidskrift 2, pp. 39—40.
Böttiger, J., 1891—92, "Unge herr Falkenbergarnes" Uppsalavistelse 1657. In: Meddelanden från Nordiska museet, pp. 3—12.

Cammiade, L. F., 1925, A primitive vehicle on runners. In: Man 25, No. 81.
Castrén, M., 1855—58, Nordiska resor och forskningar. 1—5. Helsingfors.
Catalogo della Mostra di Etnografia Italiana, 1911.
Catalogue of the collections in the Science Museum. 1926. Land transport. 1. Road transport. London.
Cederblom, G., 1923, Svenska folklivsbilder. Stockholm.
Chauvet, S., 1921, La Normandie ancestrale. Paris.
Childe, V. G., 1931, The forest cultures of Northern Europe. In: Journal of the Anthropological Institute 61, pp. 325—348.
Clemenson, G. and Kjellberg, S. T., 1933, Landshövdingeresidens och landsstatshus i Göteborgs och Bohus län. Uppsala.
Cole, F.-C., 1922, The Tinguian. Social, religious and economic life of a Philippine tribe. Chicago.
Coll, A. L., 1902, Fra Helleristningernes Omraade. In: Foreningens til Norske Fortidsminders Bevaring Aarsberetning, pp. 106—140.
Consten, H., 1919—20, Weideplätze der Mongolen. 1—2. Berlin.
Costenoble, H. H. L. W., 1905, Die Marianen. In: Globus 88, pp. 4—9, 72—81, 92—94.
Crælius, M. G., 1774, Försök till ett landskaps beskrifning uti en berättelse om Tunaläns, Sefwede och Aspelands häraders fögderie. Kalmar.

Daehne, P., 1930, Der Holzbauch. Eine fascinierende Fap-Fibel für fröhliche Gesellen. Leipzic.
Dahlberg, E., 1716, Suecia antiqua et hodierna. Stockholm.
Dahlbäck, S., 1926, Skidorna och Torne-Kalix' folk. In: På skidor, pp. 19—32.
Dalarnas hembygdsförbunds tidskrift. Falun.

Dalman, G., 1932, Arbeit und Sitte in Palästina. II. Der Ackerbau. Gütersloh.
Déchelette, J., 1908—14, Manuel d'archéologie. 1—2. Paris.
Dedekam, H., 1920, "Perspektivet" paa Osebergdronningens tapisserier. In: Kunst og Kultur 8, pp. 145—177.
Demant-Hatt, E., 1913, Med lapperne i höjfjeldet. Stockholm.
Descamps, P., 1930, État social des peoples sauvages. Paris.
des Noëttes, L., 1931, L'attelage. Le cheval de selle à travers les âges. 1—2. Paris.
Donner, K., 1915, Quelques traîneaux primitifs. Finnisch-ugrische Forschungen 15, pp. 91—104.
Donner, K., 1927, Über das Alter der ostjakischen und wogulischen Renntierzucht. In: Finnisch-ugrische Forschungen 18, pp. 115—44.
Drake, S., 1918, Västerbottenslapparna. Uppsala.
Durham, M. E., 1904, Through the Lands of the Serbs. London.
v. Düben, G., 1873, Om Lappland och lapparne. Stockholm.

Ebeling, W., 1932, Die landwirtschaftlichen Geräte im Osten der Provinz Lugo (Spanien). In: Volkstum und Kultur der Romanen 5, pp. 50—151.
Ebert, M., 1921, Südrussland in Altertum. Bonn-Leipzic.
Ebert, M., 1924—32, Reallexikon der Vorgeschichte. Berlin.
Ecsedi, I., 1926, A jégszánka. In: Értesítöje 37, p. 144.
Ecsedi, I., 1928, A bolgárok ösi földmürelése. In: Értesítöje 39, pp. 78—85.
Ecsedi, I., 1934, Népies halászat a Köpzép-Tiszán és a tiszántúli kisvizeken. In: A Debreceni Déri-Múzeum Évkönyve, 1933, pp. 123—300.
Eding, D., 1929, Gorbunovskij torfjanik. Tagil.
Edling, N., 1925, Vendels sockens dombok 1615—1645. Uppsala.
Eitrem, S., 1923, Vognen i Osebergskibet. In: Kunst og Kultur, pp. 75—85.
Ekhoff, E., 1880, Qville härads fasta fornlemningar. In: Bidrag till kännedom om Göteborgs och Bohusl. fornminnen 2, pp. 117—234.
Ekholm, G., 1921, Studier i Upplands bebyggelsehistoria. 2. Bronsåldern. Uppsala.
Ekman, S., 1910, Norrlands jakt och fiske. Uppsala.
Ekman, W., and others, 1922, Handbok i skogsteknologi. Stockholm.
Elgh, M., 1749, Om åkerbruket i Småland. Växjö 1925.
Elgström, O., 1922, Karesuandolapparna. Stockholm.
Encyclopédie ou Dictionnaire raisonné des sciences etc. 1751—80.
Endres, F. C., 1916, Die Türkei. Munich.
Engelhart, C., 1863, Thorsbjerg Mosefund. Copenhagen.
Engelhart, C., 1869, Vimose Fundet. Copenhagen.
Enquêtes du Musée de la Vie Wallonne. Liège.
Enqvist, A., 1930, De förhistoriska samlingarna i Gotlands fornsal. Stockholm.
En tur genom Österbotten, 1883. By Z. S[chalin]. Helsingfors.
Ericsson, G., 1883, Ordlista ur Åkers och Östra Rekarne härads folkspråk. S. In: Bidrag till Södermanlands äldre kulturhistoria 4, pp. 27—69.
Eriksson, M., 1925, Bondeliv i norra Uppland i mitten av förra århundradet. In: Fataburen, pp. 65—120.
Erixon, S., 1931 (a), Vägledning genom Skansens kulturhistoriska avdelning. Third ed. Stockholm.
Erixon, S., 1931 (b), Svensk kulturgeografi från etnologisk synpunkt. In: Svenska kulturbilder 9, pp. 9—50.
Erixon, S., 1932 (a), Skaraborgsböndernas byggnadskultur. In: Västgötagårdar. (Stockholm.)
Erixon, S. 1932 (b), Eldhus. In: Svenska kulturbilder VI, pp. 33—52.
Erixon, S., 1932 (c), Byar. In: Svenska kulturbilder VI, pp. 185—210.
Erixon, S., 1933, Hur Norge och Sverige mötas. In: Bidrag till bondesamfundets historie 2, pp. 183—299.
Erixon, S., 1934, Sveden. En bergsmansgård. Stockholm.
Ermans Archiv für wissenschaftliche Kunde von Russland. Berlin.

Értesítöje, A Magyar Nemzeti Múzeum. Budapest.
van Erven Dorens, 1930, De Boerenwagen in Nederland. In: Het Nederlandsch Openlucht-Museum te Arnhem. Bijdragen en Mededeelingen n:o 17, pp. 195—212, n:o 18, pp. 222—224.
Essendrop, J., 1761, Physisk oeconomisk beskrivelse over Lier præstegiæld. Copenhagen.
Europaeus, A., 1929, Uusia Kivikauden taidelöytöjä. In: Suomen Museo 36, pp. 82—88.
Europaeus-Äyräpää, A., 1930, Die relative Chronologie der steinzeitlichen Keramik in Finnland. In: Acta archaeologica 1, pp. 165—90, 205—20.

Faggot, J., and Chydenius, A., 1764, Svar pa frågan angående kärrors förbättring. In: Vetenskapsakademiens handlingar.
Fahrholz, G., 1931, Wohnen und Wirtschaft im Bergland der oberen Ariège. Hamburg.
Feldhaus, F. M., 1914, Die Technik der Vorzeit, der geschichtlichen Zeit und der Naturvölker. Leipzic-Berlin.
Fellman, J., 1906, Anteckningar under min vistelse i Lappmarken. 1—4. Helsingfors.
Ferencz, P. V., 1909, Ösegyszerü szállítási mód Erdélyken. In: Értesítöje 10, pp. 240—241.
Findeisen, H., 1934, Menschen in der Welt. Berlin.
Finland, 1923, Land, folk, rike. Helsingfors.
Finsch, O., 1876, Reise nach Westsibirien. Berlin 1879.
Fischer, A., 1900, Streifzüge durch Formosa. Berlin.
Flagge, L., 1935, Provenzalisches Alpenleben in den Hochtälern des Verdon und der Bléone. Florence.
Flateyjarbók. Ed. Vigfússon-Unger. Oslo. 1860—68.
Flor, F., 1930 (a), Zur Frage des Renntiernomadismus. In: Mitt. d. Anthrop. Gesellschaft in Wien 60, pp. 292—305.
Flor, F., 1930 (b), Haustiere und Hirtenkulturen. In: Wiener Beiträge zur Kulturgeschichte und Linguistik 1, pp. 1—238.
Flor, F., 1933, Beitrag zu den Problemen der arktischen Kulturgliederung. In: Mitt. d. Anthrop. Gesellschaft in Wien 63, pp. 53—59.
Florinus, F. Ph., 1772, Oeconomus prudens et legalis. Nuremberg.
Forde, C. D., 1934, Habitat, economy and society. London.
Fornmannasögur. Ed. Copenhagen. 1825—35.
Forrer, R., 1923—24, Die Fortschritte der prähistorischen und römischen Forschung im Elsass. In: Deutsches Archäologisches Institut, 15. Bericht, pp. 58—66.
Forrer, R., 1932, Les chars cultuels préhistoriques et leurs survivances aux époques historiques. In: Préhistoire 1, pp. 19—123.
Forrer, R., 1933, Drei primitive Wagenräder im Bernischen Historischen Museum und ihre prähistorischen Vorläufer. In: Jahrbuch des Bernischen Historischen Museums 13, pp. 16—22.
Forssell, C., 1827, Ett ar i Sverge. Stockholm.
Forssell, H. L., 1872—83, Sverige 1571. 1—2. Stockholm.
Forssander, J. E., 1933, Die schwedische Bootaxtkultur und ihre kontinentaleuropäischen Voraussetzungen. Lund.
Forseman, J., 1789, Om Dahl-Kärran. In: Hushallnings Journal, pp. 349—352.
Forsslund, K.-E., 1919—, Med Dalälven fran källorna till havet. Stockholm.
Fox, C., 1931, Sleds, carts and waggons. In: Antiquity 5, pp. 185—199.
Freuler, B., 1906, Die Holz- und Kohlentransportmittel im südlichen Tessin. In: Schweiz. Archiv für Volkskunde X, pp. 1—21.
Friedli, E., 1905—28, Bärndütsch. 1—7. Bern.
v. Friesen, O., 1922, Ett ställe i Jordanes' Skandia-beskrivning. In: Strena philologica upsaliensis, festskrift tillägnad Professor Per Persson, pp. 173—177.
Frödin, J., 1927, Bygdestudier i norra Jämtland. Lund.
Furuskog, J., 1924, De värmländska järnbruken. Lund.
Führer durch das Museum für Völkerkunde. Ackerbauhalle. 1931. Basle.

Gadd, J. A., 1871, Allmogemalet i Östra härad. Karlskrona.
Gahn, J. G., H. and H. J. and Adelswärd, J. L., 1765, En resa i Dalarna. Falun 1909.

Gaimard, M. P., 1838—40, Voyages en Scandinavie. Atlas. 1—2. Paris n. d.
Gandert, O. F., 1930, Forschungen zur Geschichte des Haushundes. Leipzic.
Gaslander, J., 1774, Allmogens i Wästbo sinnelag, seder m.m. Stockholm.
Gavazzi, M., 1929, Saonice kod pogreba. In: Lud Słowianski 1, pp. B 88—92.
Gavazzi, M., 1934, Über die Verbreitung und Deutung des Schlittenbegräbnisses. In: Congrès international des sciences anthropologiques et ethnographiques, Compte-Rendu, pp. 255—56.
Geete, E., 1927, Tryga och skidkälke i avverkningens tjänst. In: Skogen 14, pp. 517—20.
v. Gennep, A., 1913, Notes d'ethnographie persane. In: Revue d'ethnographie et de sociologie 4, pp. 73—89.
Georgi, J. G., 1776—80, Beschreibung aller Nationen des Russischen Reiches. St. Petersburg.
Gielleböl, R., 1771, Naturlig og oeconomisk beskrivelse over Hölands praestegield. Copenhagen.
Gielleböl, R., 1780, Beskrivelse over Saetersdalen. In: Topografisk Journal h. 26—27 (1800).
Giese, W., 1931, Volkstümliche Siedlung und Wirtschaft in den Monts d'Arrée. In: Volkstum u. Kultur der Romanen 4, pp. 343—377.
Giese, W., 1932, Volkskundliches aus den Hochalpen der Dauphiné. Hamburg.
Ginzrot, J. Chr., 1817, Die Wagen und Fahrwerke der Griechen und Römer. Munich.
Glasnik Zemaljskog Muzeja u Bosni i Hercegovini. Sarajevo.
Globus, Brunswick.
Godwin, H., 1934, Pollen-analysis. An outline of the problems and potentialities of the method. In: The New Phytologist 23, pp. 278—305, 325—358.
Goeteeris, A., 1615—16, Journal över den holländska beskickningens resa. Ed. by S. Hildebrand. Stockholm 1917.
Goldstern, E., 1922, Hochgebirgsvolk in Savoyen und Graubünden. Vienna.
Gomme, G. L., 1890, The Village Community. London.
Gotlandslagen, ed. by C. J. Schlyter, 1852. Lund.
Gottlund, C. A., 1817, Dagbok öfver dess resor på finnskogarne i Dalarne, Helsingland, Vestmanland och Vermland år 1817. Stockholm 1931.
Granberg, E., 1927, Med härjedalingar i färdeväg och pa handelsresor. In: Jämten, pp. 59—71.
Granberg, O., 1929—31, Svenska konstsamlingarnas historia från Gustav Vasas tid till våra dagar. 1—3. Stockholm.
Grau, O., 1748, Hushålds anmärkningar under resan igenom Upsala och Stockholms län. In: Upplands fornminnesförenis tidskrift 8, appendix.
Graves, K., 1921, Ved Halleby aa. (Danmarks folkeminder.) Copenhagen.
Grieg, S., 1928, Osebergfundet. 2. Oslo.
Grierson, G. A., 1885, Bihār peasant life. Calcutta.
Grimm, J., 1854, Deutsche Rechtsaltertümer. Second ed. Göttingen.
Grotenfelt, G., 1899, Det primitiva jordbrukets metoder. Helsingfors.
Grotenfelt, G., 1915, I Finland använda redskap för stallgödselns transport. Helsingfors.
Grothe, H., 1913, Durch Albanien und Montenegro. Munich.
Grude, J., 1891, Stölsdriften paa Vestlandet. Stavanger.
Grundtvig, F. L., 1909, Livet i Klokkergaarden. Gammeldags Falstersk Bondeliv. Copenhagen.
Gröber, K., 1925, Schwaben (Deutsche Volkskunst). Munich.
Gröber, K., 1928, Kinderspielzeug aus alter Zeit. Berlin.
Gustavson, H., 1931, En gammal gotländsk danslek och en dansvisa hos Jöran Wallin. In: Gotländskt Arkiv 3, pp. 76—74.
Gyllenius, P. M., 1880—82, Diarium Gyllenianum. 1622—67. Helsingfors.
Györffy, I., 1928, Takarás és nyomtatás az Alföldön. In: Értesítöje 20, pp. 1—46.
Gönczi, F., 1895, Die Kroaten in Maraköz. In: Ethnologische Mitteilungen aus Ungarn 4, pp. 163—175, 201—209.
Göteborgs museums årstryck. Gothenburg.
Göth, J. A., 1931, Raskens Zenobia. Stockholm.

Haberlandt, A., 1912, Beiträge zur bretonischen Volkskunde. Vienna.
Haberlandt, A., 1917, Kulturwissenschaftliche Beiträge zur Volkskunde von Montenegro, Albanien und Serbien. Vienna.

Haberlandt, A., 1926, Die volkstümliche Kultur Europas in ihrer geschichtlichen Entwicklung. In: Buschans Illustrierte Völkerkunde 3.
Haberlandt, A., 1929, Allerhand Schwerarbeit im Hochgebirge. Reprint. Vienna.
Haddon, A. C., 1908, The Study of Man. London.
Hahm, K., 1928, Deutsche Volkskunst. Berlin.
Hallström, G., 1926, En färd från Kiruna till Varangerfjorden. In: På skidor, pp. 224—257.
Hallström, G., 1929, Kan lapparnas invandringstid fixeras? In: Norrlands försvar, pp. 39—92.
Hamburgs Vergangenheit und Gegenwart, 1896—97, Eine Sammlung von Ansichten — — — 1—2. Hamburg.
Hamilton, H., 1928, Hågkomster. Stockholm.
Hammarstedt, N. E., 1912, "Släpan". In: Skansens programblad. 1 maj.
Haraldsson, M., 1893—94, Anteckningar om seder och bruk, sägner och vidskepelse i Villstads socken, Västbo härad i Småland under 1700-talet. In: Meddelanden från Nordiska museet, pp. 43—56.
Hartley, D. and Elliot, M. M., 1928 (a), Life and work of the people of England. The fourteenth century. London.
Hartley, D. and Elliot, M. M., 1928 (b), Life and work. The seventeenth century. London.
Hartley, D. and Elliot, M. M., 1931, Life and work. The eighteenth century. London.
Hartnack, W., 1930, Madeira. Landeskunde einer Insel. Greifswald.
Hasund, S., 1932, Vårt landbruks historie. Oslo.
Hatt, G., 1913, Lappiske slaedeformer. In: (Danish) Geografisk tidsskrift 22, pp. 139—145.
Hatt, G., 1916, Moccasins and their relation to Arctic footwear. In: Memoirs of the American Anthropological association 3, pp. 149—250.
Hatt, G., 1918, Rensdyrnomadismens elementer. In: (Danish) Geografisk tidsskrift 24, pp. 241—269.
Hatt, G., 1919, Notes on reindeer nomadism. In: Memoirs of the American Anthropological association 6, pp. 75—133.
Havard, H., Dictionnaire de l'ameublement. 1—4. Paris n. d.
Hazelius, F., 1913, Johan Sevenbom och hans målningar för slottet och rådhuset i Stockholm. In: S:t Eriks årsbok, pp. 1—20.
Heckscher, E., 1907, Till belysning av järnvägarnas betydelse för Sveriges ekonomiska utveckling. Stockholm.
Heckscher, K., 1925, Die Volkskunde des germanischen Kulturkreises. 1—2. Hamburg.
Hedin, A. G., 1741, Beskrifning öfver Kräklinge socken i Neriket. Ed. 1916. Lund.
Heikel, A. O., 1888, Die Gebäude der Ceremissen, Mordwinen, Esten und Finnen. Helsingfors.
Heimatgaue. Linz.
Heimskringla. Ed. Jónsson. Copenhagen. 1893—1901.
Heine-Geldern, R., 1923, Südostasien. In: Buschans Völkerkunde 2.
Heineman, F., 1900, Der Richter und die Rechtspflege in der deutschen Vergangenheit. Leipzic.
Hellström, P., 1917, Norrlands jordbruk. Uppsala.
Helminen, H., 1931, Vanhan Tammelan niityistä, heinäkaluista ja heinänteosta. In: Sanakirjasäätiön toimituksia 1, pp. 197—212.
Hembygden. Åmål.
Hennel, T., 1934, Change in the farm. London.
Herman, O., 1902, Knochenschlittschuh, Knochenkufe, Knochenkeitel. In: Mittheilungen der Anthropologischen Gesellschaft in Wien 32, pp. 217—238.
Hermans, E. P., 1918, Tjärlaks bysamhälle i Närpes socken. Helsingfors.
Hersoug, O., 1932, Fedrenegården. Oslo.
Heyne, M., 1901, Das deutsche Nahrungswesen von den ältesten geschichtlichen Zeiten bis zum 16. Jahrhundert. Leipzic.
Hillgren, B., 1925, En bok om Delsbo. 2. Stockholm.
Hilzheimer, M., 1931, Die Anschirrung bei den alten Sumerern. In: Prähistorische Zeitschrift 22, pp. 1—18.
Hirth, G., 1882, Kunstgeschichtliches Bilderbuch aus drei Jahrhunderten. 1—6. Leipzic-Munich.
Historiallinen Aikakauskirja. Porvoo.

Hjärne, E., 1917, Storkågefyndet. In: Fornvännen, pp. 147—92, 203—25.
Hoernes, M., 1882, Holzgeräthe und Holzbau in Bosnien. In: Mittheilungen d. Anthrop. Gesellschaft in Wien 12, p. 89.
Hofberg, H., 1861, Allmogeord ur Vestra Nerikes bygdemål. Örebro.
Hofberg, H., 1878, Skildringar ur svenska folklifvet. Stockholm.
Hofberg, H., 1880—81, Några drag ur det forna skogsbyggarlifvet i Halland. Stockholm.
Hoffman, E., 1853—56, Der nördliche Ural und das Küstengebirge Pae-Choi. 1—2. St. Petersburg.
Hoffmann, W., 1932, Rheinhessische Volkskunde. Bonn-Cologne.
Hofman, J., 1928, Die ländliche Bauweise, Einrichtung und Volkskunst — — — der Karlsbader Landschaft. Karlsbad.
von Hofsten, E., 1917, Beskrifning öfwer Wermeland. Karlstad.
Holmberg, A. E., 1842—45, Bohusläns historia och beskrifning. 1—3. Uddevalla.
Holmberg, A. E., 1848—49, Skandinaviens hällristningar. Stockholm.
Horniman Museum, 1925, Travel and transport.
Horwitz, H. Th., 1931, Über den Transport von Steinkolossen im alten Ägypten und in Mesopotamien. In: Der deutsche Steinbildhauer 47, pp. 39—41, 49—51, 61—63.
Horwitz, H., 1933, Die Drehbewegung in ihrer Bedeutung für die Entwicklung der materiellen Kultur. 1. In: Anthropos 28, pp. 721—57.
Horwitz, H., 1934, Rev. of des Noëttes, 1931. In: Anthropos, pp. 846—48.
Hottenroth, F., 1893—96, Handbuch der deutschen Tracht. Stuttgart.
Howitt, W., 1842, The natural and domestic life of Germany. London.
Huber, G., 1919, Les appellations des traîneaux et de ses parties dans les dialectes de la Suisse romane. Heidelberg.
Huntington, E., 1907, The pulse of Asia. Boston-New York.
Hupel, A. W., 1774—82, Topographische Nachrichten von Lief- und Ehstland. 1—3. Riga.
Hushållnings Journal, Patriotiska sällskapets. Stockholm.
Hutton, J. H., 1929, Assam Megaliths. In: Antiquity 3, pp. 324—38.
Hülphers, A. A., 1757, Dagbok öfver en resa genom Dalarne. Västerås 1763.
Hülphers, A. A., 1763, Finska resan. In: Leinbergs Bidrag 2. (Jyväskylä 1886.)
Hülphers, A. A., 1780, Ångermanland. Västerås.
Hülphers, A. A., 1789, Westerbotten. Västeras.
Hyltén-Cavallius, G. O., 1864—68, Wärend och wirdarne. 1—2. Stockholm.
Håkansson, G., 1932, Slåtter i Bleking. In: Svenska landsmål, pp. 5—24.
Hårleman, C., 1749, Dag-Bok öfwer en ifrån Stockholm — — — gjord Resa. Stockholm.
Högberg, P., 1926, Fiske i Lule skärgård. In: Svenska landsmål, pp. 5—46.
Hörlén, M., 1914, Gamla seder och bruk från södra delen av Ingelstads härad. Ystad.

Ingvorsen, I., 1918, Gammelt sjællandsk Bondeliv. Copenhagen.
Isberg, O., 1930, Till frågan om människans och renens första uppträdande på den skandinaviska halvön under postarktisk tid. In: Ymer, pp. 381—402.
Itkonen, T., 1923, Suomenlahden saarelaisten hylkeenpyynti. In: Suomen Museo 30, pp. 25—36.
Itkonen, T., 1930, Muinaissuksia ja -jalaksia. In: Suomen Museo 37, pp. 82—90.
Itkonen, T., 1931—32, Muinaissuksia ja -jalaksia. 2. In: Suomen Museo 38, pp. 51—63.
Itkonen, T., 1932, Karjalan vanhat liikeneuvot. In: Karjalan Kirja, pp. 404—13.
Itkonen, T., 1935, Muinaissuksia ja -jalaksia. 3. In: Suomen Museo (in print).

Jacob, G., 1927, Arabische Berichte von Gesandten an germanische Fürstenhöfe. Berlin-Leipzic.
James, H. E. M., 1888, The Long White Mountain or a journey in Manchuria. London.
Jekyll, G., 1925, Old English household life. London.
Jenness, D., 1932, The Indians of Canada. Ottawa.
Jirlow, R., 1928, Gamla västerbottniska bårredskap. In: Västerbotten, pp. 201—208.
Jirlow, R., 1930, Västerbottnisk säljakt. In: Västerbotten, pp. 77—95.
Jirlow, R., 1931 (a), Drag ur föröiskt arbetsliv. In: Rig, pp. 97—133.

Jirlow, R., 1931 (b), En lapsk klövjesadel och dess ursprung. In: Rig, pp. 90—95.
Jirlow, R., 1935, Gamla dagars vinteridrott i Transtrand. In: På skidor, pp. 27—46.
Jochelson, W., 1908, The Koryak. Leiden-New York.
Jochelson, W., 1933, The Yakut. New York.
Johansson, L., 1924—25, På en storbondegård i Frostviken i mitten av 1800-talet. In: Arkiv för norrländsk hembygdsforskning, pp. 56—95.
Jubileumsutställningen i Göteborg, 1923, Hantverkshistoriska och industrihistoriska avdelningarna. Gothenburg.
Jämten. Östersund.

Kalén, J., 1923, Ordbok över Fageredsmålet. Göteborg.
Kalm, P., 1746, Wästgötha och Bahusländska Resa. Stockholm.
Kalm, P., 1747—51, En resa til Norra America. Ed. Svenska litt.-sällskapet i Finland. Helsingfors 1904—15.
Kanitz, F., 1875—79, Donau-Bulgarien und der Balkan. 1—3. Leipzic.
Karling, S., 1933, Tyresö slott. In: Fataburen, pp. 67—106.
Karlinger, H., 1925, Bayern (Deutsche Volkskunst). Munich.
Karutz, R., 1898, Zur Ethnographie der Basken. In: Globus 74, pp. 333—340.
Karutz, R., 1925—26, Atlas der Völkerkunde. 1—2. Stuttgart.
Keyland, N., 1923, Seder och bruk vid dödsfall och begravning i västra Värmland. In: Fataburen, pp. 94—108.
Kiechel, S., 1586, En resa genom Sverige. Uppsala 1897.
Kiesewetter, H. C. O., 1807, Praktisch ökonomische Bemerkungen auf einer Reise durch Hollstein. Hof.
Klein, E., 1924, Runö. Folklivet i en gammal svensk by. Uppsala.
Klein, E., 1929, Skärkarlsliv i Möjatrakten. In: Fataburen, pp. 124—147.
Klein, E., 1930, Vårt äldsta näringsfång. In: Svenska kulturbilder II, pp. 131—152.
K[lei]n, E. and Ö[sterman], J., 1927, Runöbornas säljakt. In: Hävd och hembygd 2, pp. 64—75.
Klemming, G. E., 1856, Skråordningar. Stockholm.
v. Knorring, F. P., 1833, Gamla Finland eller det fordna Wiborgska guvernementet. Åbo.
Koeppen, A., and Breuer, C., 1904, Geschichte des Möbels. Berlin.
Koppers, W., 1930, Der Hund in der Mythologie der zirkumpazifischen Völker. In: Wiener Beiträge z. Kult. gesch. u. Linguistik 1, pp. 359—99.
Koppers, W., 1934, Die Indogermanenfrage im Lichte der vergleichenden Völkerkunde. In: Congrès international des sciences anthropologiques et éthnologiques, Compte-rendu, pp. 185—86.
Kossinna, G., 1915, Die deutsche Vorgeschichte. Second ed. Würzburg.
Kreisel, H., 1927, Prunkwagen und Schlitten. Leipzic.
Krieg, H., 1931, Schleswig-Holsteinische Volkskunde. Lübeck.
Kristensen, E. T., 1900, Det jyske almueliv. Appendix 1. Århus.
Kruse, H., 1934, Sach- und Wortkundliches aus den südfranzösischen Alpen. Hamburg.
Krüger, F., 1925, Die Gegenstandskultur Sanabrias und seiner Nachbargebiete. Hamburg.
Krüger, F., 1927, Die nordwestiberische Volkskultur. In: Wörter und Sachen 10, pp. 45—137.
Krüger, F., 1928, Rev. of Chauvet, 1921. In: Volkstum und Kultur der Romanen 1, pp. 197—200.
Kullander, A., 1896, Några drag ur det forna skogsbyggarlivet i Edsvedens skogsbygder. In: Svenska landsmål 11.
Kuusanmäki, L., 1928, Vanha Korpilahti. Porvoo.
Kuylenstierna, O., 1923, Svensk rokoko. Stockholm.

La Baume, W., 1924, Wagendarstellungen auf ostgermanischen Urnen der frühen Eisenzeit und ihre Bedeutung. In: Blätter für deutsche Vorgeschichte 1, pp. 5—28.
La Baume, W., 1928, Bildliche Darstellungen auf ostgermanischen Tongefässen der frühen Eisenzeit. In: Ipek 4, pp. 25—56.
Lacroix, P. and Serré, F., 1848—51. Le Moyen Age et la Renaissance. 1—5. Paris.
Laloy, L., 1902, Alte Anspannungsgeräthe. In: Archiv für Anthropologie 27, pp. 433—34.

Laloy, L., 1904, Ethnographisches aus Südwest-Frankreich. 2. Das Baskenland. In: Archiv für Anthropologie. N. F. 2, pp. 185—93.
Lannér, I., 1765, Tankar om lands culturen. Stockholm.
Larsson, L., 1912, Te byn å Levång. Östersund.
L'art populaire hongrois, 1928. Budapest.
Lassota von Steblau, E., 1590—91, Tagebuch. Ed. by R. Schottin, Halle. 1866.
Latvju Raksti. Riga 1924—31.
Laufer, B., 1910, Zur kulturhistorischen Stellung der chinesischen Provinz Shansi. In: Anthropos 5, pp. 181—203.
Laufer, B., 1914, Chinese clay figures. 1. Chicago.
Laufer, B., 1917 (a), The reindeer and its domestication. Lancaster, Pa.
Laufer, B., 1917 (b), The beginnings of porcelain in China. Chicago.
Laufer, B., 1920, The reindeer once more. In: American Anthropologist 22, pp. 192—97.
Laufer, B., 1930, The early history of felt. In: American Anthropologist 32, pp. 1—18.
Laufer, B., 1931, Some fundamental ideas of Chinese culture. In: Kroeber-Waterman, The source Book in Anthropology, pp. 535—45.
Lechler, J., 1933, Neues über Pferd und Wagen in der Steinzeit und Bronzezeit. In: Mannus 25, pp. 123—136.
von Le Coq, A., 1911, Lieder und Sprichwörter aus der Gegend von Turfan. Baessler-Archiv, appendix.
Lehner, H., 1923, Ein gallo-römischer Wagen aus Frenz an der Inde im Kreis Düren. In: Bonner Jahrbücher 128, pp. 28—62.
Lehtisalo, T., 1932, Beiträge zur Kenntnis der Renntierzucht bei den Juraksamojeden. Oslo.
Leinbock, F., 1932, Die materielle Kultur der Esten. Tartu.
Lenaeus, K. N., 1764, Delsboa illustrata. Stockholm.
Leser, P., 1927, Landwirtschaftliche Sommerschlitten. In: Ethnologica 3, pp. 38—44.
Leser, P., 1928, Westöstliche Landwirtschaft. Kulturbeziehungen zwischen Europa, dem vorderen Orient und dem fernen Osten. In: P. W. Schmidt-Festschrift, pp. 416—84.
Leser, P., 1931, Entstehung und Verbreitung des Pfluges. Münster in W.
Leuss, H., 1903, Zur Volkskunde der Inselfriesen. In: Globus 84, pp. 202—06, 223—25.
Levander, L., 1914, Livet i en älvdalsby. Stockholm.
Lid, N., 1930, Skifundet frå Övrebö. In: Universitetets oldsaksamling, Årbok, pp. 152—178. Oslo.
Liebe, G., 1924, Das Judentum in der deutschen Vergangenheit. Second ed. Jena.
Lilljebjörn, H., 1865, Hågkomster fran ungdomen. Stockholm.
Lindberg, K. H., 1921, Något om husdjur och lantbruksredskap i Skee socken i Bohuslän. In: Göteborgs o. Bohusl. fornminnesfören. tidskrift, pp. 43—56.
Lindblom, A., and Branting, A., 1932, Medieval embroideries and textiles in Sweden. Uppsala-Stockholm.
Lindblom, K. G., 1931, The use of oxen. Stockholm.
Lindgren, G., 1933, G. W. Palm. Stockholm.
Linder, A., and Berg, G., 1923, Vägledning för besökande i Dalslands fornsal. Uddevalla.
Lindqvist, S., 1918, Nordens benålder och en teori om dess stenåldersraser. In: Rig, pp. 65—84.
Lindqvist, S., 1933, Gotlands bildstenar. In: Rig, pp. 97—117.
v. Linné, C., 1732, Iter lapponicum. Second ed. Uppsala 1913.
v. Linné, C., 1734, Iter Dalecarlicum. In: Carl von Linnés ungdomsskrifter. II. Stockholm n. d., pp. 233—368.
v. Linné, C., 1741, Öländska och Gottländska resa. Stockholm-Uppsala. 1745.
v. Linné, C., 1747, Wästgöta-resa. Stockholm.
v. Linné, C., 1749, Skånska resa. Stockholm 1751.
Lithberg, N., 1918, Till allmogekulturens geografi. In: Rig, pp. 1—27.
Ljunggren, R., 1913, Ord och uttryck för åkerbruk och boskapsskötsel i Laske-Vedums socken, Västergötland. In: Svenska landsmål. 1913, pp. 37—98.
Loewenthal, J., 1918, Zur Erfindungsgeschichte von Rad und Wagen. In: Zeitschrift für Ethnologie, 50, pp. 204—209.

Loewenthal, J., 1920—21, Irokesische Wirtschaftsaltertümer. In: Zeitschrift für Ethnologie, 52—53, pp. 171—233.
Lund, J. M., 1785, Forsög til Beskrivelse over Övre-Tellemarken. Copenhagen.
Lundberg, E., 1931, Beenhammar. In: Svenska kulturbilder V, pp. 225—254.
Lundin, C., and Strindberg, A., 1882, Gamla Stockholm. Stockholm.
Luttrell Psalter. Ed. by G. Millar. London 1932.
Lönborg, S., 1907, Finnmarkerna i mellersta Skandinavien. In: Ymer, 22, pp. 65—90, 361—408, 465—504.
Löw, G., 1922—24. St. Mellösa i äldre tider. 1—2. Strängnäs.

Magasin för konst, nyheter och moder. Stockholm.
Magyar Népmüveszet, 1924. Budapest.
Mahr, O., 1934, Zur Geschichte des Wagenrades. In: Technik—Geschichte. Beiträge zur Geschichte der Technik und Industrie. 23, pp. 57—61.
Makarenko, A., 1913, Sibirskij narodnyj kalendar'. St. Petersburg.
Mallory, W. H., 1926, Land of famine. New York.
Mandelgren, N. M., 1889, Förteckning pa — — — studier, teckningar och utkast till Atlas. Stockholm.
Manninen, I., 1925, Etnograafiline sõnastik. Tartu.
Manninen, I., 1928 (a), Etnograafilisi märkmeid eesti ingerist. In: Eesti Rahva Muuseumi Aastaraamat 4, pp. 39—56.
Manninen, I., 1928 (b), Führer durch die ethnographischen Sammlungen (in Eesti Rahva Muuseum). Tartu.
Manninen, I., 1931—32, Die Sachkultur Estlands. 1—2. Tartu.
Manninen, I., 1932, Die finnisch-ugrischen Völker. Leipzic.
Manninen, I., 1934, Suomen suku. 3. Helsinki.
Marinov, D., 1901, Sbornik za narodni umotvorenija, nauka i knižnina. 1. Sofia.
Markowski, B., 1932, Die materielle Kultur des Kabulgebietes. Leipzic.
Markwart, J., 1930, Südarmenien und die Tigrisquellen. Vienna.
van Marle, R., 1931—32, Iconographie de l'art profane. 1—2. La Haye.
Martin, F., 1897, Sibirica. Stockholm.
Mason, O. T., 1894—96, Primitive travel and transportation. Washington.
Matériaux pour l'ethnographie de la Russie. St. Petersburg.
Menghin, O., 1931, Weltgeschichte der Steinzeit. Vienna.
Mercer, H., 1925, Ancient carpenters' tools, Part 2. In: Old-time New England 16, pp. 19—52.
Meringer, R., 1906—07, Das Schlittenhaus. In: Indogermanische Forschungen 19, pp. 401—430, 21, pp. 277—282.
Merwald, K., 1932, Glimtar ur Herrakra sockens historia. In: Hyltén Cavallius-föreningens årsbok, pp. 19—52.
Messerschmidt, H., 1931, Haus und Wirtschaft in der Serra da Estrêla (Portugal). In: Volkstum u. Kultur der Romanen 4, pp. 72—163, 246—305.
Meyer-Lübke, W., 1909, Zur Geschichte der Dreschgeräte. In: Wörter und Sachen 1, pp. 211—244.
Mielke, R., 1912, Äussere Volkskunde. In: Landeskunde der Provinz Brandenburg 3, pp. 3—160.
Mielke, R., 1917, Das Pfluggespann. In: Festschrift Eduard Hahn, pp. 190—208.
Mitzka, W., 1934, Volkskundliche Verkehrsmittel zu Wasser und zu Lande. In: Pesslers Handbuch der Deutschen Volkskunde 3, pp. 1—17.
Modée, R. G., Publique förordningar, Utdrag utur — — —. Stockholm. 1742—1829.
Modéer, I., 1933, Småländska skärgardsnamn. Uppsala.
Modin, E., 1916, Gamla Tasjö. Örebro.
Montandon, G., 1934, Traité d'ethnologie culturelle. Paris.
Moszyński, K., 1929, Kultura Ludowa Słowian. Cracow.
Mummenhoff, E., 1901, Der Handwerker. Leipzic.
Munsterhjelm, L., 1922, Färder i fjärran Östern. Helsingfors.
Müller, S., 1907, Nye Fund og Iagttagelser fra Sten-, Bronze- og Jernalderen. In: Aarböger, pp. 75—160.

Müller, S., 1920, Nye Fund og Former. In: Aarböger, pp. 88—111.
Mötefindt, H., 1917, Der Wagen im nordischen Kulturkreise zur vor- und frühgeschichtlichen Zeit. In: Festschrift Eduard Hahn, pp. 209—240.
Mötefindt, H., 1918, Die Entstehung des Wagens und des Wagenrades. In: Mannus 10, pp. 32—63.
Mötefindt, H., 1926, Kultwagen. In: Eberts Reallexikon.
Mötefindt, H., 1927—28, Schlitten. In: Eberts Reallexikon.

Nansen, F., 1914, Gjennem Sibirien. Oslo.
Nansen, F., 1898, På skidor genom Grönland. Stockholm.
New English Dictionary. Oxford.
Nicolaysen, N., 1882, Langskibet fra Gokstad ved Sandefjord. Oslo.
Nilsson, S., 1816, Dagboksanteckningar under en resa från södra Sverige till Nordlanden i Norge. Lund 1879.
Nordén, A., 1926, Kiviksgraven. Second ed. Stockholm.
Nordén, A., 1932, Hällristningstraditionen och den urnordiska runskriften. In: Arkeologiska studier, tillägnade H. K. H. Kronprins Gustaf Adolf, pp. 53—69.
Nopcsa, F., 1925, Albanien. Bauten, Trachten und Geräte Nordalbaniens. Berlin-Leipzic.
Nopcsa, F., 1927, Ergänzungen zu meinem Buche über die Bauten, Trachten und Geräte Nordalbaniens. In: Zeitschrift für Ethnologie 59, pp. 279—281.
Nordenskiöld, A. E., 1880—81, Vegas färd kring Asien och Europa. 1—2. Stockholm.
Nordenskiöld, E., 1930, Modifications in Indian culture through inventions and loans. Gothenburg.
Nordenström, M. N., 1769, Utkast till beskrifning öfwer Stöde socken. Stockholm 1923.
Nordgaard, O., 1932, Om opdagelsen av Norges dyreverden. In: Videnskabselskabets forhandlinger, Trondheim, 4, pp. 32—41.
Nordisk familjebok, Second ed. Stockholm.
Nordlander, J., 1914, Norrländskt skolliv. Stockholm.
Nordlander, J., 1933, Ordbok över Multråmålet. Stockholm.
Nordman, C. A., 1927. Den yngre stenåldern i Mellan-, Väst- och Nordeuropa. In: De förhistoriska tiderna i Europa 2.
Nordström, A., 1925, Luleåkultur. Luleå.
Norges jubilæumsutstilling 1914. 2. Den landbrugshistoriske avdelning. Oslo.
Norsk kultur, 1931, i samtidige billeder. Oslo.
Nörlund, P., 1926, Gyldne Altre. Copenhagen.

Oelmann, F., 1927, Haus und Hof im Altertum. Berlin-Leipzic.
Ogier, Ch., 1634—35, Dagbok. Stockholm 1914.
Ohnefalsch-Richter, M., 1913, Griechische Sitten und Gebräuche auf Cypern. Berlin.
Olaus Magnus, 1539, Charta marina. See: Brenner. 1886.
Olaus Magnus, 1555, Historia de gentibus septentrionalibus. Swedish ed. 1—4. Uppsala 1909—25.
Olsen, J., 1914, Fra Sydsjaelland. Barndomsminder fra Bakkebölle ved Vordingborg. Copenhagen.
Olsen, Ö., 1915, Et primitivt folk. Oslo.
Olsen, M., 1914—24, Eggjumstenen. Norges indskrifter med de aeldre runer. (Oslo.) 3, pp. 77—197, 268—279.
Olsson, M., 1914, Uppländska sjöbodar. 2. Redskap. In: Fataburen, pp. 36—50.
Olufsen, O., 1911, The Emir of Bokhara and his country. Copenhagen-London.
Oprescu, G., 1929, Peasant art in Roumania. London.
Ord och bild. Stockholm.
Osbeck, P., 1796, Utkast til beskrifning öfver Laholms prosteri. Lund 1922.
v. Otter, E., 1930, Som officer och storviltjägare i Turkana. Stockholm.
Oudemans, Th. Chr., 1926, Die Holländischen Ackerwagen. Wageningen.

Pacala, V., 1916, Der Bauernhof und die Alpenwirtschaft in Resinár. In: Anzeiger d. Ethnogr. Abteilung des Ungar. Nationalmuseums 8, pp. 118—135.

Pallas, P. S., 1776, Sammlungen historischer Nachrichten über die mongolischen Völkerschaften. 1—2. S:t Petersburg 1776—1801.
Pallas, P. S., 1793—94, Bemerkungen auf einer Reise in die südlichen Statthalterschaften des russischen Reichs. 1—2. Leipzic 1803.
Palmstedt, E., 1778—80, Dagbok. Uppsala 1927.
Pamfile, T., 1910, Industria Casnică la Români. Bucharest.
Papahagi, T., 1928—30, Images d'ethnographie Roumaine. 1—2. Apostol Margarit-Bucharest.
Parkes, J., 1925, Travel in England in the Seventeenth Century. Oxford.
Patsch, C., 1909, Archäologisch-epigraphische Untersuchungen VII. In: Wissenschaftliche Mitteilungen aus Bosnien und der Herzegowina 77, pp. 104—183.
Patsch, C., 1912, Archäologisch-epigraphische Untersuchungen VIII. In: Wissenschaftliche Mitteilungen aus Bosnien und der Herzegowina 12, pp. 68—167.
Paulaharju, S., 1922, Kainuun mailta. Helsinki.
Paulaharju, S., 1923, Vanhaa Lappia ja Peräpohjaa. Helsinki.
Paulaharju, S., 1927, Taka-Lappia. Helsinki.
Paulaharju, S., 1932, Härmän aukeilta. Porvoo.
Peasant Art in Italy, 1913, ed. by Charles Holmes. London.
Peate, I. C., 1929, Guide to the collection of Welsh bygones (in National Museum of Wales). Cardiff.
Pessler, W., 1914, Aufgaben der deutschen Sach-Geographie. In: Mitteil. aus der Sammlung für deutsche Volkskunde 4, pp. 147—167.
Petersen, H., 1888, Vognfundene i Dejbjerg Praestegaardsmose. Copenhagen.
Pettersson, K. P., 1917, Lantmannaredskap i Nagu. In: Folkloristiska och etnografiska studier 2, pp. 131—197.
Petterson, O. P., 1888, Lapparnas sommarlif. In: Svenska landsmål VII.
Phieler, W., 1934, Volkskundliches aus den Marken. Hamburg.
Phleps, H., 1934, Ost- und westgermanische Baukultur. Berlin.
Pitkiewiez, Cz., 1928, Polesie rzeczyckie materjały etnograficzne. 1. Cracow.
Piton, C., 1913, Le costume civil en France du XIII:e siècle. Paris.
Pitré, G., 1913, La famiglia, la casa, la vita del Popolo Siciliano. Palermo.
Pleyte, W., 1877, Nederlandsche Oudheden. Friesland. Leyden.
Pogio, M. A., 1895, Korea. Vienna-Leipzic.
v. Post, L., 1927—28, Pollenanalyse. In: Eberts Reallexikon.
Prinz, G., 1913, Második belsöázsiai néprajzi eredményei. In: Értesítöje 14, pp. 165—78.
Prinzinger, A., 1914, Volkskundliches aus Schweden. In: Zeitschrift für österreichische Volkskunde 20, p. 170.
Pulbrook, E. C., 1922, English country life and work. London.
På skidor. Stockholm.
Pälsi, S., 1916, Kulttuurikuvia kivikaudelta. Helsinki.

Radloff, W., 1860, Briefe aus dem Altai. In Ermans Archiv 20, pp. 556—97.
Rahvateaduslikud küsimuskavad, 1931, 5, Rahvateaduslikke ja rahvaluulelis küsimuisi. Tartu.
Rehsener, M., 1891, Die Gebirgsnatur in Vorstellung und Saga der Gossensasser. In: Zeitschrift für Volkskunde 1, pp. 421—431.
Reimer, Chr., 1910—19, Nordfynsk bondeliv. 1—5. Odense.
Rhezelius, J., 1634, Kulturhistoriska notiser och traditioner. Ed. by A. Enqvist. In: Fataburen 1930, pp. 17—36.
v. Richthofen, B., 1932 (a), Zur Frage der archäologischen Beziehungen zwischen Nordamerika und Nordasien. In: Anthropos 27, pp. 123—51.
v. Richthofen, 1932 (b), Zur religionswissenschaftlichen Auswertung vorgeschichtlicher Altertümer. In: Mitteilungen Wien 62, pp. 110—144.
Rieck-Müller, M., and Högberg, O., 1920, Medelpad och Ångermanland. 1—2. Stockholm.
Rietz, J. E., 1867, Svenskt dialekt-lexikon. Malmö.
Ringström, Th., 1928, Vertebratfynd i finiglaciala skalbankar vid Uddevalla. Göteborgs K. Vet.-o. Vitt.-Samhälles Handl. 33, No. 6.

Rockhill, W., 1894, Diary of a journey through Mongolia and Tibet. Washington.
Rohrbach, P., 1919, Armenien. Stuttgart.
Rokseth, P., 1923, Terminologie de la culture des céréales à Majorque. Barcelona.
Romdahl, A. L., 1905, Pieter Brueghel d. ä. und sein Kunstschaffen. (Jahrbuch der Kunsthist. Sammlungen des allerhöchst. Kaiserhauses. 25, 3.) Vienna.
Roskoschny, H., 1882—84, Russland. Land und Leute. 1—4. Leipzic.
Rudenko, S. I., 1925, Bashkiri. 2. Leningrad.
Rudenschiöld, U., 1738—41, Berättelse. Helsingfors. 1899.
Russwurm, C., 1855, Eibofolke oder die Schweden an den Küsten Ehstlands. 1—2. Reval.
Rydbeck, O., 1930, The earliest settling of man in Scandinavia. In: Acta Archaeologica 1, pp. 55—86.
Rydbeck, O., 1934, Das Pferd als Transport- und Kampfmittel in den Völkerwanderungen der Ganggräberzeit. In: K. Hum. Vet.-samf:s i Lund årsberättelse 1933—34, pp. 77—98.
Rytkönen, A., 1931, Savupirttien kansaa. Porvoo.
Rütimeyer, L., 1924, Ur-Ethnographie der Schweiz. Basle.

Sahlin, C., 1931, Svenskt stål. Stockholm.
Salander, N., 1811, Beskrifning öfver Åsleds församling i Skaraborgs län. Stockholm.
Sarauw, G., and Alin, J., 1923, Götaälvsområdets fornminnen. Gothenburg.
Sayce, R. U., 1930, The transport and the ox-waggon in Natal. In: Studies in regional consciousness and environment, pp. 69—77.
Sayce, R. U., 1933, Primitive arts and crafts. Cambridge.
Scheel, Fr., 1921, Gammal grensetrafik. In: Bygd og bonde 3, pp. 135—37.
Schier, B., 1932, Hauslandschaften und Kulturbewegungen im östlichen Mitteleuropa. Reichenberg.
Schissler, P., 1753, Jerlsö Sokns Beskrifning. Stockholm.
Schmeltz, J. D. E., 1892, Die Sammlungen aus Korea. In: Internationales Archiv für Ethnographie 4, pp. 45—65, 105—38.
Schmidt, P., and Koppers, W., 1924, Völker und Kulturen. 1. Regensburg.
Schonken, F. T., 1910, Die Wurzeln der Kaphölländischen Volksüberlieferungen. In: Internationales Archiv für Ethnographie 13, appendix.
Schotel, G. D. J., 1905, Het maatschappelijk Leven onzer Vaderen in de zeventiende Eeuw. Leiden.
Schrader, O., 1917—29, Reallexikon der indogermanischen Altertumskunde. Second ed. Berlin-Leipzic.
Schramek, J., 1908, Der Böhmerwaldbauernhaus. Prague.
Schrenk, A. G., 1848—54, Reise nach dem Nordosten des europäischen Russlands. 1—2. Dorpat.
v. Schrenk, L., 1891, Reisen und Forschungen im Amur-Lande in den Jahren 1854—56. 3. St. Petersburg.
Schröter, C., 1925, Festschrift. Zürich.
v. Schulenberg, W., 1896, Ein Bauernhaus im Berchtesgadener Ländchen. In: Mitteilungen d. Anthrop. Gesellschaft in Wien 26, pp. 61—86.
Schultz, A., 1918, Ethnographischer Bilderatlas von Polen. Berlin.
S(chultze), S., 1747, Tägtejords skötsel eller om sättet at bruka åker och äng wid Stora Kopparberget och omkring Fahlu stad. Stockholm.
Schück, A., 1933, Sveriges vägar och sjöleder under forntid och medeltid. In: Nordisk kultur 16, pp. 229—255.
Schück, H., 1923, Ett porträtt från frihetstiden. Stockholm.
v. Schwarz, F., 1900, Turkestan. Freiburg i. B.
Schweizerisches Idiotikon. Frauenfeld.
Schäfer, H., 1908, Priestergräber — — — vom Totentempel des Ne-user-rê. Leipzic.
Schöning, G., 1773—75, Reise. 1—2. Trondheim 1910.
Seebohm, M. E., 1927, The evolution of the English farm. London.
Sidorov, A. S., 1932, Eigentumsmarken (pas) der Syrjänen. In: Journal de la Soc. Finno-Ougrienne 45, No. 5.

Sirelius, U. T., 1906—11, Über die primitiven Wohnungen der finnisch-ugrischen Völker. In: Finnisch-ugrische Forschungen 6—11.
Sirelius, U. T., 1913 (a), Über einige Prototype des Schlittens. In: Journal de la Société Finno-Ougrienne 30, No. 32.
Sirelius, U. T., 1913 (b), Über das Jagdrecht bei einigen finnisch-ugrischen Völkern. In: Mémoires de la Soc. Finno-Ougrienne 35.
Sirelius, U. T., 1916, Über die Art und Zeit der Zähmung des Renntiers. In: Journal de la Société Finno-Ougrienne 33, No. 2.
Sirelius, U. T., 1919—21, Suomen kansanomaista kulttuuria. 1—2. Helsinki.
Sirelius, U. T., 1928, Zur Geschichte des prähistorischen Schlittens. In: P. W. Schmidt-Festschrift, pp. 949—953.
Sirelius, U. T., 1933, Jagd und Fischerei in Finnland. (Die Volkskultur Finnlands. 1.) Berlin-Leipzic.
Sjöbeck, M., 1927, Bondskogar, deras vård och utnyttjande. In: Skånska folkminnen, pp. 36—62.
Skansvakten. Falun.
Skar, J., 1909, Bygdeliv. Gamalt or Saetesdal 4. Oslo.
Skånelagen, ed. C. J. Schlyter. Lund 1859.
Smith, A. C., 1797, Beskrivelse over Trysild Præstegjeld. In: Topographisk Journal 19—22.
Sommier, S., 1885, Un' estate in Siberia. Florence.
Sparrman, A., 1783, Resa till Goda-Hopps-Udden. 1. Stockholm.
Sprog og kultur. Aarhus.
Stebler, F. G., 1903, Alp- und Weidewirtschaft. Berlin.
Stefansson, V., 1923, Hunters of the great North. London.
Steinhausen, G., 1893, Der Kaufmann in der deutschen Vergangenheit. Leipzic.
Stigum, H., 1933, Plogen. In: Bidrag til bondesamfundets historie 1, pp. 74—166.
Stockholmsbilder från fem århundraden. 1923. Uppsala.
Stolt, J., 1892, Byskomakaren Jonas Stolts minnen från 1820-talet. Stockholm.
Ström, H., 1762—66, Physik og oeconomisk beskrivelse over Söndmör. 1—2. Sorö.
Ström, H., 1784, Physisk-oeconomisk beskrivelse over Egers praestegiaeld. Copenhagen.
Strömbom, S., 1924, Forskningar på platsen för Nya Lödöse. Gothenburg.
Stuhlmann, F., 1914, Die Mazigh-Völker. Hamburg.
Stötzner, W., 1930, Der dahurische Karren. In: Zeitschrift für Ethnologie 62, pp. 311—320.
Sundén, O., 1903, Allmogelifvet i en västgötasocken. Stockholm.
Suomen suku, 1928. 1—2. Helsinki.
Svabo, J. C., 1781—82, Föroyaferðin. Ed. by M. A. Jacobsen. Thorshavn 1924.
Svenska akademiens ordbok. Lund.
Syrjänen, L., 1931, Heikki Hannunpojan Vermlannin suomalaisia koskevat muistiinpanot. In: Sanakirjasäätiön toimituksia 1, pp. 271—311.
Säve, C., 1852, Alskogs-stenarne på Gotland. In: Annaler for Nord. Oldkyndighed, pp. 171—207.
Säve, P. A., 1867, Skäl-jagt på Gotland. In: Läsning för folket 33, pp. 14—59.
Säve, P. A., 1869, Ordlista från Västergötland. In: Antiqvarisk tidskrift 2, pp. 158—188.
Säve, P. A., 1873, Samfärdseln på Gotland i gamla tider. In: Land och folk, pp. 33—48, 97—124.
Säve, P. A., 1891, Åkerns sagor. Spridda drag ur odlingshäfderna och folklifvet på Gotland. Visby.
Säve, P. A., 1892, Hafvets och fiskarens sagor. Second ed. Visby.

Tallgren, A., 1926, Ett viktigt bronsåldersfynd från Lappmarken. In: Finskt museum 33, pp. 78—88.
Tallgren, A., 1932, Finland vid slutet av hednatiden. In: Fornvännen, pp. 94—113.
Tanner, V., 1929, Antropogeografiska studier inom Petsamo-området. 1. Skoltlapparna. In: Fennia 49.
Tersmeden, C., 1912—19, Memoarer 1—6. Stockholm.
Teutsch, J., and Fuchs, K., 1905, Ethnographische Mitteilungen aus den Komitaten Kronstadt und Fogaras in Siebenbürgen. In: Mittheil. d. Anthrop. Gesellschaft in Wien 35, pp. 133—53.
Tham, P., 1796—97, Resa til Stockholm. Stockholm 1797.
Thede, M., 1933, Die Albufera von Valencia. In: Volkstum und Kultur der Romanen 6, pp. 317—383.

Thordeman, B., 1927, Rev. of Nörlund, 1926. In: Fornvännen, pp. 56—60.
Touring Club Italiano. Piemonte n. d.
Traill, H. D., and Mann, J. S., 1903, Social England. IV. London.
túri Mészáros, I., 1928, Adalékok az alföldi gazdálkodáshoz. In: Értesitöje 39, pp. 105—112.

Uppfinningarnas bok, 1899, First ed. 4. Stockholm.

Waern, C., 1910, Mediæval Sicily. London.
Wagner, M., 1921, Das ländliche Leben Sardiniens im Spiegel der Sprache. (Wörter und Sachen. Beiheft 4.) Heidelberg.
Wagner, W., 1926, Die chinesische Landwirtschaft. Berlin.
Vahl, M., and Hatt, G., 1922—27, Jorden og menneskelivet. 1—4. Copenhagen.
Wahle, E., 1929, Wagen. In: Eberts Reallexikon.
Walker, G., 1814, Costume in Yorkshire.
Wallin, J., 1747—76, Gotländska samlingar. 1—2. Stockholm-Gothenburg.
Walther, P., 1929, Schwäbische Volkskunde. Leipzic.
Valvasor, J., 1689, Die Ehre des Hertzogthums Crain. 1—2.
Variarum rerum vocabula, 1538. Ed. A. Andersson. Uppsala 1890.
Wegelius, H., 1825, Vöra socken. In: Budkavlen 1928, pp. 47—60, 83—91, 121—123.
v. d. Ven, D. J., 1920, Neerlands Volksleven. Arnhem.
W(engelin), E. G., 1893, Gamla minnen. Gävle.
Vennberg, E., 1925, Erik Dahlbergh. Hans levnad och verksamhet. Uppsala.
Verantius, F., Machinae novae. Venice n. d.
Vetenskapsakademiens handlingar. Stockholm.
Weule, K., 1912, Die Urgesellschaft und ihre Lebensfürsorge. Stuttgart.
Whitelocke, B., 1653—54, Dagbok öfver dess embassade til Sverige. Uppsala 1777.
Wiedemann, A., 1920, Das alte Ägypten. Heidelberg.
Wiener Zeitschrift für Volkskunde. Vienna.
Wigström, E., 1891, Allmogeseder i Rönnebergs härad i Skåne. In: Svenska landsmål 8.
Wiklund, K. B., 1899, Om lapparna i Sverige. Stockholm.
Wiklund, K. B., 1914, Urnordiska ortnamn i de södra lappmarkerna. In: Namn och bygd 2, pp. 105—120.
Wiklund, K. B., 1918, Om renskötselns uppkomst. In: Ymer 38, pp. 249—273.
Wiklund, K. B., 1928 (a), Huru länge har det funnits lappar i Jämtland och Härjedalen? In: Jämtländska studier, pp. 391—412.
Wiklund, K. B., 1928 (b), Ur skidans och snöskons historia. In: På skidor, pp. 5—86.
Wiklund, K. B., 1929, Mera om skidans historia. In: På skidor, pp. 252—79.
Wiklund, K. B., 1931, Den nordiska skidan, den södra och den arktiska. In: På skidor, pp. 5—50.
Viksten, A., 1916, Något om timmerkälken och virkets utdrifning. In: Skogsvännen, pp. 46—61.
Wilkinson, J. G., 1878, Manners and customs of the ancient Egyptians. 1—3. London.
Vilkuna, K., 1930, Vanhat veto- ja ajoneuvot. 1. Helsinki.
Vilkuna, K., 1931 (a), Suomen vetohäristä (Sanoja ja asioita). Turku.
Vilkuna, K., 1931 (b), Vehmaro 'parihärkien aisa'. In: Sanakirjasäätiön toimituksia 1, pp. 57—61.
Vilkuna, K., 1933, Var har "Codex f. d. Kalmar" utarbetats? In: Kulturhistorisk årsbok, Helsingfors, pp. 7—14.
Wille, H. J., 1786, Beskrivelse over Sillejords Praestegield. Copenhagen.
Wilse, J. N., 1779, Physisk, oeconomisk og statistisk Beskrivelse over Spydeberg Praestegield. Oslo.
Wilson, G. L., 1924, The Horse and the Dog in Hidatsa Culture. Anthrop. Papers of the Amer. Museum of Nat. History. New York.
Viollet le Duc, E., Dictionnaire raisonné du mobilier francais. 1—6. Paris n. d.
Virchow, R., 1887, Einige Ueberlebsel in pommerschen Gebräuchen. Report in Verhandl. der Berl. Anthrop. Gesellschaft, pp. 361—63.
Virdestam, G., 1923, Minnen från en gammal fädernegård. In: Hyltén Cavallius-föreningens årsbok, pp. 22—38.

Wissler, C., 1910, Material culture of the Blackfoot Indians. Anthropol. papers of the Amer. Mus. of Natural History V, 1. New York.
Wissler, C., 1912, North American Indians of the Plains. Amer. Mus. Nat. History, Handbook. Ser. 1. New York.
Wissler, C., 1914, The Influence of the Horse in the Development of Plains Culture. In: Amer. Anthropologist. 15, pp. 1—25.
Wissler, C., 1922, The American Indian. Second ed. New York.
Vitterhetsakademien, 1926, Kungl. Vitterhets Historie och Antikvitets Akademiens årsbok. Stockholm.
Volkskunst und Volkskunde. Munich.
Wrangel, F. U., 1899, Bilder från 1700-talets Stockholm. Stockholm.
Wrede, A., 1922, Rheinische Volkskunde. Second ed. Leipzic.
v. Wright, W., Fries, B. F., Ekström, C. U., and Sundewall, C. J., 1836—48, Skandinaviens fiskar. Stockholm.
v. Wulfschmidt, J. P., 1771, Bonde-Stolpe. N. d.
Västergötlands fornminnesförenings tidskrift. Skara.

Zeissler, H., 1922, Geschirre und Sättel aller Arbeitstiere. Berlin.
Zelenin, D., 1927, Russische (Ostslavische) Volkskunde. Berlin-Leipzic.
Zéliqzon, L., 1922—24, Dictionnaire des patois romans de la Moselle. 1—3. Strasbourg.
Zell, F., 1902—03, Volkskunst in Allgäu. Kaufbeuren-Munich.
Zettersten, A., 1933, Jugoslaviska skidor. In: Pa skidor, pp. 96—103.
Zoepfl, Fr., 1928, Deutsche Kulturgeschichte. 1. Freiburg i. B.

Åkesson, E., 1911, Färöarna. Stockholm.

Ödmann, S., 1930, Hågkomster från hembygden och skolan. Seventh ed. Lund 1918.
Östberg, K., 1926, Norsk bonderet. 4. Af tömmerdriftens rets- og sedvaneregler. Oslo.
Östergren, O., 1919—, Nusvensk ordbok. Stockholm.
Östlid, M., 1929—30, Kråkstad. En bygdebok. 1—2. Hamar.

CORRECTIONS

Pp. 150—151. Examples omitted from the table: *Västergötland*, Främmestad, E. u. 3960, Lyrestad, E. u. 4203; Småland, Femsjö and Färgaryd, E. u. 6796, Öja, E. u. 4301.

P. 168. — A waggon with outer supports is to be seen on a German engraving as early as 1493, Boerner, 1932, Pl. II.

P. 179 — Hatt, G. 1916 (b), Kyst- og Indlandskultur i det arktiske. In: (Danish) Geografisk tidskrift, 23, pp. 284—290.

Review

SLEDGES AND WHEELED VEHICLES: ethological studies from the view-point of Sweden. (Nordisk Museets Handlingar: 4) By GÖSTA BERG. *Uppsala: Almquist and Wiksells Boktryckeri-A-B, 1935. pp. 189, 32 plates, 38 drawings, 13 distribution maps. Price not stated.*

'The object of this work,' says its author, 'is to investigate certain problems connected with the history of vehicular transport from a Swedish point of view' but, though he is thus an avowed specialist, he never loses sight of the two facts, that Swedish transport is part of the world's transport, and that vehicles are historically important because they are an essential part of the culture of their users. He is to be congratulated on treating studies of vehicles as the ethnological studies that they certainly are.

Besides dealing very fully with what may be called the "normal" stages of slide-car, sledges, wheeled-sledge, car, and wagons, he produces evidence of a pre-sledge era of single runners dating back to Neolithic times; and he also devotes much attention to the difference between the pair-drawn and the single-draught form of cart. Much that is said bears on points that have been already raised in ANTIQUITY.

The vast wealth of evidence accumulated in this book forms in itself a permanent and valuable contribution to the literature of the subject. The plates provide nearly a hundred good photographs and reproductions. The drawings are excellent, but the value of the distribution-maps would be increased if we were told more about the methods by which they were drawn up, and if the symbols in some of them were more clearly explained. A minor defect is that several illustrations are wrongly numbered in the text.

Such theories as are expressed are, wisely, somewhat tentative. The author recognizes, as all must who tackle this subject seriously, that both wider and more thorough researches are needed before a complete statement can be made with any approach to certainty. He does, however, commit himself to the unqualified opinion that the single-horse cart had its origin in the slide-car. More often he plays the part of the research-worker, with a patience and thoroughness which compel admiration.

It must be recognized that the translator had to deal with an extremely difficult task. But this does not alter the fact that the English reader is faced by obvious mistranslations in several rather important passages; these not only baffle him in themselves, but also raise uncomfortable doubts about the accuracy of other passages. The sum total of these errors and possible errors is, however, only a fraction of the whole.

The paper and print are good, and the book, when opened, lies flat. This is helpful to the reader, particularly in a volume which one is likely to wish to leave open for comparison with other. A bibliography of the subject occupies 17 pages.

There is no doubt that this book will be of great value to anyone seriously interested in the history of transport. It will provide English readers with information that they are not likely to be able to get for themselves. It is hoped that someone will produce a similar book, dealing with these matters from "the view-point of Great Britain."

R. H. LANE

Reprint of review by
R. H. Lane (1935). Review of Gösta Berg 'SLEDGES AND WHEELED VEHICLES: ethnological studies from the view-point of Sweden'. *Antiquity*, 9, pp 497-497. doi:10.1017/S0003598X00011017.

www.ingramcontent.com/pod-product-compliance
Lightning Source LLC
Chambersburg PA
CBHW081719100526
44591CB00016B/2436